Building, Preparing and Racing Your
MINI

Bill Sollis with Dave Pollard

Haynes Publishing

First published in May 1999
Reprinted February 2003

British Library cataloguing-in-publication data:
A catalogue record for this book is available from the British Library.

ISBN 1 85960 621 0

Library of Congress Catalog Card Number 98-75401

Haynes North America Inc.
861 Lawrence Drive, Newbury Park,
California 91320, USA

Published by Haynes Publishing, Sparkford,
Yeovil, Somerset BA22 7JJ, UK

Tel: 01963 442030 Fax: 01963 440001
Int. tel: +44 1963 442030 Fax: +44 1963 440001

E-mail: sales@haynes-manuals.co.uk
Web site: www.haynes.com

Typeset by Character Graphics (Taunton) Ltd

Printed and bound in Great Britain by J.H. Haynes & Co. Ltd

Contents

Acknowledgements

This is perhaps the hardest part of the whole book to write, and that is saying something, since I have had nightmares over the whole thing.

It all started with a letter from Haynes asking me to write a book about modifying Minis for the road. Naturally I was flattered, but I knew I simply didn't have the time. Mindful that one day perhaps I would like to do it, I made an appointment and drove to Sparkford to explain why I was declining the offer. Somehow or another I was persuaded to go away and reconsider. I had received lots of advice about getting other people involved to ease the workload, and in a moment of madness I signed the contract.

Progress was pitiful. As I had correctly identified originally, I didn't have the time, and once again I drove to Sparkford to put my hands up and surrender. As a compromise we agreed upon this title, as I felt it possible. Since then I have missed every deadline ever set, and literally years have gone by. This book is only here now thanks to the patience of Alison Roelich at Haynes, who has managed to keep it alive and push me along without ever really telling me off, as she was certainly entitled to do.

When I again ground to a halt with the text sort of finished, but personally stuck over photographs and layout, Alison once more came to the rescue, bringing in Dave Pollard – a proper author – to take the pictures and tidy it all up. Well, here it is, and thank you Alison and Dave.

Going back to the very beginning, I was wholly inexperienced and the Mini Se7en Racing Club, as an institution, guided me to people who would offer honest help and advice. My racing could have ended very early without the help of Gerald Dale, who repaired my first car after its fourth race when I had crashed it heavily. Gerald did the donkey work, straightening out the floor and bulkhead, and was prepared to stop at that, charge me a very fair price and then provide telephone advice as I finished repairs and worked at becoming competitive.

As I tinkered with engines, Keith Manning and Keith Calver offered complimentary advice, and good quality service at friendly prices when required.

Sponsorship is a facet of motorsport in which I have never excelled. However, Sebron Auto Stores, my local spares shop, offered practical advice, and Steve Brown charged me only cost prices, and for many years made small but significant contributions to my budget. There can have been no commercial sense in it. Sebron actually got me some support from Duckhams, who have supplied me with oil for the best part of ten years. As the saying goes, Bill Sollis Racing uses and recommends Duckhams Lubricants.

The Rover Sport operation, now known as the Mini Competitions Department, enhanced the standing of the Mini Challenges throughout my participation. In particular Christopher Belton has assisted, indirectly, every competitor in the field, and much of the credit for the current health of the championships should go to him, along with Chris Norman of the BRDC and the committee of the Mini Se7en Racing Club.

My big break came with graduation to Miglia, when Nigel Fryatt invited me to the offices of *Cars and Car Conversions* magazine and offered support for my impending first season of Mini Miglia. One year stretched to six, and Nigel gave me the opportunity to write, encouraged me and got me started as a contributor to *Mini World*. That magazine has allowed me a huge experience of Mini driving, and has led to opportunities literally all over the world. I have enjoyed the help and support of Mike Askew and Monty Watkins during their editorships, and that of Steve Bennett who is now at the helm of *CCC*.

During the *CCC* years my small collection of sponsors has grown. They have all offered long-term support, some with financial assistance and all with product support, encouragement and interest. So, my thanks go to Mike Standring at Moss International, Peter Gibbons of Jack Knight Developments, Colin Folwell of Corbeau Seats, Peter and Colin Woollard of KAD, Ron Webb at Tarox, Andy and Doreen Myers of Mini Machine, Jeremy Rossiter of Spax, Dan Boon at NGK, Bryan Slark of SRE, Chris Tyrrell, Ian Curley of Curley Specialised Mouldings, Nick Paddy of Play Mini, all the staff at Mini Spares Centre, Chris Lewis of The Food Weighouse, Ross Buckingham of Southern Carbs, Martin Short of Rollcentre Racing, Peter Baldwin for his rolling road service, Harley at TRS, Ray Armes of Graphique Sport, Brian McGee of BM Graphics, Alan Minshaw of Demon Tweeks, Rob Walker of Rob Walker Engineering, David at Maniflow and the team at Richard Longman and Co, for an engine that finally did the job!

Whilst I did build my own Mini Se7ens, the Miglias relied heavily on Peter Vickers, who was always there, and could generally solve the difficulties which were beyond me. He is a true supporter of club racing, and someone to whom a large percentage of the Mini racers down the years owe a debt of thanks. Nick Cole is another from the same mould. I worked with him on all the KAD cars, and established a proper driver/engineer relationship. He trusted my judgements and feedback and never swayed from a determination to provide the best equipment possible, often with meagre funds. It has always tickled me that Nick has, at his own admis-sion, occasionally 'tested me out' with set-up and the like, and apparently I have come up with the goods! I suppose I've tested him, too, in times of dire need, and he's always delivered.

With Nick I made two of the trips to Japan. The Narita family showed us warm hospitality in '94 – it was an eye-opening trip and they were perfect hosts. I have established a close link with Sanwa Trading. Nori and his wife Tomiyo are personal friends now, and we often enjoy a meal together. Their business set-up needs to be seen to be believed. Driving my old cars in Japan has been great fun, and something that I hope will continue. Nori always enjoys new projects and I hope to involve him in our Historic exploits which apparently interest him as much as me.

Then there are the members of the Mini Se7en Club, whose numbers are only 300 or so, but who are rather like a huge family. I wish to thank every-one I have raced with, even those I have crashed with! It has been a pleasure.

Finally there is the Mini itself. It enchanted me as a child; it has brought me to maturity, and along the way it introduced me to my wife, Emma. What more could a man ask?

Bill Sollis

Dave Pollard extends his thanks to Colin Wilson (RACMSA), Christian Tilbury (*Mini Magazine*), Indespension Limited, Keith Ellison (Mini Se7en Club), Ken Ankers (Demon Tweeks), Ian Curley (Curley Specialised Mouldings), Steve Bennett and Norman Hodson (*CCC* magazine), John Colley and Paul Harmer.

Preface

It is a difficult task to write a book with technical content and I am acutely aware that there will be detractors – those with strong opinions as to how cars should be built, prepared and tuned. They will have valid alternative views and a right to hold them but this book is not aimed at these people – although I am sure it will entertain them. My intention is to enlighten those without expertise, the category in which I stood before I started racing.

This is not a black art. Over the years we have worked hard but without huge expenditure and all of the methods and directions in this book have been proven to work. There are of course many ways to skin a cat and this is a true account of how we did it. This took us to ultimate success and given patience and perseverance, will work for anyone.

Bill Sollis
Sevenoaks, 1999

Introduction

So you want to race?

We've all done it, sat in front of the TV on a summer Sunday afternoon watching the Grand Prix and sighing in disgust because we *know* that we could have done better. There's a world of difference, of course, between fighting the traffic around the M25 and fending off the pack hounding you into Redgate corner at Donington Park.

The odds of any of us landing a Ferrari drive for next year make winning the lottery look like a sure thing, but you *can* go racing for a reasonable budget *and* have just as much fun on the track. Indeed, with the massive commercialism now rampant in the higher echelons of motor sport, many would say that clubman racers get considerably *more* fun than the guys at the top!

Without doubt, one of the best ways to go racing is in Britain's favourite small car – the Mini. With 40 years of production and over five million manufactured (still counting), cars, spares and specialists are everywhere, and its size means you don't need a 38-tonne truck to tow it, or a huge workshop to store it in and work on it.

Perhaps one of the most important points you'll find with Mini racing is that the friendship – off the track at least – remains, harking back to the days when drivers were racing for enjoyment rather than eight-figure salaries and the chance to be a sponsor's puppet. And if you want to use it as a

springboard to other formulae and maybe even a full-time career in racing, there are plenty of opportunities available – Steve Soper and Patrick Watts are two highly successful touring car drivers who started their careers in Minis. Have I whetted your appetite? Good, now read on ...

Where to start

You can't decide to go racing just from reading this book. You MUST go to at least one race meeting (and preferably several) to get a feel for the formula; to see what's involved at first hand and to see, if nothing else, just what you would be letting yourself in for! You can also get to know a few of the characters – everyone likes to talk about their cars – and, unlike Formula 1, you won't be asked to sign a secrecy agreement for the privilege. Chat with as many drivers as you can – those at the mid-field and back of the grid, as well as the front-

At all race meetings you'll see the stickers and signs everywhere telling you quite categorically that motor racing can be dangerous, and that's just for the spectators! It follows that for drivers, the risk of getting hurt is considerably higher. Of course, the rules, regulations and basic common sense make modern motor racing, whether Minis or Formula 1, safer than it has ever been. Improved construction of race clothing, helmets, etc., and more stringent standards of scrutineering, mean that little is left to chance. But nothing and no-one is perfect and when your brakes fail into the tightest hairpin on the track, or the driver behind decides to use your car rather than his own brakes to slow him down, there's not much you can do about it. This is not meant to put a potential racer off. On the contrary, it's the element of risk that puts motor racing into the same adrenalin-boosting category as slalom skiing, mountaineering and off-shore powerboat racing. But you simply must be aware that motor racing is not the same as going for a drive on a Sunday afternoon (although ...), and that all drivers have a real safety responsibility, not just for themselves but for their fellow racers. If you want a really safe and quiet life, then seaside crazy golf would probably be ideal.

When the running of race engines is banned (at some tracks early on Sunday mornings) you'll be thankful you're not racing a Mustang!

And there's no sexism in Mini racing – anyone is allowed to push!

runners. The really successful drivers will probably be sponsored, which makes their lives much easier. However, those at the back will probably be funding their fun from their own pockets and will be more in your league – unless you've got very understanding employers who want to finance your hobby. You should find out which companies are good for supplying engines, suspension and spares, and which trailers are the best, etc. (a personal recommendation from the driver who uses a product in anger is worth a thousand adverts). If you're lucky, you'll also pick-up a few vibes as to which drivers

tend to be a little, shall we say, wild? And, of course, there may be someone in the paddock with a car for sale. The point here is that, rather than buying it from a cold garage in October, you can check it out in action to see if claims by the owner match up with reality.

Which race series?

Mini Se7en and Miglia are the two most popular ways of going circuit racing in The Most Famous Small Car, the regulation engine capacities being 1000cc and 1300cc respectively – Mini Se7en keeps the cars nearer to standard specification than Miglia. The costs are intended to be within the reach of the man in the street, and the regulations aim to define something that can be built at home using a comprehensive tool kit, personal skills and enthusiasm. Evolution has inevitably played its part in the formulae which have been around since the sixties, and in certain areas professional services *must*

be called upon, but the basic concept remains intact. For Mini Se7en and Miglia racers, the annual calendar comprises a fairly well-balanced mix of single and two-day events. Remember above all that help *will* be needed. It cannot be done alone and the human factor will

The paddock just before practice is positively buzzing with nervous excitement ...

... but not for everyone, it seems.

keep you sane when everything else conspires against you. (*See Appendix 2 for details of Mini race series.*)

Finance

It's long been the greatest bugbear of motor racing, but finance is the factor that restricts the majority of existing and potential racers. Running costs are an open-ended commitment, but the essentials can be accurately predicted, though there must always be a provision for the unexpected. I look at £400 being a realistic base figure for every race entered. This covers entry (roughly £110), tow car petrol, race petrol and consumables, average tyre wear and food for you and your team. It could be done for less, but not by much.

Unforeseen expenses may be encountered for accident damage and engine failures. These cannot be quantified, but I have always held that the driver must be aware that the worst could happen to his car and he may return home with only an empty trailer. In twelve years I have yet to witness such terrible misfortune, but there has been many a car written off, where the shell, roll cage and most of the suspension parts are rendered scrap. I seek not to be alarmist – but merely to inform you of the harsh realities of racing life.

In essence, you've got to have cash to deal with the following basic categories:

- The car (either buy complete or build your own)

Scrutineering is quite rightly very thorough, as everyone's safety depends on it ...

BUILDING, PREPARING AND RACING YOUR MINI

- Transport for race car (trailer/van, etc.)
- Safe garaging for race car
- Personal safety equipment and clothing (fireproof clothing, helmet, etc.)
- Race weekend costs; fuel there and back, B&B, food and drink, race entry fees, etc.
- Maintenance and tuning
- Repairs

As a general rule of thumb, a newcomer contemplating a full 12-race season should allow for £5,000 running costs, with a further £1,000 provision for damage repairs – no one's perfect!

Buying a car

Probably the best place to search for a suitable car is actually at a race meeting, where you can see for yourself how it performs. Failing that, such publications as *Motoring News*, *Autosport* or the *Mini Se7en Racing Club* magazine all have racing Minis for sale.

Buying an existing car is the simplest and most cost effective method of gathering everything together. When buying,

... and for most, it's a more nerve-racking time than sitting on the grid ...

... and the waiting is the worst part.

'Me and my car, a mix of safety and sponsorship. Note the chequered flag design continued from car to helmet.

mum requirement in reality. Any spares offered with the car should be useful. A tidy, well-prepared Se7en in this condition will fetch in the order of £5,000–£6,000. For a similar Miglia car, add another £2,000.

There will, of course, be cars that are cheaper, but weigh it up carefully, for in the long term these are often more costly in terms of work required to make them competitive. Regular winning cars are rarely offered, and when they are, prices will be much higher. It is very tempting to buy such a car on the grounds that it will make you, too, a winner, but you can't count on it; you need some serious talent, too!

Conversely, it is often the case that a quality driver can flatter an average car the way Michael Schumacher was able to make the Formula 1 Benetton-Ford into a regular winner against the Williams-Renault which was usually by far the better car. It's up to you to decide how the equation works and whether or not you're paying over the odds for the vehicle. Whatever, always make sure that everything which made it successful has been left on the car.

Cars in bits

There are numerous people who feel more able to build from scratch, but the cost in parts alone is considerably more than the typical used, but basically sound, runner offered for sale. Building clearly allows the initial cost to be spread, but I advise strongly against it unless you are a GP-standard mechanic with a tool kit and workshop facilities to match. This applies doubly so if you, like me, have a day job to slot in between the races!

Through the chapters of this book, costings for a new car-build can be assessed. Expect the total cost to be 50 per cent higher than the figures quoted above, and do not expect to get it all right first time. Further fine-tuning and

look for the most competitive car available, preferably as part of a greater package, which will save you time and money in other areas. For example, a driver giving up racing may be selling not only the car, but the trailer, spares, tyres, etc. into the bargain.

Six wheels with dry (slick) tyres and four wet (treaded) tyres are the mini-

Let's not forget there are other ways to race a Mini – this immaculate car is ready to go in the Classic Touring Car Championship.

modification, with associated costs, will be necessary! If you take the buying route, read this tome cover to cover before looking – you will thus be prepared, knowing where to look, and for what!

Towing the line

A trailer adds considerably to your expenses if acquired separately, so if you can include one in the package when you're buying a complete car it may well be cheaper. Remember to consider the towing vehicle, too. It simply *must* be reliable, since time and race meetings wait for no man (or woman). A family car (of sufficient size and engine power for the job in hand) will suffice and will usually carry your team, too. Plenty of people race quite happily on this basis. A trip around the paddocks will give ample illustration of the multitude of methods of transporting the essentials to the circuit. There are now many motorhomes and box trailers to be seen, lorries are increasing in pop-

ularity and beyond doubt some spend more on the support than on the racing itself! Choice will depend on budget, but do not forget that it rains quite a lot, and wet people are usually miserable people. (*See* Chapter 15 for towing in detail.)

Personal safety

The reason that so few people are hurt in modern motor racing is that great attention is paid to safety. To race your Mini there are very strict minimum standards that must be adhered to. A high quality helmet, fireproof racing suit and underclothing, etc. None of it is cheap, but it's pure give-away compared to having an accident without it. Do not think about going racing and cutting corners here – you can't. (*See* Chapter 12 for more details.)

Maintenance and tuning

Simply buying a car is the easy bit – some would even say the cheap bit! Before the big step is taken, other necessities must be considered. You'll need a reasonable tool kit (for yourself or your willing mechanic helper) and be ready to keep your race car in tip-top condition. Remember that you can't cut corners with a racing car the way that you can with a road car – anything which is not absolutely right is, by definition, absolutely wrong! Exact details of our own maintenance schedules are in Chapter 14.

The time

Do not forget that time will be demanded, both for race weekends and preparation. The costings given earlier make no allowance for labour costs; as well as the driver's contribution, you will need the help and support of a friend or two. It is my opinion that it is impossible to race successfully without the dedicated help of at least one other committed individual. You will often find that moral support is more important than practical help. I have, and will happily continue to complete all the

between-races preparation myself. Once things are well organised and the car is to the required standard, the time spent between races should be rationalised. A strict order and structure forms the backbone of my own routine, meaning that thinking is less important.

If the car has returned from its previous outing undamaged, or at least not requiring repairs, then the routine re-preparation can be easily completed in a day, or a couple of evenings. More time will have to be allowed for assembling spares, food and overnight provisions if a whole weekend is involved. The actual process of loading up should become a strict routine to ensure nothing is omitted, and should only take an hour once a system is established.

If you relish making the most of your investment in a race meeting, a Saturday/Sunday meeting can be stretched to cover both Friday and Saturday nights. You will not be alone,

Unless your name is Senna or Schumacher, the odds are you don't exactly relish racing in the wet. But you'll have to get used to it if you're going to get anywhere on UK circuits. (Courtesy Norman Hodson, CCC magazine)

the Mini Se7en Racing Club in particular having a good social atmosphere that readily invites newcomers into the fold. On the other hand, if you prefer your own bed, and don't mind an early start it is possible to minimise or delete overnight stops altogether. I have done it both ways and there are, of course,

pros and cons. You will have to weigh it up and canvass the opinion of all involved.

A final word on the time element concerns the unforeseen incident. Body damage or engine blow-ups are going to occur, and they must not be the end of the world. Yes, it's annoying, costly and

It's certainly not much fun, and even less so if you're stuck in traffic where all you can see is a wall of spray from the guy in front. Far better ... (Courtesy Norman Hodson, CCC magazine)

... to get around them and into the lead, and if you have some skill, experience and, let it be said, luck, then you'll end up with. ... (Courtesy Norman Hodson, CCC magazine)

usually totally unnecessary, but unless you can take it, playing tiddly winks may be a better way to spend your weekend leisure time! I have only once been forced to miss a race because of such a debacle at the previous outing. In the early years this was a matter of good luck, but nowadays, with the assistance of Peter Vickers, any bodywork damage my car suffers can be rectified in days not weeks – quite literally. Once again Peter is an example of the sort of help you cannot do without.

The place

So you've got the time, what about the place? A racing car simply has to be kept under cover. The minimum requirement is, clearly, a place to keep the car safely away from the elements, thieves and vandals – even a tiny lock-up garage is better than nothing, but if you can get somewhere with some room to work in, with facilities such as power and light, you'll make your racing life so much easier. Make sure it's secured by a high-quality hasp and padlock, not a £5 supermarket special. If you have an up-and-over garage door, do NOT rely on the standard lock – these are notoriously weak and easy to overcome. Ideally, invest in a lock which secures the lower part of the door to the concrete base. If you have wooden doors, reinforce the inside of them with sheet mild steel.

Of course, plenty of cars have been run from the humblest of stables, but

... the victory spoils. A very satisfactory afternoon's work! (Courtesy Norman Hodson, *CCC* magazine)

how hard do you need your life to be? I now enjoy quite spacious surroundings, but I was equally successful when confined to a single garage. Being cramped makes things a little more difficult, and puts organisation at a premium, but a race-winning car can still be prepared. Do not forget that the racing Mini is usually a trailered-to-race-meetings car, and that your trailer will need storage space too. Depending on your location, trailers can be extremely vulnerable to theft, and the effect of losing an expensive trailer has finished more than one racer's career.

Summing up

Well, having considered all these points, is it possible? I hope the answer is 'yes', and I would suggest a humble start to assess the reality of it all. Everybody in the paddock who has been at it for some time has evolved their own methods, and built up the equipment with which to go racing. It's a rewarding process, and from my current position I still relish a session of reminiscing over the early days when we hadn't any idea of what we were up to!

Where to from here?

Technicalities, rules and regulations and dry facts by the ream may make Mini racing appear to be dull and loaded down with bureaucracy. In reality this is not so – as you will see from the Prologue, which recounts my career details to date. I can assure you that the excitement and adrenalin more than balances out the rules and red tape!

Note: The prices quoted here were approximate and correct at the time of going to press.

My formula for success

Chapter 1

My own efforts at the wheel

This recollection of my own efforts at the wheel of a racing Mini is not intended as a trumpet-blowing exercise, but more to show that you don't have to start racing at the age of four and have a million-pound budget to enjoy fun on the track. And, regardless of everything else, having fun is the essential ingredient – engine preparation, body build quality, chassis tuning and suspension geometry are important technical aspects, and all require your attention, but if you're not enjoying the end result, you're getting something wrong. What has happened to me still surprises me, even today, and I have so many fond memories tied up in the events of the past 15 years or so.

On the road …

My initial enthusiasm for the Mini was probably based on our family run-around – a 1966 tweed grey 850. It was a bit rusty, and not as glamorous as the (then) new Austin Allegro, but I liked it. My interest was founded in the maintenance carried out by my Uncle Alan, who always welcomed my enquiries and allowed me a small involvement. I was probably about 12 or 13 years old when he said to me: 'Do you want to do this or shall I – but there's only one pair of overalls!' Well I did the job (ball joints, as it happens) wearing Alan's AP overalls – and I still have them! I remember that episode as clearly as if it were yesterday, and I am

not noted for having good long-term recall!

I longed for the day I would be able to drive; indeed, my friend Raphael Speed and I began developing our skills a little ahead of schedule (on a private road, of course, officer!). We acquired a Mini Cooper between us and took it apart with gusto. Regrettably it never returned to the road, but it marked the beginning of major undertakings on the mechanical front. We took the engine out and got it back in again; we cut bits off and welded new bits on in their place.

Once in possession of a driving licence, and with my own car – a 17th birthday present from my parents – I began clocking up miles and miles and miles. Nowhere was too far, and my enthusiasm was enormous. I probably drove too quickly (Emma, my wife, will tell you I still do) but never recklessly. I began to want to compete in a Mini. It was a clear desire but I had no knowledge of what was possible. Minicross was perhaps at the height of its popularity in 1984, and I began to think this was the way to go. However, fate was to take a hand.

Like many petrolheads I was a magazine junkie too, and was regularly buying a Link House title – *Auto Performance* (long since dead). In July 1984 I opened it to read about Mini Se7en, and things have never been the same since! I joined the club immediately, and then placed a wanted advert in the club magazine for a car, or the bits to build one. In the issue in which my advert appeared there was a car for sale. It belonged to Mark Cinnamon, and had a blown engine. It had been stripped and needed rebuilding. For the sum of £650 the car (part of it in kit form) was mine; I paid a further £550 for his trailer and a brand new Bryan Slark cylinder head. So I was skint but never happier. As Mark was giving up racing, he offered me the entire contents of his garage, and I suppose that was the start of what has become the habit of a lifetime. I took the whole lot, and amongst it there were sufficient bits to rebuild the engine. There was a paint mark on the flywheel which I used to set the ignition timing, and we set off for Brands Hatch and a test session prior to the first race.

... and on the track!

I had bought my licence. This was prior to the days of any form of training, so I was extremely nervous on discovering a packed test session for mixed cars. In the week before the Formula Ford Festival, chaos best describes the scene. I didn't even know how to stay out of everyone's way, but my 13th and final lap of the morning was 66 seconds. The lap record was then 59.4 and anything under a minute was special, so I was on target to achieve my aim of finishing the race and not being lapped!

The day of my first race finally arrived, 28 October 1984. I had been suffering from a cold that week and I was worried about it affecting my performance! The day went so well. I passed scrutineering but forgot to stick the pass label in the window, and Bob (Cooper) was obliged to rival Linford Christie to ensure we joined practice on time. We did, and the ten laps were very exciting. I had a spin at Druids – it felt graceful and delicate as the rear overtook the front. I qualified 19th of 23 cars and took my place towards the rear of the grid. As the red lights came on I was aware that I hadn't contemplated a start technique, and almost immediately they went green and I was away in a cloud of my own tyre smoke.

My only recollection now is that on about lap eight I was getting so excited because I thought I was going to finish. Then high drama – starting my ninth lap, approaching Paddock, the cavalry loomed large in my mirrors. I moved aside willingly and marvelled at the pack squabbling. The pace was awesome, and the car of Gary Hall slewed into the corner sideways, holding off Barbara Cowell and Russell Grady. As they disappeared into the distance I completed my last lap and took the chequered flag. Being lapped wasn't a problem because the track was still damp, anyway I reckon I was happier than both Gary Hall, the race winner, and Chris Gould, the confirmed National Mini Se7en Champion 1984.

1985 – Mini Se7en: A learning year

I only did the one race in '84 since I wanted to be eligible for the '85 Novice Championship. I spent the winter rebuilding the engine and getting to know the ins and outs of the car. My progress was steady and non-dramatic. I recall enjoying every moment of it, but looking back at the result sheets I feel genuine frustration. It's an odd mix, but knowing now that I could do it, it seems that I spent far too long proving it. Certainly, I was learning on two fronts. The driving was one thing, but the set-up and handling of the car didn't occur to me for some time. By the end of '85 I made something of a breakthrough. Another local driver, Colin Richardson, told me that the car didn't handle, and lent me his setting-up gear. The corner weights were a disaster, and sorting it all out transformed the car. The final race of the year, a Southern Championship round at Brands, yielded

third place, and with it the Novice Championship. I went into winter hibernation full of ambitious plans.

1986 – Mini Se7en: Red and white, but blue

I stripped the whole car and painted it red and white. The first real Bill-built engine was completed, and we were finished early. The opening race of '86 was at Silverstone and it was memorable. We ran at the front for the first time. Indeed on the final run down to Woodcote, the last corner on the club circuit, I moved down the outside and into second place, at the head of a three-car bunch. I played it safe as they all moved into position for the out-braking, and finished fourth, with a best lap only $^2/_{10}$ths slower than the winner. If this was mega progress, then

it somewhat floundered for the next few races as driver error saw me in the gravel trap at Brands, and mechanical failure prevented a start at Castle Combe.

It finally happened at Mallory in June. I led a national race, and I shall never forget the feeling inside as I saw Chris Tyrrell and Gary Hall take each other off and hand the lead to me. It was lap three of ten, and as we came over the line I was leading and aware that the whole crowd were looking my way. I felt an overwhelming responsibility, and spent the remaining laps looking in the mirror. I should have won that race, but inexperience caught me out and, while fumbling hopelessly for first gear at Shaws Hairpin, Peter Bonas swept by into the lead. I hounded him, but had no idea how to engineer a pass against someone who knew how to lead. Second was my reward, with fastest lap by some considerable margin.

These were joyous days and I really couldn't believe it was happening to me. Two weeks later we went down to Lydden, and I won. I can't recall a single detail of that day. Lydden races were Southern Championship events, and did not attract the 'big boys' so it was less exciting, but I reflect upon the trips down to Kent with collective affection. This was where I learned to race, to dice and, of course, to win. The venue still operates today, although I haven't raced there since the first 1000cc Mini Se7en race in 1991, when Tina Cooper beat me into second place. As I was carrying Number One for the first time, the moral of that story is that you should never get complacent.

On the '86 national scene real progress was made. The front-running pace was complemented by consistency, and at Thruxton I qualified on pole, ahead of Gary Hall and Chris Tyrrell. In the race these two got the jump on me, and tore away from the field taking me with them. Round Thruxton's flat out sweeps they travelled side by side, gesturing to each other through the side windows. I followed in wonderment. It was spoiled when Chris dropped out with a damaged valve, and I was left to watch a master at work. I still didn't know how to use my clear advantage, and never offered the stern challenge that my equipment should have allowed. I finished an elated second – now I was in the big time. On the podium after the race Gary told me to see him at the end of the year and he would tell me all about tactics! I held him to his word, and still call on him for occasional advice. That win had all but won Gary the championship, especially with the demise of Tyrrell, his only challenger.

The next race was at Brands Hatch, and on the night before, struggling with a clutch problem on Raph's car, I phoned Chris for some words of advice. It was late and I asked if he could spare me a few minutes. 'Sure, as long as you beat Gary Hall tomorrow,' was the reply. Delighted that a luminary like Tyrrell should speak to me on such terms, I told him that, of course, I would try. Well we got the clutch to work, and the following day an excellent race unfolded.

I qualified on pole again, and this time led to the first corner where Gary passed me on the outside and settled in the lead, Chris muscled by, too, and I settled down for a continuation of my education. It was a slip-streaming race, with the first dozen cars all in line, none able to pass. Then Tyrrell took the outside line through Druids and held on down Graham Hill bend. They clashed side by side at the bottom of the hill. Two hard-dicers, each refusing to give an inch; Gary came off worse with a trip across the grass. Chris gathered it all together and continued in the lead, whilst I grabbed second and Gary rejoined having lost several places. I followed hard, and was looking for a way by but couldn't find one.

My best memory is that Gary made quick work of fighting back, and was soon on my bumper. Whilst I couldn't attack, my application of the art of legitimate defending was improving, and he couldn't find a way by me. We stood on the podium together again. This time I think Tyrrell was more excited than I was, since the title would go down to the wire. Suddenly I was playing a major part.

The final national race was an anticlimax, the exact details of which I cannot recall. I finished fifth, whilst Chris beat Gary to both the chequered flag and the title. It had been some turn around, and was to be Gary's last season. He remains one of my great inspirations of those formative years. Tyrrell had regained the championship he last

BUILDING, PREPARING AND RACING YOUR MINI

won in 1974, having recovered from a huge Metro accident, and subsequent brain surgery. Chris became my close friend, helping, encouraging and inspiring me to greater heights.

There remained a few Southern Championship rounds and I was well in the hunt for the title. I did just enough to win and then wrote the car off at the last race when leading by a country mile. It should have been my first Brands Victory, but while lapping a Miglia back-marker we collided and that was it.

This had been a stunning season. Every race constituted a step forward, even the retirements were good, as the level of preparation required to be a front runner became apparent. I could now look forward knowing that I had won smaller races and run at the front of the big ones. I had already decided to build a new car for the next season, and at the end of season dinner-dance, true to his word, Gary Hall explained the finer points of tactical racecraft.

1987 – Mini Se7en: Almost there

Gerald Dale found me a good shell, and the build programme began in earnest. I can honestly say I built the entire car. I welded the rear wheel arches, made the airbox and wiring loom, and painted the finished car. It was all my own work, and it was state-of-the-art, although things have moved on dramatically since. On reflection, the stress of completing the whole thing left me grumpy towards the end, and at Cadwell for the first round of the National Championship I was pensive and nervous. A whole winter's effort would now be balanced on the edge that I was still new to. I finished seventh, pleased with the result and thrilled with the potential.

The race included a dig in the side from another competitor using strong-arm tactics to hold me back! I stayed there with my foot down, as he came across intimidatingly. I could have backed off and conceded the ground, but I wouldn't have done so in the old car, so I didn't in the new. It wasn't a conscious decision, just instinct, and ever since that moment I have never been afraid of racing a car no matter how immaculate or expensive it is. It was a pivotal event, and there followed four consecutive victories!

The first was not unexpected. Lydden was the venue and I was defending my Southern Championship. My recall of that event is nil, but the next one holds vivid memories. It was Castle Combe, with all the big boys again. I qualified sixth and raced with Chris Tyrrell, until he retired on the run down to Camp on lap six. That handed me the lead from Alan Jackson and Tina Cooper, and this time I held on until the chequered flag. I was punching the air inside the car, and struck myself a fair blow on the crash helmet. That taught me not to get over-excited, but to this day I haven't mastered it! On the slowing down lap, there stood Tyrrell, with his customary fag on, generously applauding.

Next was Lydden and another win, before Brands Hatch and the chance to race for the first time on the Grand Prix circuit. My favourite memory of this whole event was Peter Bonas cooking his oily clutch plate in a frying pan. The thing was, I led most of the race by a fair margin at times, but starting the final lap Peter was right there. Turning left at Surtees to join the GP loop, he disappeared from my mirror, his luck and his clutch plate ran out together! I won, he set the lap record, and once again dreams and reality seemed mixed!

The year unfolded with consistent front-running pace, and Chris Tyrrell building a decisive lead in the championship. I played catch-up for the latter part of the season, returning to winning form at Castle Combe. However, a couple of retirements had cost me dearly, and I wasn't in the running for the title. This was of little consequence for I had neither expected nor even considered it a possibility. Donington brought my first 'full house' – pole position, victory and lap record. It was unexpected, though the Derbyshire sweeps were superb and it remains one of my favourite places to race. The national final that year was at Mallory Park, and Tyrrell was already home and dry in the championship. I could overhaul Peter Bonas for the runner-up spot, and duly won the race, avenging the loss of a certain win in '86. It felt good. I would carry Number Two on the car for '88, and with Tyrrell stating his intention to join the Miglia ranks, a new champion would be crowned. I wanted badly to be that man.

1988 – Mini Se7en: Still the bridesmaid

In retrospect, this was to be the beginning of three difficult years, ones that tested my interest and resolve. Chris told me that he was moving up because he might not win Mini Se7en in '88, and Miglia was a better option than

being beaten in his own formula. He was a master driver and tactician. I don't think I ever really beat him, but we developed a strong friendship, and he helped me through all the trials and tribulations that make up a season of Mini racing.

So '88 was to be the year, and perhaps that billing was my downfall. It couldn't have started much better, with four wins from the first five, but from then on things soured, as they so often do in motor racing, whether it's Minis or Ferraris. I finished second four times, and third twice. There was also a retirement and, critically, a missed race when I could not get a day off work. I went to the final race needing a win, with Malcolm Joyce several places back. It didn't happen, and I was one mortified bloke!

After the race I shed a few tears; it was such a disappointment from a year that promised so much. I now think that deep down what hurt most was that only I was to blame – no-one took it away, I just lost a grip on it mid-season, and wasn't mentally equipped to reassert myself. Psychology is a com-

Castle Coombe, 4 April 1988 – leading on the first lap at Quarry. (Steve Jones)

BUILDING, PREPARING AND RACING YOUR MINI

plex subject, but it plays a huge part in motor racing, simply because the sport is so confrontational. I lacked the maturity, arrogance even, to maintain the pace and pressure over the course of a long season. Things had moved on and I had to come to terms with the changing circumstances.

I was coming away from a race having finished second, and was thoroughly fed up about it! The exciting days of stepping forward, learning and improving were over – now I was expected to produce results, every time. I'm glad to say that I came to terms with it, and made a point of playing the averages game, and being happy with consistent results. The next thing to consider was the following season. '89 was going to be a big year – I had to win it now, surely?

1989 – Mini Se7en: The machinery fights back

I decided that part of my losing to Malcolm Joyce was down to engines. I was self-building while Malcolm was a customer at Hass Motorsport, and they were operating on a higher plane – and for mega bucks! Hass was out of my league, and instead I went to Bryan Slark of SRE. I had always used Bryan's cylinder heads, and had good service from him. He was equipped with an engine dyno and had years of experience. So Bryan built an all-new engine, with a new head, and I collected it ready to fit. It was the days of *Aztec Camera* and *Prefab Sprout*, and those two albums instantly recall driving to Bryan's, usually late, delivering parts and finally collecting the finished item. I was over the grief of '88 and ready for more punishment!

It turned out to be a similar start to the previous year. A last lap retirement at Brands with a thrown fan belt handed victory to Steve Cooper, but from there I won the next four, Castle Combe on the Easter Bank Holiday Monday

being particularly significant for personal reasons. By the time we got to Silverstone on the new national circuit in May, I was leading the championship, and qualified on pole by over a second. Things were going well and I was relaxed. It all came to a shuddering halt in the race when an ambitious overtaking move from behind me resulted in myself, Steve Cooper and Dick Grimwood all leaving the track. I sustained a hefty blow in the side from Steve, who had been in heavy contact with Dick. It was a real mess, and as the dust settled I rejoined, wounded, along with Dick. Steve was left with a wheel hanging off, and went no further. Now with half a yard of toe-out on the rear the handling was quirky to say the least. I clawed my way up to sixth and left the circuit that night with major body repairs to make, and thinking that was the extent of my troubles.

Gerald Dale repaired the side of the car, and made quick work of it to allow me the time to have the whole thing right for Thruxton. This done, I arrived at the Hampshire track anxious to get the challenge back on course. Well it wasn't to be. Perhaps I should have taken the hint when I was given an entry as ninth reserve! It was a combined race for Se7ens and Miglias and I figured my chances of racing to be close to nil. Determined to race I set about trying to buy another competitor's entry, and was rescued by Nigel Muskett, a Mini Se7en regular who gave me his place. It was a generous gesture, and one which I failed to capitalise on. On the first lap of practice the crankshaft broke, causing – as always – extensive damage in the process. I loaded up the car and headed for home. I am sure the failure was a legacy of the Silverstone fracas.

The next race was six weeks away, and that period would be sufficient to get the engine back to Bryan for a complete rebuild. I obtained a new 850

Castle Coombe again, 27 March 1989 and leading Grimwood Cooper to victory. (Mary Harvey)

crankshaft from Mini Spares, and expected this to herald a return to the early season form. The championship then comprised fifteen rounds, with the driver's best ten results counting for the final standings. Though I already had three weak scores in my hand, it should not have been a problem to re-establish an attack. The remainder of the year was an unmitigated disaster. Only at Brands did I figure at all, and that was having thrown the best of my old bits together for a mule engine. The next best result was eighth, and in the end I gave up and missed the penultimate round at Pembrey. My final position was fourth, and it could have been the end of my racing days. I wasn't downcast, however. Unlike the bitter disappointment of '88, this was a mechanical not emotional failure and I set about regrouping for the new decade.

1990 – Mini Se7en: Champion at last!

I was surrounded by bits, but using the best of the old and some new components I had two engines ready before the first race. This was unprecedented, and I set off for Cambridge and Peter

Baldwin's rolling road. Motor racing is nothing if not surprising, and I came back down the M11 with just the one engine, the spare had expired spectacularly whilst pulling 7,000 rpm in top gear! Peter was swinging the distributor in when the blow-up occurred, and I saw him leap backwards as he disappeared in a cloud of white smoke. The crankshaft had broken, allowing a now less restrained piston to hit the head and shatter. The small end of the rod made short work of junking the bore and then part of an escaped gudgeon pin was fired out the back of the gearbox, emptying the oil on to the exhaust and producing a huge white cloud. All very spectacular and, as it turned out, the beginning of a theme that lasted the season!

Each meeting heralded promise, but the early races offered nothing but failure. We opened at Brands, and I led for nine and a half laps before parking up on Cooper Straight on the last lap. The water temperature had got higher and higher throughout the race, and I stopped as the motor began to tighten. No points! At the next round, Thruxton, I led comfortably again until a heavy misfire intervened near the end, and Eian Riddiford swept ahead. I coaxed it to the line in second place thankful of some points. Next we drove all the way to Pembrey in deepest South Wales. I liked the circuit but retired mid-race when the bottom pulley fell off! I gave my chief mechanic (me) a lengthy bollocking.

So next we went to Castle Combe, another favoured circuit, and I stuck it on pole (as they say). The race was going well until I was launched into the scenery by a colleague attempting an ambitious overtaking manoeuvre. With friends like that …

Damage to the car was extensive, but I was fine, and once again I headed for home empty-handed. The cost of professional repair was more than I had available to spend. So, encouraged by Tim Sims, I purchased a Portapower kit, and with Tim's help set about pushing out the crumpled floor. Using little more than common sense, hammers and the hydraulic jacking kit we pushed and pulled, and the car resumed a normal shape with relative ease. I had no option but to miss the Donington Park round that followed a week later, but we were ready for Silverstone in June. I had finished just one of the first five races, and things were not looking good. Graham Penn led the championship having won the last three in a row, while I languished in a lowly tenth place.

Graham added a fourth straight win at Silverstone but I was second with a new lap record, confirming for me that our amateur efforts at crash repairs had been successful. A week later I won at Mallory, with Graham second. Next stop was Cadwell Park in Lincolnshire. This was Penn country, and I had to start beating him soon if I was to stand any chance. He took the pole and looked confident. We began the race with my nose to his tail until I was caught out by an abandoned sump of oil on the entry to the Gooseneck. I had a huge sideways moment, lasting all the way down the hill into Mansfield corner! It was a heart-stopper, but I gathered it up to resume in second place but with the pack all over my rear bumper, and Graham now literally out of sight.

This became an inspired drive for me, one that I readily recall with clarity. I shook-off the squabbling pack and began a relentless chase. He came into sight and the gap narrowed and narrowed until on the last lap I was close enough to challenge. Finding a way by would be another thing altogether, and so it proved. My only hope was to chase a mistake out of my prey, and it came on the mountain when Graham's car jumped out of gear, and I tapped the back of him. It wasn't hard enough to damage his car or his control of it, but it broke my oil filter housing, and cut the ignition dead. I coasted to a halt two corners from the finish, whilst Graham notched another victory. Things were desperate. I had three scores from the first eight races, and would need top-three placings at all remaining races to have even a chance of the title. This was the last year of 850cc Mini Se7en, and my chance of the championship seemed to be escaping.

If the front of my car was dented, my own resolve was not, and we reconvened at Brands Hatch, my home track. I equalled the lap record for pole position, a second clear of Eian Riddiford. There was no doubting the pace, just the reliability. I won the race, which was a relief, but the most significant fact was that Graham was pushed down to fourth by Neil Johnson and Dick Grimwood. This was what I needed.

Snetterton was next – not my favourite venue, for the corners are less challenging and the straights are boring. However, it rained for practice, heightening the odds. It was a disaster;

we bunched and mistakes were plentiful. I was trying not to take any risks, and my actions had the opposite effect. In a misunderstanding, my good friend Guy Sims hit the offside rear corner and spun me into the gravel at Russell. I was mortified and climbed from the car feeling that my season was over. I expected the damage to be extensive, preventing me from taking any further part in the meeting. The session was red-flagged and my car was pulled from the gravel. Incredibly the damage was superficial, and I was rescued from my worst nightmare! I had even qualified third despite missing the restarted section of practice. Guy was on the front row – bless him! I won the race and Graham was second, so we would be at Silverstone next, Graham leading the championship with 80 points from Neil Johnson on 71 and me next on 52. The maths said it was possible, but I was coming from a long way back.

Silverstone marked the return of Michael Jackson to Mini Se7en with a brand new car. I hoped that he would increase competition at the front. He duly did. Eian Riddiford was on pole, his knowledge as a Silverstone instructor used to good effect. Graham was next, then Michael and myself. This had the makings of a close race but the field actually got a bit strung out, and it was a straight fight between Mike and I. He took a debut victory for the new car and I lowered my own lap record but Graham finished only ninth! Things were hotting up just a touch!

The next race was at Oulton Park, and I will always recall this as the day that made the year. I had already replaced one cracked crank, and during the race in Cheshire the engine began to display the roughness that indicated the crank was in trouble. The race had settled down with Johnson and Jackson disputing the lead. I was close behind, with Graham Penn some way back in fourth place. I cut the revs, short changing everywhere, and survived in third place by $^2/_{10}$ths of a second. Once back in the workshop the engine was stripped, and the crank subjected to my usual crack testing. Suspended at the primary gear ring on the nose of the crank, between thumb and forefinger, the crank is struck lightly with a ball hammer. A good one rings like a bell, and holds the note for some time. A cracked crank has a dead note that doesn't ring and the Oulton Park example was as bad as I have heard. It was consigned to the bin.

Seven days later we were back in action at Castle Combe, a circuit where there is no substitute for horsepower. The engine was rebuilt with another crank, and qualifying was excellent. I was on pole by over a second, and feeling confident. Graham Penn was fourth on the grid, and although I was still 16 points back in the championship race, the dropped scores element meant that my position was becoming stronger with each race I finished. I don't think that either Graham or Neil Johnson really understood that at this stage. In the race I couldn't repeat the pace of the morning qualify-ing, having to drive a tactical race. I still won, with Eian Riddiford following me home in second place with a new lap record.

Two rounds left, the gap was down to ten points and the next race was at Brands Hatch where we were part of the Cellnet Superprix. It was home soil for me, and a tense race gave me victory over Michael Jackson, now well and truly on the pace in his new car. I was ecstatic, at last the waiting was over, and only a single race remained. Snetterton was the venue, and all the mathematics could be worked out. I stood a single point behind in the Mini Se7en title chase, but would only drop a single point. This meant that a sixth place finish would do it for me. Intriguingly, if I finished second I could win the prize Mini which had looked all year to be going the way of Owen Hall in Mini Miglia.

I don't recall any pre-race nerves, but the car was subjected to a thorough round of preventative maintenance.

… and the first of the following season in the new 1000cc National Mini Se7en Challenge formula. Here, I am getting the jump on the pole position man, before … (John L.E. Gaisford)

Everything that had ever let me down was scrutinised. Qualifying was a tense affair. The race was for Mini Se7en and Miglia mixed together, and I was cautious with the slower Miglias which were easy meat through the corners but came roaring back down the straights. I was the third fastest Se7en in the middle of the mixed grid, and things were looking good. I can recall this race as well as any I have contested. Once the first few laps were done and things settled down it was a three way scrap between Mike Jackson, Neil Johnson and me. I could have sat there in third place and that would have won the championship. Part of me wanted to do that, but the more dominant part continued to race and I held second com-

fortably, knowing this was good for the prize Mini. On the last lap we ran flat out as usual down the Rivett Straight. I was in Mike's tow, and pulled out into the breeze to attack on the outside. I drew level and slightly ahead as we entered the braking area. Here I was vulnerable, and for a moment I knew I was risking everything needlessly. Truth is, I put myself where I had to be to win, but only in the knowledge that Mike Jackson was someone I could trust not to turf me off. He didn't and I led the three-car train home.

Crossing the line, my emotions were a mixture of joy and relief. Six seasons had taken me from novice to champion, and I honestly felt that I had achieved everything I had ever desired in motorsport. Back in the paddock I shook up a bottle of bubbly, overwhelmed by all the congratulations from rivals and competitors, some of whom I hardly knew. Spare a thought though for Graham Penn. He had led for the lion's share of the season, and had it snatched at the end. I knew well the feelings he experienced.

1991 – Mini Se7en (1000cc): New formula – same champion

One thing was clear, Mini Se7en was to become a 1000cc formula for '91. The engine spec had been developed on a dyno, tested in a car, and now everyone would be building a new motor for the next season. This gave me the perfect follow up to my 850cc Championship, and I would carry Number One on the car. The days of fragile 850 cranks were at an end, and I for one wasn't sorry!

These were momentous days for the Mini Challenges. The introduction of the Rover 216GTi Championship with full factory backing saw the creation of Rover Sport to oversee the running of the series. The Metro Challenge and the Minis came under the family wing, and this meant big changes in status, whilst the Mini Se7en Racing club still maintained control of its championships. It was a marriage made in heaven, and the British Racing Drivers Club assumed responsibility for organisation of the championship calendar. Gone were combined races, suddenly we were at the best venues with the big meetings. We had Formula 3 and British Touring Cars to support us!

The winter preparations concentrated solely on the new engine build. I remained satisfied that the chassis could do the job, despite its somewhat advancing years. The new engine ran on Peter Baldwin's rolling road in Cambridge, it was the only visit for the whole year, and if 82bhp peak wasn't spectacular, then the spread of power was.

Having won the last National 850 race I was super motivated to win the first National 1000cc event. Further to that I was carrying Number One and it felt good. The race took place at Mallory Park which isn't one of my favourite circuits. A defensive race leader here can be difficult to dislodge, since real overtaking opportunities occur only when a mistake is made. It turned out that I was that defensive leader. Kelly Rogers had qualified on pole, but I got the jump at the lights, defended the lead robustly and duly won the race. Fairy-tale stuff, but it was clear that the Rogers car, built and run by Peter Vickers had an advantage that would make it even harder to beat at some of the other circuits.

Next we moved to Brands, my home track, where I took pole position and won the race. It was controlled stuff, and I was certainly on a roll. What was already clear was that the change of engine had not affected the popularity of the formula. The club had expected a steady start, with grids smaller than the 850 days. The first two races had filled the grids and disappointed some reserve entries! The Rover Sport association certainly was helping, and already it was safe to declare the package of changes a huge success.

Round three was at Brands, too, but before then I fulfilled a promise to Ben Edwards which was to change my Mini career dramatically. Ben was a good friend, and had raced on the international stage. He was a some time contributor to *Cars and Car Conversions* magazine, and fancied a drive in the Mini reckoning that the magazine would run a feature on it. So on a damp day at Brands he did a dozen laps or so with Norman Hodson taking the snaps. I didn't think a great deal about it. Truth is, nobody had driven my car before, and I only let Ben do it because I trusted him. I didn't for one minute imagine what this would lead to over the next twelve months. I concentrated on the season, and went back to Brands Hatch, super confident.

Motor racing has a habit of pricking bubbles, however, and as a reminder of this I qualified eighth! Things didn't improve in the race, and eventually I retired with drop gear failure, brought about by disintegration of the idler gear bearing in the gearbox case. I wasn't sure why we were off the pace for the weekend, and at Castle Combe for round four I again qualified a second off the pace, this time in fourth place. The race was the usual slip-streaming humdinger, and I won by the scant margin of 0.35 seconds! It put the challenge back on track, and we headed next for Lincolnshire and Cadwell Park, one of the most exquisite venues in the country. Built originally as a motorcycle track it is narrow and twisty with little run off area, and not a single gravel trap! Racing there has been described as 'a thrash down country lanes' and this is entirely accurate. Qualifying went well, resulting in pole position, with Eian Riddiford next up and starting to mount a serious challenge for the championship.

The race was wet, and I was not on the pace. Phil Manser and Riddiford escaped, with Eian getting the result. Neil Johnson was quicker than me, too, and fourth was the best I was going to get for the long trip north. I was two seconds off the wet pace, and back in the workshop we sought reasons why. I checked the suspension set-up thoroughly, made some minor revisions and headed for Silverstone hopeful of a return to form.

This was Eian Riddiford's home circuit, and he was an instructor there, too. He also led the championship by two points, and duly stuck it on pole. I was almost two seconds slower in eighth place and puzzled – to say the least. In the race it rained again, and

although I got to fourth, that was as far as it went. Again we weren't on the pace, and answers were needed urgently if we were to stay in contention. There was one thing super clear, however – the grids were now burgeoning, with reserves at most rounds, and even the odd qualification race being staged where possible.

Back in the workshop, and thoroughly dried out, we reached a conclusion on our poor wet pace. There was one simple factor, our wet tyres (Dunlop CR65s) were old and hard, and having completed a full check of the set-up, we were sure that new rubber would put us back on the wet pace. I bought two new CR65s for the front, and ironically we never used them!

We were back on form at Donington, another of my favourite tracks. Qualifying was conclusive – we were quickest, and it was repeatable. The race was really exciting; from a good start I led well until on lap three at Coppice the car cut dead, six Se7ens streamed past as I cursed my luck! As a last dying hope I flicked the ignition switch off and back on again, and, hey presto, we were running again. I was some way back now but there was time and I relished the challenge. I quickly caught the bunch, and began to pick my way through. The car never missed another beat, and I homed in on Paul Brown who was clear in the lead. I could almost see him looking at me in his mirror, and certainly he expected me to pass him! I did, and won the race with a lap record too. This was the turning point in the season for me, I was now leading the championship, and had a non-finish score to drop included in that. I did feel for Paul who looked a winner that day, but ended up second. There were five races left, and seven days later it was back to Silverstone.

The championship was now pretty much a two-horse race, between Eian

Riddiford and myself. Eian used his circuit familiarity well to secure pole, and once again I couldn't approach that pace, qualifying fifth. Once the race got underway, however, that counted for little, as a mass brawl for the lead developed. Through it all came Dave Braggins for his maiden win. A string of fastest laps had at last been topped by the big result. I was probably equally delighted with my second place just ahead of Eian to extend the championship lead.

After a five week break, and some exhaustive maintenance we returned to Castle Combe, and I was quickest in practice. The championship was getting closer. In the race Braggins did it again with his second win in as many races. I followed him with Eian in my wheel tracks. The next race could be the one to decide the final destiny of the championship. It was back at Silverstone, and Eian Riddiford had an all-new engine in an effort to boost his challenge.

We both went well in qualifying, and took front row grid slots, but at last I had overturned the territorial advantage to nick pole whilst Eian settled for third. In a Mini race the pole counts only for prestige, the nature of the races is that anybody from the first ten could easily lead at the end of the first lap, so I was concentrating my thoughts on a good race strategy. Whilst I was thinking, frenzied activity was underway in the Riddiford camp. The new engine was being hauled out to make way for the original unit which was complete, and carried as a spare. They were very pushed for time, and as we drove to the assembly area they were still working. Eian did take his position on the front row, and started the race. However, on the first lap he was out with loss of drive, and it really began to swing my way. I won the race, and with two rounds remaining a single sixth place would seal it for me!

I returned to Snetterton for the first time since my championship victory in 1990, with a simple-looking task to make it back-to-back titles. Again my practice pace was not up to much, fifth place being the result. Eian was fired up, knowing he needed to win both remaining races to have any chance at all, and from the front row that was what he did. I was next, winning the championship and another prize Mini Cooper, with one race still to go. Eian and I shook hands in the pit road shortly before the race commentator, none other than Ben Edwards, conducted the post-race interviews. Eian told his tale, and then Ben asked me about the race, the years and another championship. He was, of course, well on the case with my own situation and he asked me what I would be doing next. Until that precise moment I had given it not a single thought. I replied by saying I would be in Mini Miglia next year! It was a shock to me if no one else, but I felt it the only thing to do. Mini Se7en had been everything I had ever wanted in motor sport, but I could have out-stayed my welcome with another title defence, and perhaps a fresh challenge would be interesting.

There was the matter of the final round of the Mini Se7en National Championship at Donington, supporting the British Touring Car Championship. It was a casual affair, I didn't enjoy having nothing to play for and the crank exploded as I launched from the start line!

The big news was that following the Snetterton interview with Ben, *Autosport* had included a news snippet in their columns outlining my plans for 1992. Not special in itself, but it prompted Nigel Fryatt, Editor of *Cars and Car Conversions*, to ring me. The Ben Edwards feature on my Mini Se7en car had been included in the first issue of *Mini World* – published as a one-off by the staff of *CCC*. Nigel explained that

Mini World had been so successful that the magazine was going to do another, but that it was very keen to make clear to the readers of *CCC* that Minis would still feature in their favourite monthly read. Nigel invited me to his office to discuss this matter, and shortly afterwards offered me sponsorship for my first season of Mini Miglia. Was I pleased? – Is the Pope Catholic?

And that was the end of the first chapter of my race career. It had been a journey through uncharted territory, bringing success beyond my wildest dreams, a full understanding of race engineering and its application, and a lifestyle of continual pressure and effort that was exceedingly rewarding.

Intent on racing a Mini Miglia, I began with relish the task of identifying the most economical way of equipping myself with the most competitive machinery possible. Converting the Mini Se7en was never an option, for in its five seasons it had worked hard, and been crashed a few times. Also, things had moved on and weld-in cages were appearing. I had a modest amount of savings that I was prepared to invest, and also the proceeds from two championships!

I offered the Se7en for sale, and quickly a deal was struck, but before that there was a last outing for the car. I had promised Bob Cooper, my perennial helper, a race, and now was the perfect opportunity. He bought himself a licence and we headed for a test day at Snetterton. Bob displayed the nervousness that I could recall so vividly from my own first test session, and I felt fully qualified to help and direct him. The first few laps were slow, and on about the fifth he was well overdue. He finally appeared – much to my relief – but with wheels full of mud after a big spin into a field. Bob looked physically sick as he explained that he didn't really fancy racing after all! I got him back

into the car and he began to enjoy it before we left.

Bob's race was to be a winter round at Brands, but it turned out to be a letdown. He qualified, albeit close to the back, but we had to withdraw the car because of low oil pressure which we diagnosed as a shell bearing failure. Bob was disappointed (although not too much!), while his mother was thoroughly relieved, and smiled for the first time that day! So Bob's race never was, and he's turned down numerous offers since. I was quietly pleased, since I was not going to lose my valued mechanic to the racetrack where he would have become a rival!

The Se7en was bought by Orbix Motorsport, and was fully rebuilt by one of the company's employees, Danny Boulton – who went on to race the car several times before it was sold to Japan. Imagine my amazement when I parked right next to it five years later at Tskuba circuit just outside Tokyo, when Emma (my wife) and I were there for a Sanwa Trading track day as personal guests of Nori Yamagata and his wife.

Getting back to the quest for a Miglia, I looked at what was available on the second-hand market. By far the best was that belonging to Gerald Dale, who had been helpful to me as a Mini Se7en novice. This car was originally built by Brian Walsh for Danny Allpress, who won a few national races in it. Gerald had acquired the car and run it for a season, maintaining it to the highest standards. It had a Hass Motorsport engine and dog box with a Zytek programmable ignition system, the latest Spectrum wheels, plenty of spares and an excellent Cannon trailer. It lacked only the weld-in cage, but Peter Vickers stood ready and waiting to help, and the car was soon mine.

I raced it twice in the '91 Winter Series at Brands Hatch, exactly as Gerald sold me the car. It performed superbly, and I won first time out against an admittedly less than strong field. My lap times indicated that I was right on front-running National pace. For my second outing I was delighted to see that Ian Gunn had also entered. As an established front runner he would give me a real idea of my standing. He beat me into second place, but I was delighted, for until I got stuck in the reverse gate going from 2nd to 3rd I had held a good lead. I took the car home completely unmarked, planning an extensive strip and rebuild, with Peter lined up to multipoint the cage and repaint the shell.

I had one last race in '91 at the wheel of a Se7en owned by Steve Bell and Mickey Bray, who had shared the car for their first season and wanted an idea of its competitiveness. The car wasn't the best ever, but I won, beating Kelly Rogers by the smallest margin, exploiting my intimate knowledge of Brands and the confidence that comes with winning regularly. I haven't raced a Se7en since – but never say never.

1992 – Mini Miglia: the same but different

We were ready early for the start of the '92 season. Nothing had been left to chance. Every part of the car had been rebuilt, and Peter Vickers had contributed massively. The car was now red, white and black in deference to *CCC*, and these were confirmed as my racing colours. Fortune also smiled on us, as the National Championship kicked off at Brands. We tested there first with an all-new suspension set-up based on the Se7en. It was superb, and I was $^{2}/_{10}$ths under the lap record, and feeling there was more to come! Peter was there, and his enthusiasm and pride overflowed. I was riding the crest of a wave into the first race.

The heavens opened before the start of practice, and we bolted on the wets and made the suspension adjust-

Leading on the first lap at Cascades, Oulton Park, 1992, followed by Wager (going off), Cable, Allen etc. (Steve Jones)

ments that Gerald had advised. Bob treated the screen to ensure it didn't mist up – always a big worry. Visibility didn't fail us, but the gearbox did! The wet session went well. I was determined not to fall off, and approached with caution. As my confidence increased, so did the pace. At no stage did I consider taking any risks, so there was only the thought of the missing first and second gears on my mind as I drove back to the paddock.

The diagnosis was a simple one. Everything at the gear lever end felt right, but apparent engagement of 1st and 2nd brought us no motion. These were the days of remote change casings, and beyond any doubt the bolt securing the 1st/2nd selector fork to its rod had dropped out. In the wet conditions, using 3rd to exit Druids had probably helped with the traction, but for the race – with its standing start and likely dry track – repairs would be necessary to permit our further participation that day. We were unbolting the engine when the time-sheets were issued. Pole position was mine! – but we could afford little time to celebrate.

Word went round the paddock and, as well as receiving congratulations, help was at hand if we needed it. It was a one-day meeting so we had about three hours. With the engine out and oil drained, Gerald advised us that the offending bolt could be retightened easily if we removed the diff assembly to provide access. We discovered that the bolt had fallen out altogether, but Gerald again stepped in and fished it out with a magnetic probe! In no time the complete unit was back in the car, and slicks were fitted with time to spare before we were called to the assembly area.

I can remember clearly that I didn't expect to lead at the end of the first lap. I was intent on a good finish more than anything. I must say that I was disappointed to be in fifth place at the end of the first tour! However, I was confident and driving well. I passed Richard Wager on the brakes into Paddock, having dummied up the outside then switched inside. I was having the drive of my life. Passing didn't seem difficult until I came to Myk Cable, the reigning Miglia champion. He despatched me ruthlessly on to the grass on the way into Druids, and I was left to gather it all up and consider an alternative approach. I was soon back on Cable's boot lid, and he was living up to his reputation as a hard and determined racer. My chance arrived when Myk and I came upon a back-marker into Graham Hill Bend. Cable saw it late and had to lift, while I was one step ahead and altered line sufficiently early not to have to back off. I was closing on the leader rapidly and momentarily went for the inside. Seeing that this was too easy for Cable to defend, I switched outside and was soon level as we approached Surtees. My position on the outside looked untenable, and as I was considering how best to minimise the effects of the impending crash, all my prayers were answered at once. Cable lifted, instantly giving me a car length, and I turned in and scrabbled round on the dirty bits to emerge in the lead as we turned into Clearways. Cable promptly drove straight through the Clearways gravel trap, and emerged to finish fifth. I proceeded to the chequered flag and victory! With it came the fastest lap of the race, and although I didn't know it at the time, the passing move at Surtees had been noted by the discerning BRSCC marshals who award their Post 2 trophy annually to 'The most entertaining driver of the year at Brands Hatch'.

It was going too well, and I knew that harder times would be ahead. Round 2 was at Donington Park, one of my favourite tracks. I qualified second fastest to Cable despite never escaping the traffic. The race was hectic. A misfire affected my first lap and I dropped to fifth, then I went off at the exit of Redgate starting the second lap, and fell to seventh. In the process the left rear wheel took on a whole load of toe-out, making the car an oversteerer, to say the least! I fought back to fourth, and then half spun at the Old Hairpin trying to fight the back end! I was pleased to see the chequered flag that day, and fourth place was a major bonus from a day that could easily have yielded nothing. So, then, the championship lead, and off to Snetterton for Round 3.

The fantastic good fortune ground to a halt at this meeting. Three laps into qualifying, the cam sprocket fell to bits with dire sounding consequences. It turned out to be a lucky escape, with only bent pushrods to be replaced. This was achieved before the start of the race, but at eleventh on the grid I was, for the first time, truly in the middle of the field – which happened to be where my race finished, at the first corner!

I probably hadn't warmed the rear tyres sufficiently on the green flag lap, because when a car ahead slewed sideways in the first corner sort-out I was obliged to lift. Already steering towards the first apex, the car snapped sideways, and I was still on the power with full opposite lock as I took an exit stage right. The infield at Riches is a farmer's field, and the crop was several feet high. The car was effectively ramped into the air, and I can recall to this day the sensation as first it all went quiet, then, still flying, the car was upside down

Being followed into the first corner at Brands on 19 July 1992 by Myk Cable, who at the end of the season secured the championship. Gearbox problems had put paid to my chances. (Steve Jones)

and only the belts were holding me in! There was a huge crash as it hit the ground upside down, and then further silence as the car bounced and righted itself before landing heavily on its wheels. That final touch-down winded me badly, and I couldn't catch my breath as I climbed from the car and instinctively stepped away from it. Marshals were running towards me from all sides, and I just managed to utter the phrase 'I'm all right' as I struggled to draw breath. In a matter of moments I had recovered and was able to survey the damage. It was a remarkable escape, the roof was heavily dented, and the rear suspension was showing large amounts of toe out, but other than that there appeared to be little amiss.

Peter Allen won the race, and my championship lead was gone, but Peter Vickers was my saviour of the day!

We loaded the car on to the trailer, and Peter towed it straight back to his workshop. By the following morning the roof was cut off, and I arrived with a roof skin from Mini Spares to find Peter, tools in hand ready to press on! On Thursday *Autosport* was published, and with our race report there was a picture of my car post-accident. It was up to the roof in corn, and I was standing beside it. The camera had caught me as I pushed my fingers through my hair having removed my helmet, and it looked just as though I was holding my head in my hands! The caption read 'Mini Miglia man Bill Sollis

My points tally in 1992 wasn't helped by my losing it at Riches and attempting to make a corn circle in the infield on the first lap of the May meeting at Snetterton. (Courtesy Autosport)

BUILDING, PREPARING AND RACING YOUR MINI

can't believe his crop damage bill.' A good line, I thought. Further, to prove that there are viewing public, some weeks later I received a video via *CCC*. It had been sent in by a reader, and was footage of the crash. Great effort had gone into a coloured sleeve showing my car, and the title on the spine was 'Bill's Spill'.

Ten days later, Bob and I set off early for Cadwell Park. Set in rolling Lincolnshire countryside, this is a fantastic race track, and one at which I had enjoyed good fortune in the past. The Mini Se7en lap records for 850cc and 1000cc stood to me, and I needed to bounce (pun intended) back from the shunt at Snet. We did fourteen laps – that was all it took. I was feeling confident, the car felt perfect and we were quick – close to the long-standing lap record. In the afternoon I did a few laps in Mike Standring's car. I was pleased to be asked and to be able to help Mike, and he was subsequently quicker.

There remained only the long drive home, but the van, my faithful Volkswagen, had been reluctant to make it to the circuit that morning and it was requiring some attention before we could leave. On top of that I had a monster headache, so, although relieved at the results on the track, I was burdened with mundane difficulties. In stepped Steve Bell, and after a few minutes of explanation he reached a diagnosis and slid under the van. The inline fuel filter was under suspicion, and it proved to be the problem. It took Steve less than 20 minutes to have us on our way, and Bob drove the full distance home with me sleeping off the headache!

The meeting at Cadwell was excellent. I qualified on pole $^6/_{10}$ths clear of the field and under the lap record! The race was a tactical battle which I never looked like winning. Richard Wager did the honours, followed by Myk Cable. I was delighted to be third, back in the

hunt, free of drama and with a new lap record too!

Silverstone was next – and another lesson. This time I was well off the pace in qualifying. I couldn't put the car where I wanted it at all, and eighth on the grid was the result. We went all over the suspension, but nothing seemed wrong, so it was almost as a guess that we put two new tyres on the front in the hope that it would help. It certainly did. The car was transformed, pin-point accuracy was back, and fourth seemed a decent result. One thing was clear, though. To beat the top men – Cable, Wager, Allen and co – I needed to be more than just quick. Tactics were winning the races, and a cool, forward-thinking head was needed. There was learning to be done, because these cars were so quick that instinct was often the deciding factor. I needed to sharpen up and become a bit harder! These were fun days, though. I was loving every minute of it, and exceeding the expectations of those around me. There was no pressure!

Next stop was Oulton Park, and again we tested. Valuable it proved as I qualified second to Cable, on the front row. At last I started a race well and led the first lap. On the second the clutch disappeared completely and I struggled on beasting the gearbox. I dropped to second, then third, but held on to the finish. I was promoted to second since Peter Allen was penalised for missing the chicane, and we left the circuit happy. Cable was building a good championship lead – but that mattered little to me.

The next two races followed a familiar pattern. We were right on the pace, but so was Cable, and at Castle Combe and Brands Hatch he led me home. If Cable was looking good to retain the title, I was becoming the closest challenger. Next we went back to Snetterton, scene of earlier disasters. This time it went well. I was on pole, under the lap record and Cable completed only a single lap of practice, failing to qualify and taking no further part in the meeting! The race, filmed by Anglia TV with on board footage from my car, was given excellent terrestrial TV coverage. It was an epic: only Len Brammer and I were in contention but there were a couple of passing moves on each lap. Len had huge experience to draw on, having won both the Se7en and Miglia titles, and is as hard as they come. I raced fair with him, and he with me, as we both examined the weaknesses in each other that could be exploited to gain victory. I was in second place starting the last lap. This was where I wanted to be, and intended to attack out of the tow down the back straight. Len defended it with maximum aggression, for he too was intent on the win, and I had to cede at the Esses. There was only the Russell Chicane left as an opportunity, but here it would be difficult and with high risk. Brammer covered the inside as I expected and compromised his speed as a result. I lunged to the outside as we neared the braking area, and to my amazement Len was on the anchors early. Instantly a car length up I turned in, for a millisecond I had the race won, until Len locked up his brakes and shot straight on across the front of me, through the gravel trap only to emerge the other side, gather it all up and lead me over the finish line. I half expected him to be penalized, and if I were a harder-headed guy perhaps I would have protested. The truth is, I didn't think it a deliberate ploy, I had enjoyed a superb fair scrap and was unwilling to end the day in the Steward's room.

Leaving Snet, I was tied on points with Cable and one behind Peter Allen who would lose out on dropped scores, so I had a very real chance of championship success at the first attempt. The next meet was Mallory Park, and crucially Cable returned to form. He took

pole and I joined him on the front row less than $\frac{1}{10}$th behind. The race followed the pattern of many before. Cable won, Richard Wager was second and I finished third. Again I took fastest lap – there was little doubt that mine was the quickest car/driver package, but I lacked the tactical thinking and ultra hard edge I saw in Cable. Let's not forget, though, I was having the time of my life, riding the wave and enjoying it all – exciting times.

The penultimate National round was at Silverstone, and a Cable victory would seal the championship a race early. I had an inspired weekend. From fourth on the grid I led by lap three with Cable, Brammer and Wager scrapping behind. It was fraught, but I was not displaced and the victory laurels were backed up by those for the Crompton Lighting Driver of the Day! Even better news was that Brammer had won the scrap for second, pushing Cable down to third. That put us level on points, but Myk had less to drop than me, so the maths was simple. I had to win at Donington and have Cable finish third or less. A repeat of the Silverstone result would do it!

I thought hard over every component that had ever let me down, and redoubled my pre-race weekend preparation programme. I towed the car into the Donington paddock confident that it could do the job. But could I? Maybe nerves got the better of me in qualifying, I managed only one proper lap, and that for fifth on the grid, the outside of the second row. Cable's teammate Steve Young was on pole, with Myk alongside, and I suppose I began to dismiss my chances.

As the lights switched to green I got a perfect start. There was no wheel spin, no bog down, just perfect traction. Instinctively I was looking to get inside the car on the outside of the front row, but suddenly aware that the start was good enough, I switched to the outside of the whole front row, passed them all and led out of the first corner! It was a magic moment, and proof to myself and others that I had the 'bottle' for the job. I led for two laps. Cable was in third place behind a resolute Ian Gunn, and I was in position to win the title! It didn't last long. On the exit of Coppice I went to change from 2nd to 3rd as usual, except that 3rd gear was having none of it. Three attempts finally got the gear in but I was already down to fifth. Fighting on I got to the Melbourne loop, where once again the upchange from 2nd wouldn't go in. This time I was hit by Owen Hall and half spun. I completed the lap in 13th place and pitted next time round. This first season of Miglia was finished, just like the 3rd/4th gear selector fork! This was no time for sadness, however, the season had exceeded my wildest dreams and, with Peter Vickers behind me and itching to build a new car for '93, I was looking only forward.

There was more to '92 than just the Miglia stuff. The relationship with *Cars and Car Conversions* magazine had started wonderfully. I had written a fair amount for the magazine, and even been asked to test drive some readers' cars and write up my findings. My publicity rating had soared, and with it came an invitation from Duncan Heard to share his FIA European Historic Touring Car Championship attack. Duncan had prepared his own car, a '65 Cooper S. The races were hour-duration with a driver change, and it was me who got the call totally out of the blue. We raced at Silverstone first, in the Christie's Meeting, which would later become the Coys Historic Festival. Finding our way through the new procedures that accompanied international racing, I thought we did a good job. From the middle of a very mixed grid we lasted the duration, fighting high water temperature throughout, and I snatched second in class on the last lap.

Some hours later we were excluded for minor technical infringements: under weight and too much valve lift, but that failed to cloud an interesting new avenue.

Three weeks later I raced abroad for the first time. Sharing the S again with Duncan, Bob and I drove through the night to the Nürburgring in Germany for the 'Old Timer Grand Prix'. This was another huge Historic festival, and to me an eye-opener to the huge new world open to Mini competitors that I had not known existed. It was another memorable weekend. We qualified fifth, and Duncan started the race. He handed over to me from eighth twenty minutes later, and I began a charge, settling into the rhythm, enjoying the car and the track. Bob was showing me position and the gap to the next car, and relentlessly we clawed our way forward. There was a growing group on the pit wall now, and with five laps to go I was P3 and +6 seconds. The chase was on. Without doubt we were lucky, since the leader, who was beyond catching, retired. So, the guy I was chasing for second was now in front, and we had a whiff of victory. It sounds unrealistic, but it really did happen: I was finally on his bumper coming down to the second to last corner – the Veedol Chicane. He braked earlier than I expected, and I was instantly alongside and ahead. I rounded the final corner to the waiting chequered flag, but it was outdone by the huge response from the pit wall. A memorable event.

Further variety was added with a race at Oulton in the new and hugely popular Beetle Cup. It was a quirky thing to drive, and my car was no match for the best, but I was generally satisfied with tenth place at the finish. The most exotic invitation of the year came from Jamaica. I joined Peter and June Baldwin and a group of their friends in the middle of their winter holiday at Discovery Bay. Peter raced each year in

By the 1993 season there was a growing collection of sponsors – my thanks to all. (Mary Harvey)

a Metro BDA, and I was invited to share the car in a race meeting at Dover Raceway. In common with Jamaican lifestyle it was laid back to say the least. The prep was average, but the track, scenery and company was superb. I retired from my race with a shredded cam belt – but it didn't seem to matter a whole lot!

The final scoop in a wonderful year was winning the BRSCC Post 2 Marshals' Trophy. It seems they didn't forget our race there early in the year, and the trophy was, and still is, a magnificent piece of silverware adorned with many of the country's true club racing heros. I am honoured to be among them.

Winter '92 was busy. An entirely new car was built, Peter Vickers was instrumental, guiding and directing the whole project. Rollcentre designed and built an all-new bespoke weld-in cage that set new standards in driver protection, and ensured a super stiff shell to receive all the suspension loads. Only the engine, gearbox, gear lever and knob and rear number plate were carried over from the old car. When Peter had finished the shell and completed the subframes and boot floor, I took the car away and finished the suspension, brakes, steering, plumbing, wiring, installation of engine and box and set up. We shook the car down at the Rover

test day held at Silverstone. The car looked fantastic and promised much. There were a few niggles, vibration that originated in the exhaust and a long brake pedal, but reliability was good.

We tested again at Brands where, still struggling with the brakes, I was comfortably under the lap record! Peter attended that test, and I shall always recall his obvious, overflowing pride!

1993 – Mini Miglia: End of season crash

The first two races were at Thruxton (in horrible rain) and Donington. I won them both! At Thruxton the margin was 9.5 seconds, and I was alone for the whole race, finding things easy in a car that worked well on wet tyres and with unblemished visibility that was denied the rest of the field. Things were closer at Donington where I won a tense battle with Ian Gunn, exchanging the lead several times.

There was a cloud on the horizon, however, and only a fool would have missed it. I refer to Chris Lewis, back in a Miglia for the first time since injury sidelined him in '86. Chris had a reputation for buying the very best equipment, and generally racing on a no-expense-spared basis. Although he had nothing particular to show for the first two races, I had little doubt that he would soon figure strongly.

The threat didn't materialise at Combe, but my fortunes took a downturn. The previously dependable engine suffered mysterious detonation, and I struggled across the finish line in eighth place with the engine tightening with each revolution. I had led into the first corner and come out in seventh place following a lurid half spin. Starting lap nine I was third and fancied my chances, but the race was a lap too far.

Upon inspection, three of the pistons had picked up, and one of the bores was heavily scored. The head gasket had blown, too. We concluded that it was a simple matter of running too hot. Most of the lap at Combe was flat out with average speeds a tad under 90mph. In the traffic throughout, I had been robbed of clean cool air, and accordingly at the next meeting we sported not only new pistons and a liner, but a standard Mini side radiator plumbed in series with the Metro front cooler.

Water temperature never exceeded 60°C (140°F) at Silverstone, but the Lewis steam-roller showed itself for the first time with pole and the win. I finished fourth with fastest lap – which was little consolation. Having started so well, the pressure of letting it slip was starting to build.

Hope was restored at Oulton Park. I qualified on pole – first time in the new car. Having lost out at the start, the race became a battle between Ian Gunn and myself, and having been on the grass at over 100mph and survived it once, I finally conceded that Ian's car was too wide and settled for second. By now, Chris Lewis could not win the championship with four poor results recorded. Never one to give up, though, he won the next five races. I took three poles and three fastest laps, with two seconds, a third, a fourth and a retirement. While Chris was winning as he pleased, the championship was shaping between Ian Gunn and myself. I will always look back on that retirement at Brands as the day I opened the door for Ian because at that stage I was looking good. From pole at Brands I clashed with Richard Wager half way round the first lap, and that was that.

Whilst still in a strong position I now had to finish the remaining races. There may not be a conscious decision, but it must make a driver in that position a shade less aggressive, and the loss of that facet cannot be quantified. Chris's run came to an end at Snetterton one cold wet autumn afternoon. Ian and I again battled head-to-head in treacher-

ous conditions, and finally I took the upper hand for the final round by finishing second ahead of him.

Again, I prepared thoroughly for the final race, mindful of my previous failure at Donington. This time the venue was the Silverstone Grand Prix circuit. We tested on the Friday, and damp conditions blighted the day, but I felt I had a handle on the thing. On Saturday I was nervous. This had come to mean such a great deal to me that I was becoming my biggest opponent. Perhaps I was too intent, I needed chilling out a bit, but I certainly couldn't see that at the time.

Because the Silverstone GP circuit was licensed by the FIA, pole position was placed on the left, and hence on the outside for Copse, the first corner. This was the choice of the Formula 1 boys, because the left for them was the clean side of the track and therefore offered the best traction for getaway with 760-odd horsepower. For every single saloon car driver it meant that fastest in qualifying got the third best starting slot, and the third fastest qualifier got the best starting position – the right-hand side to give the inside line at the first corner. I decided ahead of qualifying that I wanted to be third quickest.

Bob had watches on the expected top four, and there were also pit lane monitors to check the positions of the whole field. On the sixth lap, with rain still falling, I set the third best time, and when I came to start my seventh lap, seeing the board, I simply cruised round. I repeated this for the rest of the session and duly took the chequered flag to signal the end of qualifying still in third place. Good planning, eh? Well no, in fact, because two cars bettered my time on their last lap and I was fifth on the grid!

Come race day it was dry, I needed only to finish fifth, even if Ian were to win. I couldn't afford a retirement,

Hammering into Quarry at Combe on 3 May 1993. Behind me, Richard Wager (far left) is beginning to lose the battle against cold tyres and moments later he collided with John Lee (second from right). (Steve Jones)

however, so again nerves were undeniably a factor. In two years of Miglia I had not finished lower than fourth when running properly, so I wasn't concerned about pace, but lack of familiarity with the GP bits in dry conditions was a concern. I predetermined that I would run a safe first lap and take no chances. We were looking at a 20 minute race, so there was no rush. In hindsight, it was a bad plan. Caution at Becketts allowed a swarming pack on to my tail for Hanger straight, and these were guys who I didn't normally have around me. I never arrived at Stowe. Inexplicably, I was hit in the right rear wheel, turning me sharp right from where I crossed the shallow grass verge to the track and slammed into the bare Armco at unabated speed. It was a huge impact and on my side. I estimate the speed (without exaggeration) to be over 100mph! During the moments from being turned sideways to striking the barrier I was filled with desperation at

the loss of the title – following the impact I was literally delighted simply to be getting out and walking away.

Naturally, I have many memories, and particularly vivid ones of that weekend, but none of them is bitter. For one thing, Chris Lewis was the fastest driver by far that year and only failed on reliability, and that would always have been a shadow on the title had I won it. Further, the support and consolation offered me by my fellow competitors and friends following the incident was magnificent. I looked on as they loaded my trailer with the wreck. Once again Peter Vickers quickly and properly repaired the car, and we did a winter round later that year to prove that the car was straight again, and to get me back in it as soon as possible. That drew a line under the 1000cc era, since 1994 would herald the 1300cc engine regs into Mini Miglia. The next challenge was mapped out and it was time to move on.

BUILDING, PREPARING AND RACING YOUR MINI

This had been another good year for racing other cars. The continuing relationship with *CCC* opened doors that usually were only accessible with large sums of money, and I enjoyed every moment of it.

Ray Armes, the reigning Rover 216 GTI champion was contesting the National Saloon Car Cup in a Rover 220 GTI. There were a number of two-driver races, and although I wasn't considered for the first, I got a late call to join Ray for the Willhire 24-Hour race at Snetterton. As it turned out, I hardly drove the car before the start of the race, and even then we failed to finish, but it was a tremendous experience. My first stint lasted 2hrs 23mins! After 20 minutes I was really lost, but somehow the next thing I knew I was

called in on the radio, having completed 90 laps! I was running right on the pace, and consistently. The stints were deliberately long to maximise our chance as we had much larger fuel tanks, and this was the only way we could challenge the faster Astras that dominated the class. My third and final stint before our retirement at 07:00 hours included the sunrise. It was a beautiful mid-summer morning, and surely one of the finest experiences of long distance racing.

I shared the car once more at Silverstone in a two-hour race. Again, the car was retired towards the end, but not before I had set the pace quite comfortably. Nothing was said, but I don't think that was appreciated, and I wasn't asked again. Whatever, I will always be

Driving for KAD in the Winter Silhouette Series lent variety to my racing. This chilly scene at Snetterton in November 1993 shows me executing a tricky overtaking manoeuvre which ultimately proved successful. No. 92 is a Honda Civic, believe it or not! (Steve Jones)

grateful to Ray for giving me a chance to drive a professionally run car in a proper team set-up.

After the crash at the end of the Miglia season there was little time to dwell on things, as a new opportunity stood before me. I had become involved with Kent Auto Developments (KAD), a new small manufacturing company near Ashford in Kent. They had produced their own twin-cam 16-valve cylinder head for the A-series engine, and numerous other Mini components, and they had offered me their brakes to try on the Miglia. This was the start and, headed by Nick Cole (a founder member of KAD and an experienced race engineer), a competition programme was planned to publicise the company and its products. I had agreed to drive the car, and a second-hand monocoque chassis built from the remains of two Formula 3 tubs was located. It had been fitted with an eight-port A-series engine and, after careful inspection, KAD bought the car, and began preparing it for the 1993 Winter Silhouette Series to be staged over four weekends in November at Brands Hatch and Snetterton.

The whole KAD team, guided by Nick, worked flat out, and finally we went testing at Snetterton four days before the first race there. I recall so clearly the sound of the engine when it first fired in the pit garage. A short stroke 1300cc engine, all steel, it was intended to rev to 10,000rpm, and it sounded like a Formula 3 car. I drove nervously on to the circuit, and began to wind the thing up. It drove well, and I quickly got a feel for it. The lap record for these cars stood at 1min 18.9sec to Norman Lackford, who I would be racing against in the Winter Series, so we knew the score. Numerous stops to fine-tune the chassis seemed to produce results, and on my 23rd lap I cracked the psychological barrier, stopping the watch at 1-19.9. Nick held out the 'IN' board, patted me on the back and said, 'Time to go home.'

The races were memorable. On our debut at Snet we finished fourth overall and first in class. Next was Brands and that was better still, second overall and class winner again. Back at Snet, and this time we were beaten by Lackford, finishing second in class and fourth overall. It meant the whole thing went down to the wire at Brands where double points were on offer as it was the last round.

The nature of the tight, twisty Kentish track meant that the nimble 1300cc class could challenge the big bangers which never handled so well, and we were again looking for overall victory as well as the class win.

The race came down to a straight scrap between Norman and myself, and we were leading the field. He made an early break, and I spent the first three laps recovering from a bad start. From fifth I made it to second to Lackford by the third lap. Finally, on lap seven I was within striking range. It was clear that the Mini was vastly superior through Surtees and into Clearways, and I attacked there, passing with ease, and establishing myself at the front. I needed to defend resolutely into Paddock where the BDA grunt was greater than our own, but ours was the best package and I duly won, securing the class and overall championship honours. This was to be the beginning of a lengthy and enjoyable association with KAD.

1994 – Mini Miglia: New engine and a first trip to Japan

1994 promised to be another busy year. The new 1300 Miglia engines would need much effort to develop and finalise the spec, and we were ahead of the game, starting early and using all the right bits. At the rolling road, power looked excellent, and we started testing feeling confident that we had got the engine right. While testing at Mallory

A highlight of 1994 was the 'Fastest Mini in the World' race held over the August Bank Holiday at Silverstone as part of the celebrations to mark the 35th birthday of the Mini. I'm seen here leading Peter Baldwin to victory. (TGS Photo)

less than two weeks before the first race there, we had a massive and unexpected blow up. There was no warning, just destruction. I was on the back straight pulling about 7,200rpm in top gear when it let go. Big-end bolt failure was suspected, but such was the extent of the damage that I was never wholly sure. It became clear that my choice of bolts had been unwise. Everyone and his dog, I was told, used ARP bolts and nuts, and they were 100 per cent reliable. Well, it was a bit late to tell me that, and it was a hard way to learn the lesson, but since then I have used nothing but, and with total reliability. Never attempt to economise with bolts!

If there is one Miglia season to forget it was this. The single highlight was Spa-Francorchamps. It was the first Mini Challenge race abroad in my time, and at a quite magnificent track. The racing there was superb, and I finished second – my best result of the year. Truth is, it was more than just the racing that made my weekend, and Spa will always be a special place for me. So, what went wrong that year? We never got the engine back to where it appeared to have been in the beginning. I was unable to get anywhere near the rolling road figures, despite countless trips to Cambridge – where Peter Baldwin operates the rolling road. I chased my tail hard for little reward. It was my first winless year since 1986, and I had to make do with four podiums from 12 starts! Consistency was still there, and I wasn't outside the top five once, so third overall was the end-of-season result.

Even in other cars the results were slow to come. I had been rather let down on the Historic front, but intent on maintaining an involvement, I approached Andy Myers who runs Mini Machine, and he volunteered on the spot to prepare a car for me! I raced it three times, sharing with Tim Sims, a friend and Mini Se7en racer who shared my affection for the Mk1 Mini. He had good mechanical sympathy and was prepared to work with me to hone the car into a winner. We went to Zandvoort in Holland, the Coys Historic Festival at Silverstone and the Old Timer Grand Prix at Nürburgring. We didn't manage one finish. I think it's called character building, and neither Tim nor I were inclined to give up easily.

The single shining result of the season came at Silverstone in August, scene of the 35th Birthday celebrations for the Mini. Conceived in the mind of Nigel Fryatt, Editor of *CCC*, I played my part in the organisation of the elaborately titled 'Fastest Mini in the World Race'. The idea was much publicised in *CCC* and *Mini World* in the six months leading up to the race. Many individuals set about preparations, but the two companies that made the thing work, KAD and Jack Knight Developments, set about their own 'works' teams.

Nick Cole was personally responsible for the design, construction and development of the car that I drove. It was an all-new alloy monocoque design, strong, safe and robust. Power was from a new 1400cc engine developed from the 1300cc unit that had proved itself in '93, and we were ready to begin testing well ahead of schedule. This turned into a nightmare. Countless times we trekked to Snet for a day's testing, and each time we left with more questions than answers. We had got the chassis to work fairly well, but the car never ran for long enough to properly perfect the set-up, as engine and gearbox failures continued to halt our progress.

Nick gave this project his all, rising at 4a.m. and working late into the evening. He was, in effect, doing two full days' work every day, seven days a week in the run up to the 'big race'. We were due to race on the Bank Holiday Monday, and on the Friday before there was an official test at Silverstone. My team-mate was Ben Edwards, TV motorsport commentator, professional racing driver and friend. He was driving the Narita-Garage car that I had driven in Japan in May, which had been shipped over from Japan especially for this race. Martin Short and Peter Baldwin were driving the two works Jack Knight Developments (JKD) cars, and they were a shade quicker than us, no doubt. That didn't seem too bad, until the engine let go again. It was a big-time blow-up, rendering most of it scrap metal. Many men would have laid down and cried, but Nick didn't have time for that. Whilst all the cars and the kit remained at Silverstone for the whole birthday weekend, Nick drove back to Kent and used the two full days available to build a brand new engine! Now, that is no small feat, especially when you see the detail that goes into preparation of the block and pistons, in particular.

Well, Nick returned, and duly installed the new engine. It was brand new, there was no time even to loosen it up on the dyno; so, prudence would be required in qualifying.

We did 16 laps of the National circuit, and the car didn't miss a beat. Having given the first half dozen to running in, we then worked down to a best time $^4/_{10}$ths short of Baldwin's pole time. I would line up third, Martin Short also going quicker than us by a margin of $^3/_{10}$ths. The car had never run that far without a problem before, so we

BUILDING, PREPARING AND RACING YOUR MINI

*Sometimes it snows!...
Practice at Mallory Park in
1994.* (TGS Photo)

were all delighted. The Captain (my favourite tag for Nick) had a smile all across his face for the first time in a month, and there were only a few hours now before the race itself. Cleaned, polished, checked and re-checked, the car was declared ready to race. I had already finished third in the Miglia – which was a good result for '94 – and Art Marcus of *CCC* was driving that in the Fastest Mini race, so I had a fair bit to think about. In the end I delegated all responsibility for looking after Art to Bob and Pete, and concentrated all my efforts on the Black Car – as it had become known!

Perhaps it was nerves, but I told Nick not to expect me to even look for the lead before lap eight. We formed up on the grid, and I was very conscious that I hadn't done a standing start in this car. Breaking the transmission at the start would have been a bad plan, so I opted for a safe getaway, confident that any places lost could easily be made up over the 12 racing laps. In the end I got to Copse in third place, and for three laps Peter, Martin and I ran as a three

car train, each machine black, and in close formation it was an excellent sight – the photographs truly do it justice.

Martin's challenge was the first to falter. Smoke began to show from his car and, although he was still running, I slipped by eventually. Peter had built a small lead as I exercised my patience. It took a couple of laps to close the gap, and finally I was with the Mini Silhouette guru. Peter had more experience in this sort of car than any man alive, and I wondered how to make a move. My car was better on the brakes, and I could carry more speed in the fast corners where superior chassis balance looked to be giving me an edge. I was still pondering my options when, through Woodcote, Peter momentarily slowed. I thought he'd missed a gear, and looked to the inside for Copse, where he defended ruthlessly, so I switched outside without losing momentum. Committed to that we rounded Copse side by side, and at Maggotts the lead was mine. It took half a lap until I felt I had resisted the counter attack. Peter didn't let me settle

– his experience was evident, and perfectly fairly he made it very difficult for me.

Just as I was beginning to believe I could hold on, Peter seemed to fade, dropping away a little to remove almost all the pressure. The pass had come on lap nine and there were only two left. Would the car make it? Everything was within correct parameters on my instruments, and I kept pushing. On the last lap, Peter disappeared from my mirrors. It turned out that his diff was suffering, and this was the cause of the apparent missed shift that gave me the sight of an opening. He made it to the finish, still in second place, but it was long after I had taken the chequered flag to much rejoicing from the pit wall. It had been a marathon effort, and all the credit should go to one man – the Captain!

The final recollection from '94 was my first trip to Japan. Accompanied by Nick Cole and, in effect, representing KAD, we spent a week as personal guests of Mr and Mrs Narita, proprietors of Narita Garage. I tested their Silhouette KAD twin-cam Mini at Fuji, and raced there, too. I took an easy victory in what amounted to little more than a demonstration. Their company, and the evenings spent talking Minis and drawing illustrations and diagrams of ideas and innovations, are fond recollections.

So, back to reality. How was I to rectify the appalling state of the Miglia competitiveness. Throwing a large chunk of money at it was neither appealing nor possible. So, careful analysis of the shortcomings was called for.

I focused on three areas. The pistons were standard Rover items, and although reliable were perhaps a little heavy. The cylinder head was returned to Bryan Slark, who said it could be improved for the 1300 spec and he would major on enlarging the exhaust ports, and finally, as was becoming *de rigueur*, I decided to fit an electric water pump and dump the standard belt-driven one. That was it – a winter's work!

We got to the rollers and, hey presto, loads of power. With 130bhp on Baldwin's rollers, I was more than a little pleased. I reckoned that we should be able to mount a challenge, but Chris Lewis was back to defend his title, so it certainly wasn't going to be easy!

1995 – Mini Miglia: Dicing with Chris Lewis

This was the year of the 'Best of British' package, and 'Racing Ahead', and part of the initiative was to reduce qualifying time, because it bored the public, and increase race time. Accordingly, at four of our 12 meetings there would be double-headers – two races for the price of one – and the championship would be decided based on the best 13 scores from 16 races. Reliability would have to be good to stand a chance of winning.

In the first three races I registered two thirds and a second. Alarmingly, Lewis had three straight wins. Further, I hadn't won a National Miglia race for two years, and it was hurting. Perhaps it was a chance remark, but Stewart Drake referred to the use of medium compound tyres on the front. I had, until then, been using hard compound on the left front. So, for Brands Hatch I tried it. I qualified on pole and led every lap of the race, and unusually there were 15 of them! My consistency was stunning after the first two laps – the greatest spread on times was $^4/_{10}$ths of a second! Lewis followed me home but I was truly back in the hunt. My tail was up and I was believing again! Our next race at Silverstone was the first of the double-headers, and finishing position in the first determined start position in the second. In the first race, normal service resumed as I followed Chris over the line, so we both started from the front row for what was the sixth round of the championship.

BUILDING, PREPARING AND RACING YOUR MINI

...other times the sun shines. On form and leading the field at Luffield Corner, Silverstone in 1995. (Mary Harvey)

I had a spell in front at the beginning, but eventually Chris eased through. I was right there, though, and on the last lap out of Copse Chris went slightly wide and compromised his exit speed. This was my chance, braving it out through Maggotts gave me the line into Becketts, and out on to the back straight I had the lead. Chris towed up alongside on the outside and began inching ahead. Approaching the braking point for Brooklands I think he would just have made it across in front of me but his hesitation allowed me to even it up again under braking. There remained only the stadium complex, I was neat and tidy, and out of Luffield 2 Chris again towed up on me. I tried to make him hesitate by delaying covering the inside which he surely knew I would do. He looked inside I duly covered it and he went outside, that moment robbing him of some momen-tum – but was it enough? We crossed the line side by side, I was just ahead – by half a bonnet! That was tactical racing at its very best. There was respect on both sides and the closest possible racing with no contact. I was proud to have taken part, and winning it was superb. Obviously someone else thought so, too, as I was awarded The Crompton Lighting Driver of the Day.

Two weeks later we were back at Spa. It is a magic venue, and the Mini is perfectly suited to the circuit. We had a great weekend but it was the first of another four ultimately unsuccessful races, as it was wins I desperately needed. I finished second at Spa, the race was wet and Chris didn't figure at all. I received another wonderful trophy and headed for home.

At Castle Combe we had another double-header, and disaster struck on the way to the circuit. My ever-faithful

Mini-Miglia dicing with Chris Lewis at Brands in 1995. Chris had won the first three races of that season, and in desperation I tried new tyre compounds for this race. It worked. I started from pole position and led every lap of the race and, as you can see here, spent most of the time looking in the rear-view mirror! (Mary Harvey)

Volkswagen surrendered to head gasket failure, ending a long and pleasurable relationship. Getting there was an epic, only made possible by a mercy mission from my mother-in-law (thanks Åsa), who towed the trailer down and dropped us off. Qualifying was poor, and the first race was a wash-out as a result. I finished fourth, while Chris won again. The second race that day, in hindsight, could have been the one that cost us the title that year. It became a straight fight between Chris and I. It was the usual hard but fair battle; he had the grunt but I wanted it really badly. On the last lap into Quarry I squeaked up the inside, hideously late on the brakes and largely out of control, to nose ahead. I needed to regain control before the apex to make the move stick, and I just managed it. Politely I put my car where Chris wanted to go on the exit, and held him back through the next corner. There were two corners left and one long straight. I was sure it was mine if I could get a good exit from Tower and Camp. Tower was perfect and I checked the mirror on the exit, Chris was a length or so back and it looked OK. The straight seemed to last forever, and he inched up alongside on the outside, eased ahead and pulled across to take the line for the last corner. It was his race again. What did I have to do to win? I could, of course, have despatched him to the grass on the last straight, and I would have won, but that was not and is not the way I want to win. Anyhow, it would have spoiled a racing relationship that I valued more highly than the extra point. Back to the drawing board – this thing had got to go faster!

The answer, I decided, was ram air. Chris had a huge air scoop behind his front grille which ducted a 5in hose. The cold air was fed into a sealed collector box on the carburettor. Whether it was simply that cold air was going in, or whether the pressure helped I don't know, but it was the only realistic way I could think of improving the car.

Myk Cable had produced what amounted to a clone of the Lewis set-up, and I duly purchased one. It robbed me of position for my oil cooler, and feeling that gambling was the only way to go, I raced at Mallory without the oil cooler. It didn't look good in practice, the oil was at 120° within eight laps, and I was only fifth on the grid. I took a hit in the race, which damaged the suspension, and finally retired having run a big-end bearing on the last lap – I guess the gamble didn't pay off!

So, we sorted out the oil cooler by hanging it below the front valance, and won the next three races – an epic at Thruxton and two tight affairs at Brands. I led every lap but four from those three races! It meant I was still in there, but clearly the underdog.

Three races remained – a double-header at Snet and the Silverstone final. At Snetterton, fortune favoured me strongly, although I won neither race. In the first, on my way out of Russell Chicane, finishing lap three, I snatched the gear lever to change up to second, and snapped the lever clean off in my hand. That was the end of my season, as a retirement meant it was mathematically impossible to steal the title. I drove up the Senna Straight smashing the steering wheel with my fist. The field streamed by, and I toured round towards the pits and retirement. As I got to Russell, out came the red flags to stop the race, so I duly pulled up on the start line, following procedures, aware that this could be a dramatic reprieve. After much confusion, the result was declared, since the leader had completed five laps and therefore 50 per cent of the race distance. Because the back markers – of which I was one – had only completed four full laps, the result had to be taken one lap before that, so it was the positions at the end of three laps that determined the results! Accordingly, I was classified second and Chris fourth! Crazy rules and massive good luck, so I was still in it.

Back in the paddock, Phil Manser's mechanic took his gear lever out of his road car for me to borrow, and we judiciously straightened out the steering wheel which I had inadvertently bent inside out! The following day we raced over the full distance, and Chris duly won. I followed him home, calculating the position on the slowing down lap. Quite simply, at Silverstone I had to win – nothing else would do. If that happened and Chris finished fourth or lower I would be champion.

All I had to do was go flat out. Emma didn't consider for a moment that I wouldn't win. It was just a case, apparently, of what Chris did! Well, I stuck it on pole, as they say, with Chris only fifth. We wondered what we had to do to get it declared a result! The race went according to Emma's script: I led away from pole and was never seriously challenged. This approach is worthy of comparison with the debacle at Silverstone at the end of '93 when caution cost so dearly! I was a strong driver mentally now, better able to cope with all the pressures. I watched the race behind me in my mirror literally. Twice I looked ahead only just in time to save myself from taking to the grass. My result was never in doubt, the car was perfect. Chris never got to second place even, but in the four-car group that was battling he held third for most of the race. Twice he was down to fourth, and I wondered if any two out of Drake, Curley and Baldwin could do the job for me. Well, would you believe it, Chris sneaked over the line in third place 0.45 seconds ahead of Ian Curley, and so ended another campaign. I wasn't too disappointed, since I knew that I'd done all I could. I had won the second half of the season clearly, but by less of a margin than Chris had won the first! We were separated not on points – here we were level – but on number of victories, Chris winning by seven to my six! I was the first to shake his hand, and I will always recall that a dodgy move on the last lap at Combe might have done it for me. I'm glad I didn't go that way, and I count Chris as a good friend.

It had been an epic battle, and I had got the best from my equipment – it just wasn't quite enough. I had done little other racing in '95, although I had again made the trip to Japan, this time at the invitation of Mr Nori Yamagata, owner of Sanwa Trading. Nori had sponsored the KAD Fastest Mini, and after the race he bought the car and had it flown to Japan to go on show. I was invited, along with Nick and Colin from KAD, to go and drive the car at Suzuka in a demonstration. I gratefully accepted and enjoyed the most famous

Japanese track. Nori expressed an interest in buying the Mini Miglia also and, mindful that Peter Vickers was once again keen to build a new car for me, we agreed a deal.

It was the right move; the car had been crashed heavily once and had had a couple of minor bumps. Sure, it drove perfectly but the repairs had caused the weight to creep up. There were new ideas in Peter's head, and who was I to argue? When I delivered the car for shipment I was truly proud that it looked so good after three years of hard battling.

1996 – Mini Miglia: New car, new problems

I bought a new body shell through Rover Sport, and Peter duly cut it to bits! This was going to be a superlight car, under the weight limit so that the ballast could be placed where we wanted it. Peter had been working on modern Super Touring cars, and this was the source of much of his inspiration. It was to be the same deal, he would do the shell, subframes, fuel tank and a mega-neat exhaust system; I would then build up the car to completion.

External pressures meant that, for both of us, progress was slower than it should have been. I had an engine and 'box to prepare, and intended to have all the suspension built up ready to simply hang on. Well, it wasn't working out like that, and at Peter's end the pressure seemed even greater. His deadline was finite, he was going to Daytona for something of a busman's holiday. This brought about a conclusion and I collected the car at the end of the first week in February. It looked fantastic, there was groundbreaking design in the shell and cage construction, and the subframe installation was superb, with comprehensive additional mountings. This was going to be a super-stiff, strong, safe car and with pride it was placed in the centre of my new workshop, for work to commence.

Further domestic disturbance meant that I seemed hardly able to get a single uninterrupted day building the car. Bob was there every spare minute, and often he worked alone. In particular, his solution to our pedal packaging problem was excellent. Working in tight confines searching for only slight realignment is uncomfortable, time-consuming and, quite frankly, at times very irritating, but Bob started and finished the job.

It was nearly finished when we took it to the Rover Test Day at Silverstone. This really was to be a shakedown only, as some areas were incomplete and lashed up just to get the car out. Bob and I did an extremely late night, got a couple of hours sleep, and then we set off early for Silverstone. This was the first time that we used the Dastle Racebox, hitched up to the Transit. Ten minutes into the journey Emma offered to drive, so I gratefully swapped over and immediately fell asleep. I woke an hour and a half later, just as we were getting off the M40. Emma was working hard, as much above 50mph we had a weaving rig on our hands – or rather hers! It had obviously been something of an effort, and Bob and I had been blissfully unaware!

We unloaded the car, and the crowds gathered simultaneously. The events of the next three weeks, before the first race of the year, are still vivid in my memory. At a specially convened Committee meeting of The Mini Se7en Racing Club, of which I was (and, indeed, still am) the Chairman, I was informed that the car was illegal, and would be declined a scrutineering ticket. This was possibly the greatest shock of my life since I had been assured only one week earlier that the car was OK, after a detailed inspection in my workshop!

If I wished to defend the car's legality, and Peter was adamant that it com-plied fully with the regs, then my position as Chairman was untenable. I felt that I would have to resign to fight my case. I didn't want to do this, and duly sacrificed a defence of the car. I didn't attend the first race, instead Peter set about removing his fabricated rear wheel arches and re-installing standard ones that he would then have to modify as was standard practice. This was a difficult job, as the roll cage complicated matters, but Peter stuck it out, still disappointed that it hadn't been defended properly. If it had been a car in which I had no involvement I would like to think I could have sorted it out in the conciliatory way we usually worked as a club. There was, however, a section of the committee, who just wanted it out, and I'll leave you to decide on their motives!

I always have been a fighter, and I wasn't going to give up like that. The second race was at Thruxton two weeks later, and the car still wasn't ready. At the infamous committee meeting I had stated, rather confrontationally I will admit, that perhaps someone would lend me their car. Well, I was delighted that Owen Hall, National champion of 1990, having finished third at Silverstone, offered me his car for Thruxton. There was a small fee to pay, but I considered it wholly fair and a decent offer. Owen would transport and prepare the car, I simply had to turn up and drive!

It was a fascinating day. The car had a very different set-up from mine, but I was a good fit in it, so I joined the circuit for qualifying in a completely unknown quantity. It was so different that it required a new driving style. Super smooth steering inputs were called for, and earlier than would have been necessary in my car. For the first six laps I was languishing in the bottom half of the grid. On lap seven I made it to fifth, to the obvious delight of my pit crew. I now had a feeling for the machine, and for the last lap I was pushing hard. That yielded second position and a front row start. I felt strangely vindicated! Owen, too, was delighted. He shared the technical secrets of the car with me and I was open with him on my own preferences. One or two of his suggestions I adopted from that day forward for my own car, and I will always recall the weekend with pleasure. The race was a bore, really. I didn't have the straight grunt to battle with the two break-away leaders, so although I stayed more or less in touch I was never going to threaten them. Still, I headed home with a third place trophy intent on having my own car out for the next round at Brands.

We made it, Peter putting a massive effort into something he didn't believe needed to be done, and keeping a sense of humour about it all. Brands set the pattern of the year. I qualified second, and finished second. I had a lap record as consolation but it was the defeat that got me. It wasn't losing, after all I had followed Chris for several seasons and never had a problem with it. Indeed, I marvelled at his consistency and willingness to fight clean and fair. Brands was the first time I felt I had lost to someone who was making mistakes ahead of me that I was unable to exploit. It could have been a fifty lap race, I was never going to win it.

And there went another season. After a retirement at the next race, I had seven straight podiums, culminating in glory at Spa, the race of the year for me. I started from pole, which was a pleasure in itself. The big drama was the weather, though. It was dismal, as it can be in the Ardenne. The track was damp – or wet, depending on how you saw it – but it wasn't raining. Somehow, though, at Spa the trees hold the damp down. We watched the previous race on the monitors in the control tower to get a feel for the whole track, and I walked away certain that it would have to be slicks. In my mind was the race the previous year when Peter Baldwin's was the only car to start on slicks in clearly worse conditions. He had been right with the lead pack until his crankshaft broke. On the way back to our awning, I poked my head into Peter's, and confirmed with him that slicks it was – he was already bolting them on! To my amazement, in the assembly area we were the only two – every other car had treaded tyres.

Pole didn't do me any favours. Ian Curley made another of his monster starts from the third row, and led through Eau Rouge for the first time. Over the first lap it became clear that this was to be a three car race between Peter, Ian and myself. We seemed evenly matched despite the differing set-ups. By lap three a dry line was emerging, and the slicks were starting to work normally. Ian could fight no longer, and I led with Peter hard on my tail. I remained under pressure for five laps until the chequered flag came out for me. Peter was less than a second behind, and the joy we all felt at having at last won a race in the new car, and at Spa of all places, was immense.

Back to the maths then, and believe it or not I still had a chance of the championship at the final race. It was similar but worse than last year. This time I had to win, but with Stewart Drake outside the top five, so it was unlikely – but do remember that from exactly his position I had lost out in '93! Well, we went to Silverstone, I stuck it on pole, then led the first lap only to burst an oil pipe at Luffield 2 and spin off big time on my own lubricant! It was a fitting end to a season that is largely best forgotten. Peter Baldwin actually won the race, and in doing so secured the runner-up spot, leaving me in third place. For the record, Drake finished third and won his championship.

The Japanese excursion for '96 had been different from those before it. This time just Emma and I were invited to join Mr and Mrs Yamagata. It was much more of a social rather than a technical week, but we had a great time, ate plenty of raw fish, and enjoyed all the Japanese delicacies. We also went to the track – this time Tskuba, just outside Tokyo – where I drove the Black car and my old Miglia. That was an emotive day, especially when we pulled up beside my championship-winning Mini Se7en used between '87 and '91. This was purely a chance encounter!

One day Nori mentioned that he had ordered a Richard Longman Mini Miglia engine, and wondered whether I would like to use it for a few races. I could hardly believe my ears, and sought confirmation that I understood him cor-

rectly. There was nothing else to say; I accepted and looked towards the new season with increased expectation. Good to his word, all I had to do was deliver my gearbox to Longman's workshops, and in due course the whole assembly, dyno'd and ready to fit, was there for collection.

1997 – Mini Miglia: Bingo! National Mini Miglia Champion

The first race of '97 was at Oulton Park. The field was relatively small but, as usual, the competition up front was tough. Chris Lewis was out in a brand new car, built to the usual high standard, whilst Baldwin, Drake and Curley were all up for it. I was $^3/_{10}$ths off the pole time, and in fourth place as a result! The race didn't go well for me. I was running fifth when Baldwin and

At the beginning of the 1997 season, after a disappointing result at Oulton Park, some hard work saw us on pole at Silverstone, $^9/_{10}$ths ahead of the field. Despite a hard challenge from Richard Wager (seen here close on my heels) I was rewarded with a victory and a new lap record. (Mary Harvey)

Wager tangled and departed, so I duly finished third and totally gutted. The truth is, I had expected to bolt in this engine and trounce the field, and it wasn't going to be like that. I had a lap record as consolation, and left the circuit compiling a list of shortcomings to be addressed before Silverstone and the next round.

We worked on the suspension, set-up, brakes and cooling system. Refocused, we turned up at Silverstone and dominated the weekend. I was $9/10$ths clear on pole, fought hard with Richard Wager for the first half of the race before his challenge faded, and took a new lap record to complete a clean sweep. That is how good the car was – totally spot on!

My impending marriage to Emma was now only two months away, and I wondered if this would be my last win as a bachelor. I was dead excited about everything the year held in store for us, and we both went to Castle Combe, the last race before our big day, wanting to close the first chapter in fine style!

I qualified third, for a front row start, but as the cars collected in the assembly area the heavens opened. The entire field returned to the paddock to hurriedly fit wets, and change set-up. Many were short of help, but we had a man at each corner, and Bob inside to treat the screen with Rain-X.

We made it to the grid, and I got the best start and led the field away. I thought I'd got it sussed, and was half expecting to simply drive away, given my clear view, as opposed to the cloud of spray the pack were contending with. I didn't allow for Richard Wager, however, and he appeared on the outside, going much faster than me into Tower – a fearsome corner in the dry, let alone the wet! I saw no way he could avoid crashing, that was until he threw the car sideways – doubtless with his right foot still buried on the gas – rounded the corner on full opposite lock and four

wheel drifting and set off towards West Way. We circulated in close formation for the entire race. Richard didn't drive defensively, just as quick as he could and I never had any chance of challenging without hanging my neck out by miles! I was $4/10$ths behind at the finish, the next car driven by Peter Baldwin was 18 seconds back!

I had enjoyed an excellent race, and now my thoughts were wholly on the weekend of 24 May 1997. On the Saturday Emma and I were married, the day was perfection. Our wedding car was a 1966 Austin Cooper S – Mini Machine had found the car for me and over a number of years completed a full restoration to their own exacting standards. This was my wedding present to Emma, and we rose early on Sunday morning and drove to Brands in the S for Round 4 of the National Challenge on the Grand Prix circuit! In effect, it made the wedding a three-day event before we went on honeymoon, and a script writer wouldn't have dared to set out this tale. I qualified on pole, but there was no time for celebrating yet. The car was running high on oil temperature and, with a long race ahead and Spa to follow, measures to increase cooling were called for. Peter Vickers stepped in to sort this out once and for all. In the paddock, using only hand tools, he fabricated a superb alloy ducting to collect air from behind the grille and pass it through the oil cooler.

We had the honeymoon suite at the Brands Hatch Thistle that night, instead of the normal sleeping bags in the box trailer, and raced early the next morning. I lost the lead at the start, but reclaimed it at the second corner and eased away from the field to win the race. It was a fantastic weekend. We had a drinks party in the paddock for all our friends from the Mini Se7en Club, and left for a ten-day honeymoon, packaged to get us home in time to leave for Spa – fittingly the venue for Round 5.

The bubble had to burst somewhere, and so it did in Belgium on the first qualifying lap! The water pump belt broke, and it was not lost on me that a lap earlier would have been the last one at Brands. We were surely blessed that day!

The Spa weekend was my least competitive of the year. From fifth on the grid after the second qualifying session, I finished fourth. It should have been third but the car coughed for fuel on the last lap, letting Peter Baldwin by. Still, nearing mid-season I comfortably led the championship. The engine had made a huge difference to the overall package. It was so strong that I was often in a position to dominate a race, rather than hang on and wait for someone's mistake to give me an opportunity.

I won the next two races at Cadwell and Donington, in what was becoming an exclusive battle between me and Ian Curley. Ian reasserted his claim at Pembrey, jumping from fourth on the grid into the lead at the first corner. The track was damp and greasy but we were all on slicks and the dry line was only a Mini wide. Ian drove superbly. I tried everything I could to push a mistake out of him, but it never came and I was second behind a deserving winner. Ian's consistency meant that he was still well in the hunt, and I could not afford to relax. I won the next race at Mallory, but this was the hardest fought of the year and there was no margin at all. Ian seemed to be stronger than me at the end of a race, and I was working hard to identify any weakness that I could rectify.

Snetterton was next, the tenth round of a 13-race championship. I checked out the maths, and if I won with Ian third or less, it would be job done with three races to spare! As had been the case several times before, it was not a

A green flag start from pole at Brands Hatch, 26 May 1997. I'd been married just two days and so car carries 'Just married' livery!

case of could I win, more what would happen behind, but I was determined to keep to myself the championship position since I was sure that no-one else would have worked it out. Well I did win, and for most of the race Ian was second. Exiting Russell on the last lap, my lead was such that I could afford to slow down and look properly in my rear view mirror. To my delight Baldwin led into Russell as I neared the finish line, and at long last it was all over. I was the 1997 National Mini Miglia Champion, and it was my pleasure to announce this to the commentator at the post race interview. Indeed no-one had been aware, but I received honest congratulations from Ian and most of the rest of the Mini Se7en Club, so it seemed to me! More than anything it was such a relief to have done it at last – now I could relax.

Three races were left, and Croft was next. This was Lewis country, deep into Yorkshire and the first time the Minis had headed up there since my involvement in the club. Chris very generously donated £2,000 to the club to be shared among all the Mini racers as start money, and having spent many days testing at the track and with guests in attendance he wanted victory badly – indeed I think he probably expected it.

I didn't test as there wasn't the need now, and I was amazed to qualify comfortably on pole on my fourth lap! I did another two laps that were quick enough for pole, and as my notes from the day state, we were on 'shagged tyres', too. It became a two-car race between Chris and I, after Baldwin and Curley were eliminated at the first corner. I led throughout, and Chris tried everywhere for the first half of the race before settling down and following dutifully. I was in no doubt that he had a plan for the last lap, and so it transpired. At the last two corners, the attack came and with unexpected force.

I took heavy blows down both sides of the car, but still came out of the last corner to win by a scant margin. I have to say I wholly disapprove of such tactics, and was pleased they had failed. It was also out of character for Chris, with whom I could not recall exchanging paintwork previously. However, it wasn't going to spoil the day, and I steered away from the controversy that the commentator seemed intent on pursuing at the post race interview. Chris and I discussed the matter, agreed it would not happen again, and our friendship and respect for each other survived. He also gave me a couple of his used tyres that I was in the habit of buying, which I felt was some compensation!

Two races left, and the prize Mini Cooper still to be decided. Steve Bell was dominating the Se7ens and it looked likely to go to the last race. The penultimate round was at Silverstone, and Ian and I fought out a monster battle. He led most of the race, but by lap seven I was close enough to challenge. Ian got out of shape at Brooklands, and it took a further two corners to work myself alongside and crucially inside for the run towards Copse. I exited ahead for the first time, but immediately Ian was past again. I simply couldn't fathom what I'd done wrong, but the next corner was to tell. As I braked and changed down, the engine let go – big time! It later transpired that the steel crank had broken, and with it went the block, two rods and pistons, camshaft, gearbox casing, drop gears and flywheel housing. Really, only the head survived, albeit with a couple of bent valves, and I was left to wonder how I could contest the last race, only seven days later.

Since it was Nori's engine I informed him by fax and awaited a response. It was difficult to see where an engine was going to come from in such a short space of time, and I phoned Chris Lewis to ask him if I could borrow his car

The big day 24 May 1997. My present to Emma – beautifully restored by Mini Machine.

complete! He agreed, so there was one avenue. Steve had won the Se7en race, so the prize Mini would be settled at the last round. Quite simply, if Steve won, and he was racing first, then I had to win too. If he failed to win, and anything in the top six would still seal the championship for him, then I didn't even need to start. In the end I didn't need to take up Chris's offer, as clear instructions came from Japan – 'Bill must race, Richard Longman will build a complete new engine.'!

Well, Jack Knight built me a new gearbox in one day flat, and Sid, Richard's A-series expert, set about a new engine. I got it all back on Friday evening, Nick Paddy collecting the engine from Dorset, as I was at work, and had it in and running that night with Nick's help. The following day, Saturday, Ross Buckingham who runs the rollers at Southern Carburettors and Injection ran it in and did a power check. The engine was spot on –

indeed, better than the last – and we arrived at Thruxton better prepared than I dare have guessed a week previously!

I stood among the massed ranks of the Mini Se7en Racing Club at the Thruxton chicane and watched the Se7en race. Steve had a spell in the lead, but was clearly intent on the championship more than the car. I cannot recall the victor, but it wasn't Steve, so the car was mine, and I had yet to race. I felt a new pressure – that I must win to justify the efforts of everyone who had contributed to the week of slog.

Ian Curley and Richard Wager had a couple of laps each in the lead, until I headed the field on lap five. Thruxton is a difficult place at which to make a lead stick, but such was the intensity of the battle between Curley, Wager and Baldwin that I escaped and stretched the legs of the car to set a new lap record.

MY FORMULA FOR SUCCESS

Occasionally, the racing boot is on the other foot, as in 1998, when ex-Mini-racer Patrick Watts got to try out my Miglia car. Despite knowing that Patrick is a top-flight, works Peugeot British Touring Car driver of many years experience, my expression says it all; please don't bend my car! (Courtesy Paul Harmer, CCC magazine)

Well, that was my last Miglia race. I hadn't considered the future until that point, but now it seemed time to stop. I had completed six full seasons of Miglia racing and enjoyed it all through the various ups and downs. In each season, except '94, I had gone to the last race with a chance of championship victory, and only in this the last season did I win, albeit with three races to go this time. I had drawn immense satisfaction from it all, as economy was always a necessity, and at no stage was it ever at any cost. I had the very best engine that money could buy for the final year, but I still only used two new tyres for the entire season – and Bob won those at the Dinner and Dance raffle! Perhaps my most competitive year, and certainly the season in which I extracted the most from my equipment,

was '95, running my own engine and still on a distributor! I was at a distinct technical disadvantage, but I nearly did it.

Now, I will never say never, and indeed perhaps I will return to Mini Se7en or Miglia, or race the new Mini when it appears in 2000. For the future we will be returning to the FIA European Historic Touring Car Challenge in a '65 Cooper S, and it is towards this project that my energies are focused as this is written. I hope to remain a part of the Mini Se7en Club, as a member and Chairman as long as I am required, and will never forget that what I started as a youthful kid has become part of the fabric of my life. If you have a fraction of the fun I've had, I can assure you it will be good value for money.

Bodywork

The Mini doesn't have a chassis, rather it is a monocoque with two subframes to carry the engine/gearbox assembly and suspension. What we will consider here is the steel body shell.

Choosing a shell

The shell is the single most important part in the construction of the car. It is the skeleton on which everything else hangs. It is designed to withstand the rigours of road use and, when new, is a comprehensive structure that in its own right is ideal for competition. It does, of course, suffer the effects of atmospheric attack – the elements and the rock salt used on winter roads form an aggressive partnership that corrodes steel with devastating effect. To build an effective competition car, the body shell chosen should be in the best possible condition. A new shell is neither necessary, nor possible for some formulae, but the objectives should be the same whatever the intentions.

At least seven different saloon shells have been made since Mini production began in 1959. Many differ only in detail, but the most obvious and significant dividing line occurred in 1969 when the last of the Mk II shells, with sliding front windows and external door hinges, was built. Up to then the car had evolved only slightly from the original, and although models are now scarce, for historic racing and rallying the correct authentic shell is mandatory.

The new design for the Mk III cars incorporated a new door, with later type door catches and push button handles. The windows were one piece and wound up, at the expense of the huge door pockets on earlier models. The new door called for revised 'A' posts and internal hinges. It was a logical progression and the door locks and handles were significantly better, but just a little of the original charming character was left behind.

The Mk III style shell has undergone numerous detail modifications, including revised front subframe mounting, enlarged front section of the transmission tunnel, and changes in detail of the floor pressing pattern. But essentially the latest version is unchanged in a quarter of a century.

My current Mini Miglia car (at the time of writing), complete with the magic number 1 on the side. Note the distinct lack of visible painted bodywork – the car isn't there to look pretty, it's a mobile billboard for sponsors who can help pay your racing bills! Though it may seem a bit obvious to say it, it's a fact that a car that looks good will attract more sponsors than a rough-looking car, regardless of the way it performs on the track. Obtaining sponsorship is often hard work and you'd be well advised to study it carefully.

The view from the front is all about low-down, wide and latent aggression, though the basic Mini shape is still there. To save weight and add strength, the entire front end comprises two carbon fibre mouldings. The bonnet ...

For Mini Se7en, Mini Miglia, Modified Saloons or any other formula without restriction on age of shell, youngest is generally best. Ideally, you should seek an undamaged shell, free from rust and repairs. To achieve the latter, look at three years old or less. Of course, you *may* find the one-lady-owner and never-driven-on-a-wet-day car, which at ten years old will be as good as new, so judge each shell on its merits and assume nothing.

The easiest option is, of course, a new shell. If you are eligible for the Rover Sport Privateer Scheme, these can be purchased, without sound-deadening, seam-sealer and underseal, for around £1,000, including doors, boot and bonnet all painted in primer. This is outstanding value for money and saves hours in preparation time.

The final option is to search out the best you can in a dismantler's or salvage yard and make the necessary repairs. Whether you choose to replace rot or repair accident damage should be balanced against the skills at your disposal. Heavily crashed cars are for the professionals only, and if a dismantler is pushing it on, the chances are it's too far gone.

Those are the choices for the contemporary stuff. For historic series the requirements are more specific. Hardest of all are the FIA-administered classes where the car must be an original example of the correct age, with log book, chassis and engine numbers all original. Strictly speaking, only the original shell with which the car was factory manufactured will do, although without doubt anomalies do exist.

There are other more realistic historic formulae which call for the period *appearance* rather than strict and complete originality. The Mk I, produced between 1959 and 1967 featured external door hinges and sliding front windows, a narrower rear window and delightful oval rear lights (which required a different pressing in the rear quarters). The Mk II version retained the hinge and window features, but featured the larger rear window that is current today, together with larger rear lights.

Whatever you choose, the preparation criteria are the same. The shell should be stripped completely and a thorough inspection carried out. It can be rolled on to its side to look closely at the underside. All the underseal must be removed – there are no special tricks here, it's just a tedious scraping job with much patience required. Later shells had sound-deadening applied to the inside of the floor pan, and this also has to come off, using similar methods. It should now be possible to assess which, if any panels require repair or replacement. Look closely in all the usual places, sills both inner and outer, door step panels, rear subframe front mounting captive nuts, and the front and rear bulkheads. Ideally these areas will all be serviceable. If so, the shell should be as good as a new one once fully prepared. The peripheral panels are less susceptible to early attack, and matter little in terms of the finished structure of a race shell.

As usual, careful reading of the regulations will indicate the extent to which modifications are permitted. For the historic route the shell prep will be a complete restoration to original spec, including all the steel front panels, and boot floor, etc. In contrast, the modern Mini Challenge shell requires a whole host of standard modifications, including an integrated roll cage to comprehensively enhance the torsional rigidity. As always, it is essential that the established rules and practices are complied with, and I will repeat the statement that you should NEVER attempt to build a car from the rule book without first looking at examples in the paddock at race meetings.

Preparing a Miglia shell

As an example, I will explain the preparation of the ultimate shell for Mini Miglia, but do check the limitations applied to your chosen formula before starting work. The bare shell, stripped of underseal and sound deadening and

... is secured by three quick-release pins and can be off in seconds, leaving good access ...

... to the engine bay for tuning and running repairs.

The entire front section, including the wings and arches, is all-of-a-piece. On some cars, it's secured by quick-release pins, but on mine there are a few screws to undo before …

… it can be lifted away to reveal …

repaired where necessary, is now ready for the preliminary works prior to the installation of the roll cage. The rear wheel arches, regardless of wheel diameter or width, will require modification to permit the achievement of sufficiently low ride height. The outermost section turns downward before joining the rear wing, and this can be cut away. A steel strip should be cut to size and

… what's beneath – I thought it hadn't been pulling too well, lately! During the winter lay-off, the engine has been removed for work, leaving the car in its present state. At this point, it's an ideal opportunity to ensure that all is well in terms of structural rigidity, etc. Note the large standard door mirrors, something I prefer rather than …

welded in to bridge the gap to the rear wing. The wing itself should be cut away, leaving sufficient material to fold under and weld into the new section of higher arch. The inevitable distortion should be made good with filler. The rear seat back stops a little short of the rear wing, and this gap should be closed to form the firewall that the bulkhead must provide. This can be done in glassfibre, although the preferred method is to let in a steel strip and spot weld this to the rear wing,

ensuring integrity for the firewall even in the event of a shunt in the side.

Bulkhead air box

Moving to the front bulkhead, an air box will be required to provide some breathing space for a Weber carburettor (the more or less acknowledged standard carb for a Miglia or Se7en engine). This will have to be let into the bulkhead and effectively sealed for firewall integrity. Before doing this the front parcel shelf must be removed. The style

… this type which are smaller, if more trendy. It's a personal preference.

At the rear of the car, things look surprisingly standard. The number plate is free so I use it for a bit of fun and personal promotion – and why not!

More weight is saved by making the boot lid from carbon fibre and, again, it's quick-release.

All the glass can be replaced by Perspex if required. Personally, I prefer to have a laminated glass windscreen because you can actually see what's going on, rather than just getting a general impression through a scratch-covered haze! The side windows, though, are Perspex.

The bulkhead air box has become pretty much de rigueur nowadays. This one is particularly extravagant, but serves the same basic function as the others – to channel cool air to the voracious single Weber 45DCOE.

box tube can be welded into the bulkhead to form the outline shape, and this can be skinned in aluminium or steel sheet. Again, the choice of roll cage should govern the decision process.

With the air box complete, the interior can be finished and the cage installed. A multitude of minor tasks should be addressed. The floor holes can be closed with steel welded patches or rubber grommets; it's a matter of preference – closed and painted looks neater, but the grommets can be removed to drain the car of water if necessary! Similar holes throughout the car will have to be closed in either way, but do remember the need to create firewalls front and rear – rubber will *not* do.

A number of brackets will be required and generally these must be made up by the individual car-builder. The steering column will have to be supported as the standard mounting will have been discarded with the front parcel shelf. The simplest method is to incorporate such a fixing into the roll cage on a suitable transverse tube. If it is desired to have the rod change gearshift assembly inside the car, a mounting should be provided for this. The battery and fire extinguisher position should be determined now, so that the necessary fixing holes can be made. The seat will need to be chosen and offered up. Mountings should be provided for both the seat and the driver's harness (*see* Chapter 11). Having installed brackets where required, there is the small matter of all the fixtures and fittings needed for a road car but surplus to requirements on a racer. There is weight to be saved here and, as the only cost is time, it's definitely worth doing. Heater brackets, cable retainers, rear door pockets and headlining retainer can all be disposed of. Its fiddly and time-consuming, but if you keep all the bits to weigh at the end,

of air box you choose depends on several considerations. If you intend to use a standard six-point bolt-in roll cage without additional reinforcements, then minimise the metal that is cut from the front bulkhead in order to retain the structural support it offers. This way, you can retain the standard mounting position for the wiper motor, although space for catch tanks is reduced. Much more fashionable in recent years is the full-width version, allowing ample space for the carburettor and some air ducting, or even a ram air system which is also a recent and valuable development (*see* Chapter 8).

Installation of the full-width air box weakens the bulkhead, and so cage reinforcements in this area are essential. There is no right or wrong way to build the air box. I prefer to use light gauge steel sheet, as this is easy to cut and bend and can be welded neatly, both to make the box and to attach it to the bulkhead. This construction can be self supporting, and will minimise the weight introduced. Alternatively, steel you'll be well-pleased with the weight you've saved.

Roll cage

A roll cage is a requirement under the safety regulations, and will help protect the driver from injury in the event of an accident. Full details of cage design and fitment requirements are shown in the RAC 'Blue Book' and you should select your cage with these in mind.

Racing saloon car construction soon evolved the rollover cage to enhance the stiffness and torsional rigidity of the shell, and this is now a major consideration in its design. The modern fully welded-in safety cage not only affords the driver a massive degree of protection, it also enhances shell performance – when you can achieve safety *and* speed in one fell swoop, you really can't complain! If your regulations permit it, the choice should be an easy one. Inevitably, price will influence the decision, but if there is a single area on the car where the budget should be stretched, this is it.

The minimum standard is a six-point cage with a diagonal above the driver's head and a single lateral door bar to

The all-important roll cage fits inside the car to protect the driver from all directions. Here, you can see how the strong tubes criss-cross the doorways, linking to a strong upright at the 'A' pillar which carries on across the four corners of the roof.

A slightly different cage, but serving the same purpose. No driver wants to get that close to the other competitors!

It also extends across between the two 'A' pillars. Note the padding to protect the legs in the event of a shunt.

At the rear corners is a complex array of welds to cage tubes leading every which way. The cage extends through the rear bulkhead and across the boot top to protect the fuel tank. Note the holes punched and swaged to provide a stiff yet light-weight reinforcing panel.

protect the driver. This will do the job, and indeed a car thus equipped can still be fully competitive. The term six-point means that there are six points where the roll cage is attached to the shell, these being the feet on the main hoop, the front legs and the back-stays. Each attachment point must be reinforced with a steel plate, at least 120cm^2 in area and 3mm thick. These plates

should be welded to the body. Each foot is then bolted through the relevant plate and the body using high tensile bolts – three on each of the main feet and two on the back-stays. The door bar is a bolt-on item, available individually, and most cars featuring this type of cage fit a further door bar to the passenger side and transverse between the main hoop at tunnel level, and the front hoop at a little above knee level. The latter makes a good steering column support.

The concept of the bolt-in cage was extended by the introduction of a basic version with many additional reinforcement tubes welded in and a total of 19 points of attachment to the shell. Each attachment point requires either a reinforcement plate or a welded-in threaded boss. This cage is a big step forward with double door bars each side, and a crossed diagonal to offer real protection to the driver, and forward attachments to the front bulkhead for stiffening. It remains a bolt-in item, and this marks a big difference from the next step. A fully welded integral safety cage has its roots in pure race car construction. The cage is built up, one tube at a time, within the car and welded together. There are no bolts whatsoever, and the tubes are fashioned to run close to, even touching, the main structural elements of the shell. The front hoop runs right along the 'A' panels and the main hoop is tight to the 'B' post. The lateral tubes follow the sills and roof lines. All along the length, each tube is welded to the shell. It takes little imagination to realise that the finished job is extremely stiff. The cage is in to stay, and it will offer the greatest protection to both the driver and the shell in the event of an accident, but if the car is written off – which will take some doing – the cage goes along with the shell. It is fitted once and can never be removed, unlike the multi-point bolt-in version. These are the choices. Having raced all types,

I would not consider anything except the fully welded integrated version.

The front end

Next consideration is the front of the car. If new or good condition steel panels are fixed, I find it hard to justify chopping them off for the sake of it. The inner wings should be sacrificed if the regulations permit, and in an instant there is excellent accessibility to make the car manageable with a fixed front end. Many cars have a removable front section comprising front panel and wings. These are commonly available in glassfibre, and more recently as a carbon fibre item from Curley Specialised Mouldings. The latter is the best solution, offering weight-saving and durability. Metal panels may be retained as a detachable assembly or fixed for the ultimate bump resistance. If you opt for detachable, do make sure they only detach when you wish it. Many a race has ended early with the bonnet or even the whole front end obscuring the driver's view.

Front subframe

Further consideration, under the bonnet, should be given to subframe stiffening, and mounting and bracket positions. The front subframe effectively hangs on the cross-member built to support it, with the rear feet to attach it to the floor/front bulkhead area. If the latter area is not reinforced and tied to the roll cage, then the subframe will be allowed to pivot about the cross-member, generating instability and weakening the floor. Under these conditions the front of the subframe should be triangulated to the cross-member to stop any movement. This is, of course, unnecessary if the cage includes support to the original mounting points. Provision should be considered for a front radiator. The A-series Metro version is located by small lugs, and the front section of the subframe can be extended to provide holes for the lugs to sit in. A suitable header tank will also need bracket provision. The matter of engine stabilisation should be considered. The flange on the bulkhead for the standard stabiliser is worthy of additional welding, and some argue that this should be replicated on the nearside to provide even-sided support. Think also of position and mountings for oil cooler, catch tank, wiper motor, emergency pull for battery switch and fire extinguisher – and additional ignition components.

The doors and boot

The doors can be relieved of the inner panel which is normally obscured by the

Much of the workings and metalwork from the inner door is removed for lightness; so, fitting a carbon fibre panel like this not only makes it look prettier, but also puts back some of the rigidity lost in the process.

Another vital piece of safety equipment is the fire extinguisher. Things get plenty hot under that carbon fibre bonnet and the result of a shunt plus a damaged fuel line is not likely to be pleasant. This is my own extinguisher which is plumbed in to release the extinguishant under the bonnet. It can be triggered manually from here inside the car or …

… by a marshal from a clearly marked switch on the outside of the car.

These automatic Tri-Flo systems are typical of those easily available from race supply specialists. Expect to pay between £250 and £1,000 – a lot you may think, but though there are plenty of areas where you can save money on your car, fire safety is not one of them. (Courtesy Demon Tweeks)

My office! Not the most extravagant of environments, but one I like and, from last season's experience, one which certainly works well. Note the yellow mark on the steering wheel in case things get very crossed-up and I need to know where the front wheels are pointing.

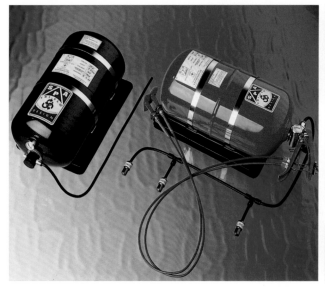

interior trim piece; or, if the regulations permit, glassfibre replacements may be considered. The boot is where the fuel tank should be housed. It is not permitted to retain the original tank, except in historic racing, since the filler neck is susceptible to damage. Proprietary replacements in alloy or plastic are commonplace, and several designs exist according to the boot floor. If the original is to be retained, a circular version to sit in the spare wheel well, fabricated in alloy, is a good bet. If you wish to remove the floor and install an alternative, there is weight to be saved and the option of fabricating a replacement or using a Curley carbon moulding which will hold a conventional rectangular tank. Do consider carefully the weight of the tank when full – and your cornering speeds – and ensure that adequate tank retaining straps are provided. This is, of course, an area of acute concern for scrutineers. If you opt to keep the original floor – and there are merits in doing so: less time and

Ian Curley's car is a
dramatic comparison with
its space-age carbon fibre
dashboard and world-
rally-car-style layout.

Compare the design with
that of my first Miglia –
raced to 2nd in the
National Challenge 1992.
(Courtesy John Colley)

Fancy footwork quite literally, as Ian's pedal cluster first saw service in a Footwork Formula 1 Car. He's pondering how he can squeeze its engine under the bonnet!

money, increased support to the rear subframe mounts – the standard battery box may still be used, but think of cutting the bottom out and making it less deep for ground clearance, and ensure that it won't cause difficulty in mounting the rear anti-roll bar.

Spraying the shell

Finally, the shell must be painted. The theme throughout the build should be 'do it once and do it right'. All other parts can be improved upon as progress is made, but the shell should be right from the off, as subsequent tweaking is not really possible. Treat finishing and painting in the same way. Try to minimise the filler used – it costs weight. Certainly, some will be necessary to achieve satisfactory appearance, but don't get carried away. Paint is an expensive commodity, so do the job properly and use (or get an expert to

use) two-pack paint. It does not come off when brake fluid gets spilled – which it will! – and the shine is superb (especially if Peter Vickers applies it!). Note: The two-pack paint process involves using highly poisonous chemicals, and it is essential that specialist air-fed breathing apparatus is worn. Unless you are equipped with a purpose-built spray booth and said apparatus, this really makes two-pack spraying a professional-only job.

Look behind you

In racing, you need to know where the other cars are, particularly those behind you – they're trying to get in front! So, mirrors are another important concern. I have raced cars with the tiny, sexy mirrors like those you see on formula cars, which look great – until you want to know what's behind! I always choose the standard door mirrors; they are easy to fit, robust and give a side view in the correct perspective. There's another benefit to fitting standard mirrors – when you lose them through another car getting a little too close, they're simple and cheap to replace! The standard interior mirror also works well, provided it is secured properly and not subject to vibration. For some time I used a large commercial door mirror, of the type normally found on lorries, as an interior mirror and this proved effective, giving a wide angle of view. When fitting the interior mirror, particularly if you are seated low in the car, remember that the ideal mounting position will be lower too, otherwise your rearward view will be foreshortened.

Wheels and tyres

At this point, you'll have a wonderful basis for a race car, but you'll be going nowhere without some wheels and tyres. Depending on the formula you enter, you will be restricted in some way on both. In Mini Miglia, for example, the maximum wheel width is 7.5in and for tyres – treaded wet weather and untreaded slick dry weather – 10in wide Dunlops are currently the control tyres for both Miglia and Se7en racing. Steel wheels are cheaper and easier to come by, but alloy wheels offer a useful weight-saving for their extra cost. There are plenty of retail outlets for suitable racing wheels, or you could buy second-hand. If you're taking the latter route, extreme care is required, as wheels lead a hard life on a racing Mini. It's clearly vital from a safety point of view that the wheels are not cracked or damaged in any way – and hairline cracks take some spotting. If you're not fully au fait with the subject, take along someone who is, or save up a little longer and buy new wheels. Remember that with some formulae, you'll need wet and dry weather tyres which means (for all practical purposes) two sets of wheels and at least one spare for each.

Tyres are Dunlop 160/490 x 10 regardless of the wheel rim size you choose, up to a maximum of 7.5in. These are 7in KAD rims with slick tyres whilst ...

... these are slightly smaller 6.5in Spectrum rims with treaded rain tyres.

The rain tyre in more detail showing the grooves which allow it to channel the water away.

In an effort to show just how really tough modern racing wheels are, I wrecked one specially for this book. Honest! Actually, this was one of the results of my major accident at the end of the Miglia season in 1993.

Chapter

Suspension

This is perhaps the single most important element in the Racing Mini. A slightly under-powered car that handles well will always outperform a powerful ill-handling machine (drivers being equal, of course). This is a point proved time and time again in Mini Challenge racing, where even from the grandstand the way a car's suspension is working can be judged.

The handling characteristics of the Mini distinguished it from ordinary cars from the beginning of production in August 1959. It was revolutionary for its gearbox, located in the sump and beneath an engine that had been installed transversely. It was front-wheel drive, and the wheels, which were a smaller size than had been seen before, were located, literally, at the four corners of the car. The sceptics had a field day, but objectivity returned once the car had been driven. It drove superbly and, indeed, it rewrote the law for car designers.

The system was, and still is, very simple. Front and rear subframes carry the power unit, transmission and suspension complete. The subframes themselves are of steel fabrication – the front one lasts forever, while the rear is known by probably every owner as a weak point in terms of susceptibility to corrosion. Unfortunately, the lateral members formed perfect ledges on which to store road dirt, salt and grime and, when mixed with moisture, rust was the only possible result. Certainly it was a weakness for long-term service-

ability, but replacement is both inexpensive and relatively straightforward. The most important point is that it works well as a suspension carrier.

Basic suspension types

As usual, there are a few types to choose from. The Mini began with, and has now reverted to, a dry suspension system. The spring is in the form of a rubber 'doughnut' which locates in the subframes. In the period 1966–1969 the car was fitted with a Hydrolastic system, which used displacers, inter-connected front to rear. They were pressurised with a fluid that carried the weight of that corner of the car, offered a damping characteristic, and by pushing fluid from front to rear and vice versa kept the car level as it traversed bumps in the road. The wet and dry subframe types are not interchangeable; and, for competition, dry is the better choice. In 1976 the mounting of the front subframe was revised. A single, large diameter bolt was used to secure the subframe tower to the cross-member, and the rear legs were attached to the front floor area by rubber mountings. The changes were all aimed at introducing a rubber element to each mounting to reduce the transmission of noise to the passenger compartment. The rear subframe has remained unchanged in its dry form.

Subframes

The race car builder must look carefully at strengthening the subframes and improving the mountings as both are cheap to accomplish and offer notable improvements in performance. The front frame can be MIG-welded around all the tower seams, and strengthening gussets around the front tie bar mountings and towers are useful against the effects of continued kerb-hopping moments. The rear frame needs gusseting where lateral legs meet the front transverse member.

The mountings, front and rear need to be relieved of all the rubber elements. It is possible to simply replicate the standard rubber mounts in alloy, and proceed with standard components, since all such bushes, spacers and mounts to achieve this are commercially available. The alternative is the fabrication of brackets and extensions to the subframes. This is neater, involves fewer components and, if done proper-

ly, is stronger. MIG-welding skills will be required, and it should be remembered that regulations may call for the original mounting point to be used, although permitting alteration of the method.

Next move is to consider additional mountings, if permitted by the regulations. Bolting the rear transverse member of the front subframe through the bulkhead is easily achieved using a bolt and spacing washers, and helps to maintain stability. The rear subframe will benefit from a similar mod to the front transverse member, drilled through and attached to the rear seat squab bulkhead.

My own Mini Miglia, built new in 1996, is equipped with the most comprehensive additional mountings yet seen – the work of Peter Vickers and Tony Baskerville. These do require a

This photo shows the basic layout of the front subframe, engine, gearbox and transmission assembly on a standard car. It is important to understand fully how the standard car works and fits together before you start to modify it.

Key
1. Engine/transmission oil drain plug
2. Oil filter
3. Front suspension tie bar
4. Disc brake calliper
5. Driveshaft outer CV joint
6. Front subframe
7. Subframe rear mounting
8. Offset sphere type inner CV joint
9. Gearchange extension rod
10. Battery positive cable
11. Steering tie rod outer ball joint
12. Lower suspension
13. Exhaust bracket

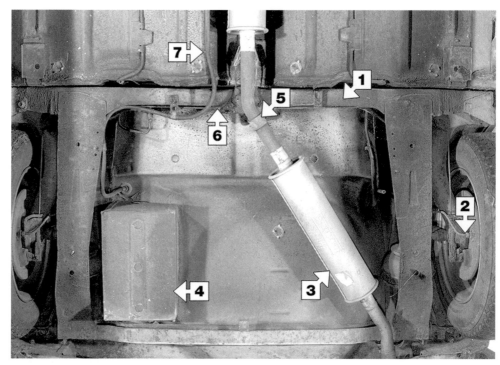

And at the rear, it looks like this. On a race car, many things are changed, with the battery making its way inside the car, along with brake and fuel lines, and a race exhaust system being fitted. As long as the basic subframe, front and rear, is retained, much work can be done to both strengthen and stiffen the frames.

Key
1. *Rear subframe*
2. *Rear brake wheel cylinder attachment*
3. *Exhaust rear silencer*
4. *Battery box*
5. *Exhaust mounting*
6. *Handbrake cable guide*
7. *Battery positive cable*

This diagram shows the standard front and rear subframes. Reinforcement is necessary, but the basic layout and dimensions must remain the same.

Key
1. *Front subframe*
2. *Rear subframe*
3. *Screw*
4. *Washer*
5. *Bolt*
6. *Washer*
7. *Packing piece*
8. *Washer*
9. *Nut*
10. *Screw*
11. *Washer*
12. *Pressure pad*
13. *Support pin*
14. *Bush*
15. *Mounting*
16. *Washer*
17. *Nut*
18. *Screw*
19. *Screw*
20. *Washer*
21. *Screw*
22. *Washer*
23. *Bracket*
24. *Nut*
25. *Washer*

little more skill with hand tools, but the results are worthwhile.

Dry suspension

The dry suspension system is attractive for its simplicity, and, if clearly understood, installation and setting up is a straightforward task. The springs on a Mini are rubber doughnuts and there is much less that can be done than with a car on coil springs. To quantify the options on springs, there are a few variables. First, the standard rubber doughnut offers a cheap starting point, and there are plenty of competitive cars running on them. Used ones are best, as they will have already settled. For the complete beginner it would be wise to begin with a softer, more forgiving set-up, with a view to trying the

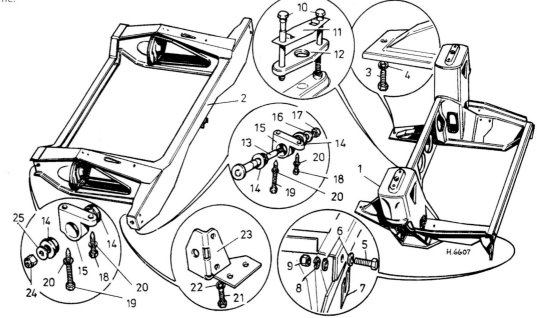

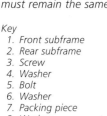

BUILDING, PREPARING AND RACING YOUR MINI

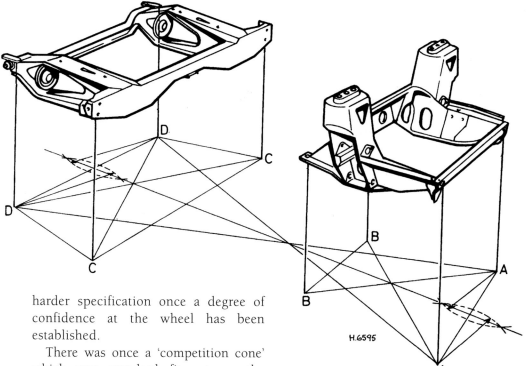

H.6595

Clearly, in order to make
the car track true, the
subframes must be
correctly aligned to the
measurements shown
here.

Key
AA Width between centres
    of the front subframe
    front mounting bolts =
    660.4mm
BB Width between centres
    of the front subframe
    rear mounting bolts =
    412.65mm
CC Width between centres
    of the rear subframe
    front mounting block
    bolts = 1,282.7mm
DD Width between centres
    of the rear subframe rear
    mounting block bolts =
    977.9mm

harder specification once a degree of confidence at the wheel has been established.

There was once a 'competition cone' which was standard fitment on the Innocenti Coopers. It has a squarer face for the alloy trumpet to push against and is therefore more resistant to compression, and hence stiffer. This has been re-manufactured by the Mini Spares Centre and is commonly described as Competition or Innocenti. This fuller profile offers less give, hence the spring's rate is increased, i.e. the load required to achieve a given compression is greater. I prefer the harder doughnuts, and use them on all four corners. Some drivers use a mix, hard at the front and standard at the rear. The Hilo, and Adjusta-ride trumpets also offer an increase in spring rate because of the wider seating face that bears on the doughnut.

So, with stiff doughnuts and Hilos or Adjusta-rides, you have the maximum practical spring rate, and with properly set-up dampers and rear anti-roll bar, the Mini will handle extremely well; it will have excellent grip, perfect traction and minimal body roll.

When locating the front doughnuts in the subframe, gravity works against their retention in the correct place, and the simple measure of a self tapping screw through the top of the frame into the doughnut top ring will ensure they do not become displaced, unsettling the set-up. Similar measures can be applied at the rear.

Suspension struts (trumpets)

Spring rate is further influenced by choice of suspension strut – commonly known as the trumpet (because of its shape). The standard item is cheap and does the job. However, variation in ride height can only be achieved by shortening (or lengthening with spacer washers). Thoroughly worthwhile is the use of Hilos or Adjusta-rides. These are replacement trumpets with the facility to alter length whilst in situ. They also feature a larger seating ring which bears against the doughnut, hence increasing the spring rate. Adjustable trumpets should only be omitted from the build if the regulations dictate, otherwise the extra, modest expense will save hours in the all-important setting-up process, and ensure that perfection can be achieved, where otherwise compromise would be made.

Looking just at the front now, the final major influence on spring rate is choice of top suspension arms. You will be aware that the knuckle joint fitted to the thin end of the trumpet sits in a nylon cup in the top arm. It may, however, have escaped your notice that wet and dry top arms differ slightly. Although outwardly identical, the wet version has the socket for the knuckle joint a little further outboard – away from the pivot pin. This results in a reduction of the leverage ratios, giving an effective increase in spring rate. Identification of wet arms is fairly straightforward, since the drilled hole through which the damper must be bolted is in fact undersize – $5/16$in as opposed to $3/8$in – since on a wet car without dampers this serves only to bolt on the bump stop. With the era of wet cars now well passed, it may be a lengthy search at breakers' yards, but it's worth the effort. In contrast, although rear radius arms vary between wet and dry cars – and should not be mixed – the leverage ratios are virtually the same and there is nothing to choose between the two.

When the fundamental chassis characteristics are sorted to your liking, fine tuning is the next priority.

Ride height

The final consideration before assembling these parts to the subframes is that of ride height. The adjustable trumpets do permit standard height suspension to be raised and lowered. However, Mini Challenge ride height is below that achievable by adjustment, and modifications are necessary. The alloy body of the trumpet may be shortened at the threaded end with a similar amount being removed from the centre shaft. The top of the centre shaft should also be relieved of the ring that prevents excessive heightening. If the doughnuts are fitted with the central threaded boss, this may also be removed since it

will restrict the adjustment, and at such low heights a suspension compression tool will never be needed anyway. For race use, dispose of the rubber boot that covers the threaded section, since the maintenance schedule required for this type of car will ensure that all is kept clean and well lubricated.

With these components all assembled to the subframe, consider next the lower suspension arms and tie bars. These control the position of the lower ball (or swivel) joint, and in turn the camber and castor angles. These are the guts of the suspension geometry, and the ability to adjust and optimise them is essential to the handling characteristics of the car. The standard parts are rubber mounted, and for racing use the compliance these offer is not helpful, with a vagueness in feel and excess play developing from rapid wearing. The first and most simple improvement is to replace these bushes with any of the hard nylon type replicas which are available from many tuning sources. This will improve the feel and resistance to deformation under load. The hardness selected should suit application, hardest for race use with only small suspension travel, and remember that the bush must provide some movement to allow the arm to move within its range.

The next variation on this theme is the stretched bottom arms, with nylon bushes. These are supplied with the intended camber angle set, and although they are a step forward it's only a small one. The real solution is infinitely adjustable bottom arm and tie bars incorporating rod end bearings. Usually these are modified standard parts with bearing sizes that assure reliability, and long life. The bottom arms have the inner end cut off and a threaded sleeve welded in place into which the joint is screwed and secured with a lock nut. The welding should be of the highest standard and this is certainly not a DIY modification. The tie bar is relieved of its standard front mount, and a female joint is screwed on. This is secured to the front of the subframe by a U-shaped saddle and cross bolt. The ultimate bottom arms are those that are adjustable in situ – the time saved at the setting up stage easily justifying the added expense. Mine were made by Selby Engineering. The inboard end has a collar into which a sleeve nut fits, and this carries the joint. Turning the sleeve nut whilst the suspension is still assembled achieves camber change.

Rear suspension

The rear suspension is a whole lot simpler and less complicated to adjust. Variation is required in camber of the rear wheels, and their tracking relative to each other. All of this can be achieved using the bracket that fixes the outer end of the radius arm. Proprietary adjustable brackets are available to allow camber alteration. This is achieved simply by slotting the hole that the radius arm shaft passes through, and creating a sliding washer that can be clamped in a position to set the camber angle required. Adjustment of track is less clever, and relies on the use of spacing shims that are placed between the camber bracket and the subframe. These are made up using thin steel sheet, with the holes slotted out so that they can be slipped in without the need to remove the bolts. These spacers have the effect of toeing out the track, meaning that the front (toe) of the wheel is trained outward. The standard setting is 1 degree toe in, while race settings are between parallel and 2 degrees toe out. So, a number of shims may be required, and the final angle will be a product of the driver's feel during testing (*see* Chapter 3 for more details on this subject).

Dampers

Dampers are often incorrectly referred to as shock absorbers. (The shocks that the car receives, transmitted from the road through the tyre and wheel to the suspension are actually absorbed by the spring – or doughnut. The action of any spring is to oscillate at a reducing frequency until balance is restored. If the car's spring oscillated, the vehicle would not have time to recover from one bump before the next appeared and handling would be a disaster. The damper, therefore, is perfectly described, as it damps out any oscillation to the extent that, if it is tuned and rated correctly, the spring deflects once and then resumes its normal attitude.) Essentially, the damper performs a straightforward task, but the problem is that the nature of the bumps differs and, when racing, there are kerbs and undulations as well as the driver's style

Dampers are an area for considerable development and investment. These are some of the best around, Quantum double-adjustable (bump and rebound), lightweight gas-pressurised. In the right hands they are almost infinitely adjustable but require plenty of time, patience and experience to get the best from them. Moreover, their wide range of adjustment also provides much more room for the amateur to tie the car in knots – metaphorically and literally! If you haven't the knowledge (and don't know a man who has), then it's probably better to stick with something simpler until you have.

At top is the Spax GP double adjustable damper, and below is the TraxSpax single adjustable unit. (Courtesy Norman Hodson, CCC magazine)

For greater travel, I used modified top damper mounts, seen here on the left, alongside a standard mount for comparison. (Courtesy Norman Hodson, CCC magazine)

On the left is a standard 'doughnut'. On the right, the square-shouldered racing variant from Mini Spares is much harder.

to consider. As a result, the requirements of a damper vary from circuit to circuit and driver to driver; and the subject is steeped in mystique and misunderstanding.

Given an understanding of what a damper does, size is the next consideration. The space in which it must fit is determined largely by the ride height. If the car is a lot lower than standard, either shorter dampers or, at the front, modified brackets will be required. Determine first the fitted length with the car at race ride height. The damper fitted should be about

70 per cent closed, giving 30 per cent bump (compression) travel and 70 per cent droop (extension) travel in use.

Off-the-shelf items, such as the Gas Spax Adjustable dampers, are available in lowered height format, do the job well and are simple to set-up. They do not offer excessive stiffness, so I usually run the front fully hard in both Mini Se7en and Mini Miglia. To demonstrate the point on dampers, I have won National Challenge Mini Miglia races on Gas Spax.

TrakSpax are a logical and effective progression, with many stroke and body lengths to choose from making compromise unnecessary. They have a single adjuster for bump but are full size bodies with rose joints top and bottom (to eliminate the compliance suffered in rubber bushed dampers). Valving can be varied at the factory to the customer's request. There are two Challenge specification dampers, valved to suit front and rear, and sized to fit the car without undue difficulty. I find that the TrakSpax offer greater consistency in extended periods of use, with greater stiffness at the top of the adjustment scale.

For the accomplished driver/engineer there is the Spax GP range, which gives many stroke and body length options. They are double-adjustable and built to

order with valving to your specification. I have used them on the front in Miglia with excellent results. The setting-up process requires some patience, a disciplined test programme and a systematic approach, but the design is such that following simple step-by-step moves the set-up can be finalised in a couple of hours. The secret is to start with zero on both bump and rebound. The rebound is increased first by a step at a time, all the time leaving bump at 0. As the rebound stiffness increases the wheel will decline slower from the arch, so you are looking for the first sign of loss of traction on the inside front wheel when cornering. The intention is to set the rebound as stiff as possible, but not so that traction is affected. If the valving is right this should fall in the mid-range of adjustment. If it does not, then the dampers can be altered

This photo shows the GP damper on the nearside of my 97 Miglia car – note the trumpet in the tower to the left of the damper. Technically not as advanced as the Quantum, but very able units and adjustable to suit most occasions. I ran TraxSpax at the rear because they're simple, effective, reliable and consistent. The pairing isn't cheap, but it was a major contributory factor to winning the championship. Nevertheless, many drivers run with single adjustable and, as the saying goes, it's not what you've got, it's what you do with it.

back at the factory. Once the rebound setting is finalised, bump is next. This is more difficult to describe, it is more a case of feel. Increase stiffness to personal preference, and take care not to go too far – you are looking for control over bumps, but not to jump them!

I have raced, and indeed won, at National level with all three types. It is hard to exceed the value for money offered by the Gas Adjustables, but each step up offers progress. Currently I use GPs on the front of the Miglia and TrakSpax on the rear, this represents value for money and gives consistently outstanding results. Similar equipment is available from other manufacturers, and good results have been demonstrated, but I cannot express a personal opinion as I have never used them myself.

Anti-roll bars

Anti-roll bars are the final piece of hardware to be considered. Mini Se7en in the 850 days was pretty much roll-bar free. Most cars used bump stops – harsh ones at that on the rear – to get the rear suspension to go pretty much solid, readily inducing oversteer which did most of the cornering. This was a very basic method which worked well, complemented the tyre performance, and was good enough to win.

Rear bars became widespread in the 1000cc Mini Se7en formula, where greater torque encouraged a more precise and tidy style. Their contribution to the package was two-fold. They certainly help turn-in if combined with a measure of rear toe-out. However, the true function is to increase stiffness by forcing both wheels to act together.

The bar is rigidly mounted to the chassis and its arms are connected to the suspension each side so that the bump and droop forces generated each side are fed into the bar. The bar reduces roll by increasing the spring rate. The rate is increased because, to allow bump travel, the side under compression by transfer through the bar, must compress the spring on the side that is not loaded, as well as its own. Also, the connection side-to-side, in theory, keeps the car even in terms of height, but the Mini will defy this theory, and has always been seen to lift the inside wheel well clear of the ground.

A number of factors affect the stiffness of the bar, notably the thickness of a solid bar, or the diameter and wall thickness of a tubular version. The length of the legs has a direct effect by altering the leverage that the suspension applies to the bar, and hence its willingness to twist.

Using a front bar in Mini Miglia strikes me as a little odd. Theory would suggest that a front-drive car would only use a bar with a limited-slip differential (LSD) to complement it, since compressing the spring on the unloaded side will increase the likelihood of traction being compromised on that wheel. An LSD will control that, but a conventional differential will drive the easy option, meaning a complete loss of traction. Where they have been used in Miglia (and I have driven Richard Wager's car), I can only assume that the torsional stiffness of the bar is low, hence the unloaded wheel does not pick up and break traction. Where the front bar proved useful was on the KAD twin-cam Silhouette machines which were running LSDs. Ultimately, I have driven all configurations, and all work well, but depend very much on a complementary chassis set-up.

My cars have always featured the Myk Cable Developments rose-jointed and fully adjustable anti-roll bar. The range of adjustment available means that a driver can learn the principles and then increase stiffness to preference, and in this way only one bar will ever need to be purchased. The bar is solid and $5/8$in diameter.

Steering

In principle the steering mechanism of the mini is straightforward. Relatively few components are used, adjustment is easy, and probably only the concept of rear wheel steering will be new!

The standard rack and pinion system

The Mini features a rack and pinion type steering system, the whole assembly, including the track rods, being referred to as the 'steering rack'. This is an item that I do not and would not consider tampering with. In the event of accident damage or free play caused by hard use, replacement of the whole assembly is the only totally safe option. Choose between second-hand, reconditioned exchange or brand new. From bitter experience I always select the latter option, having more than once suffered rapid deterioration of the alternatives, and then faced the lengthy task of removal and replacement on a built up car.

My preference for steering set-up is to stick with standard components. Do ensure that the rack used is a Mk II onwards version (Mk I Minis had a slightly different rack and a larger turning circle) and that it is in perfect order. The track rods should be carefully checked for straightness and zero play in all planes.

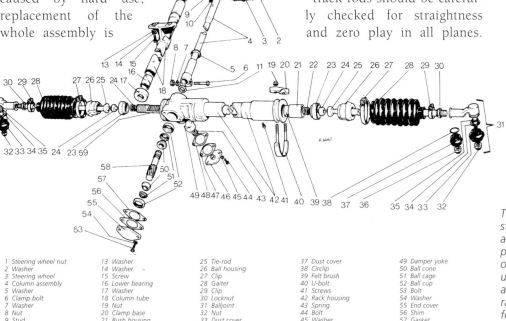

1 Steering wheel nut	13 Washer	25 Tie-rod	37 Dust cover	49 Damper yoke
2 Washer	14 Washer –	26 Ball housing	38 Circlip	50 Ball cone
3 Steering wheel	15 Screw	27 Clip	39 Felt brush	51 Ball cage
4 Column assembly	16 Lower bearing	28 Gaiter	40 U-bolt	52 Ball cup
5 Washer	17 Washer	29 Clip	41 Screws	53 Bolt
6 Clamp bolt	18 Column tube	30 Locknut	42 Rack housing	54 Washer
7 Washer	19 Nut	31 Balljoint	43 Spring	55 End cover
8 Nut	20 Clamp base	32 Nut	44 Bolt	56 Shim
9 Stud	21 Bush housing	33 Dust cover	45 Washer	57 Gasket
10 Locknut	22 Thrust spring	34 Circlip	46 Damper cover	58 Pinion
11 Oil seal	23 Locking ring	35 Washer	47 Shim	59 Rack
12 Upper bearing	24 Ball seat	36 Nut	48 Gasket	

The standard Mini steering system is rack and pinion and particularly good straight off the shelf. I prefer using standard parts, and always replace the entire rack system if a fault is found – you can't afford to make mistakes in this area!

The standard mounting to the body shell is strong and reliable and the U-bolt fixing allows the rack to be rotated, altering the steering column angle. The angle can be changed to suit any preference, and should be set finally with the driver seated in the definitive position, and belted in.

The hub assemblies are standard and use tapered roller bearings to Cooper S spec, with Cooper S CV joints, driveshafts and inner couplings. Also standard are the top and bottom ball joints, top arms and steering arms (although some drivers bend or space the latter to achieve a difference in bump steer). The bottom arms are non-standard because they are rose-jointed, which takes away the movement inherent with rubber bushes, and also provides a way of adjusting the camber. When it comes to tie bars, there is a choice; many owners opt for the rather attractive tubular versions from specialists such as Manx racing. However, I like to stick with the standard, solid steel items which seem to me to work better when bumping over kerbs, etc. They are fitted with a rose joint at the front for adjustment of the castor angle.

Bump steer

Bump steer is a self-explanatory term, and one that the race Mini demonstrates. Alteration of the camber angle, and more significantly the castor angle, changes the inclination of the bearing hub and hence the angle of the mounting face for the steering arm. The net effect is that if you plot the wheel direction throughout the range of suspension travel, you will discover that it changes dramatically despite the steering wheel remaining fixed. A variety of solutions have been applied to this problem, and having eliminated theoretical bump steer completely from my car by steering arm spacing, within a single race I had reverted to the original set-up because it felt better!

In order to assess bump steer, support the car on axle stands and remove the doughnut and trumpet from the front suspension. Ensure that the steering cannot move, and with the road wheel removed check that all the wheel studs are exactly the same length, or that with sleeve nuts screwed on their projection beyond the drive flange is equal. If the hub assembly is now raised through the range of travel permitted by the damper, bump steer can be assessed. To do this, place on the ground either a hardboard or cardboard sheet that my be drawn on. This must be taped down so that it cannot move. A flat piece of alloy plate now held against the sleeve nuts/studs/hub face and allowed to rest on the base will make a projection line which should be drawn on the base. A series of lines can be built up by moving through the range of suspension travel. Whilst assessing bump steer between full bump and full droop, remember that the actual travel in use is probably less and therefore the effect is not so great. However, the theoretical requirement is to have none whatsoever. To eliminate the bump steer, it is necessary to alter the angle of the track rod, back towards that which it would display without the increased castor and camber angles. I am unwilling to bend the steering arms. The results are rather unpredictable and several attempts may be made, each calling for the steering arm to be heated and cooled. My preference is to space the steering arm from the hub face. In order to establish the amount of spacing necessary, plain washers are used in increasing numbers until the bump steer is eliminated. Once the size is established, a spacer can be machined to include the dowels that ensure the arm cannot fret on the hub face. Finally, longer high tensile bolts complete the job. Repeated on both sides, the car should now be free of bump steer, provided that the existing ride height and geometry are respected. As stated, try this yourself, as the theoretical advantage cannot be argued. However, in practice, I felt it offered nothing.

Steering arms

The steering arms are a current production part and can be purchased new at modest expense. When you consider the loads that they are subjected to, particularly with a slick-shod car, second-hand items will be less attractive. Many people still search out the Cooper S arms, which are considerably stronger. However, they are inevitably old and it is impossible to gauge how they have been used; so, at the very least have them crack-tested, and inspect them regularly for signs of distress.

Rear wheel steering

So, the matter of rear wheel steering should now be addressed. Certainly we are not dealing with true four-wheel steering, but the rear tracking when used with an anti-roll bar may be set to assist the turn-in qualities of the Mini. Quite simply, if the rear wheels toe out a little when only one of them is on the ground then the car will be steered outwards on that side. This is a characteristic that will give a sharper feel to the turn-in, providing the driver is expecting it and has the experience to maintain control with a feeling that the back of the car has stepped out or even gone sideways. This is not something to try first time out, rather it is one of the small tweaks that makes the difference between front-running and midfield pace.

Tracking

The measurement of wheel tracking is most easily achieved using Dunlop optical gauges, and is expressed as the angle between the pair of wheels in degrees and minutes (60 minutes make one degree). Do remember that the gauges are intended to be used at the front of a car, and when used at the rear the indicated toe-in will in fact mean toe-out and vice versa. Having established a reading, alteration is the next step. There are a number of methods of doing this. You may slot the inner hole for the radius arm shaft and make a sliding adjuster, but adjustments will alter the ride height and the corner weights. It is preferable to move the outer end of the radius arm, and this is easily achieved by shimming out the radius arm bracket using shims cut from thin steel plate. The tracking figure measured by gauges does not, of course, tell you whether the rear wheels are pointing correctly ahead. The gauges may read parallel, but both wheels could be pointing to the left (or right). This can easily be assessed by placing a straight edge against the side of each tyre and looking along it to see the projection relative to the front wheel. This will indicate which side should be shimmed to achieve both the degree of toe required on the rear and the relationship to the forward direction of the car. The amount of rear tracking will be dependent on driver preference, but I suggest that you work upwards from a half of one degree towards a maximum of two degrees.

Finally ensure that all of the steering components are subjected to a spanner check before each and every outing. It takes only a short while but is worth plenty in terms of driver confidence.

Chapter 5 Brakes

The braking system on any racing car is arguably the single most important system fitted to it. The limiting factor for the brake system on a racing car is the grip level of the tyres themselves and not the performance capacity of any component making up the brakes.

Brake choice

Historically, the Mini started life under-equipped in the braking department. With drums all round, the car was just about adequate for road use, but any tuning or competition applications soon over-stretched them, and this was recognised when the first Mini Cooper, introduced in 1961, was fitted with disc brakes. The discs were 7in diameter, and proved to be hopelessly inadequate, but did pave the way for the Cooper S 7½in diameter discs and more effective callipers which were fitted

Classic Miglia set-up. 7.9in solid Tar-Ox disc with KAD 4-pot calliper and carbon metallic pads. Superb performance! (Courtesy Norman Hodson, CCC magazine)

with servo assistance. At last real brakes were available and this set-up works well to this day.

For racing or fast road purposes, then, at the very least 7½in 'S' discs and callipers are a must, but there are now a multitude of superior alternatives.

Of all Mini racing formulae, Mini Se7en is the most restricted on brake systems. 'S' discs and callipers are permitted, and these should be your choice, as any of the lesser options are worthless. The rear brakes must be single leading shoe drums, and these in effect are under utilised to eliminate the risk of locking the rear wheels under braking. With the Mini Se7en weighing around 560kg, the servo is unnecessary,

the result being a firm and effective pedal.

Rear brake regulators

The matter of effort to the rear is addressed by the fitting of an adjustable regulator – this simple device reduces the pedal effort to the rear brakes, as weight transference (or dive) to the front under braking, can cause non-regulated rear brakes to lock-up. However, it is important to achieve a balance between locking up on the one hand and barely working on the other. There are several ways of achieving the balance required.

The standard rear regulator already reduces the effort applied to the rear

They're serious lumps of metal, something that can be seen more clearly in this close-up. (Courtesy Norman Hodson, CCC magazine)

Mounted at the rear of the cabin is the brake pressure regulator. The rear brakes must work, but most drivers adjust them so that there is virtually no braking effect at the rear – locked rear wheels under heavy braking do nothing for one's confidence when racing!

brakes, and by dismantling and weakening of the spring (achieved by sawing off one or more coils) the pressure at which the rear brakes are shut off will reduce. A step further, but still using the standard regulator, is to use an adjustable version (commercially available from Mini Spares), and this is my preference. The final option is the fitment of a Tilton regulating valve, a more expensive proprietary item that may be installed to permit adjustment whilst racing. There is one further alternative, that being to use a twin master cylinder layout, where the front and rear brakes each have an independent master. This will be covered later in this chapter.

Front brake uprates

The serious hardware is for enhancement of the front braking capacity. The disc choices vary in both size and type, vented and non-vented. Calliper options are production or after-market – 2, 4 or even 6-pot versions in alloy or steel. Consider first the regulations specific to the championship you wish to contest. Mini Se7en is very restricted while, in comparison, Miglia is relatively free. As well as official regulations, the other restrictions are those of wheel size and, of course, the size of budget available.

The Mini Se7en set-up based on standard Cooper S components works well and is good for 100bhp maximum, beyond which temperatures and hence performance will become marginal. The next step is to use Metro discs, either solid or vented as fitted to the Turbo model. These will need to be fitted with the late Mini drive flange. These discs are supplied in 8.4in outside diameter, and for most of the calliper options will need to be turned down to 7.9in to fit under a 10in wheel – this is definitely a job for a specialist. The choice between vented and solid is a much discussed subject. I have used both, and lately have opted for the reduced weight offered by the solid version, and I experienced no deterioration in performance as a result. The theory of the vented disc is that the increased surface area for heat radiation, enhanced by superior air flow will keep the disc and the calliper cooler, providing more capacity. For Silhouette type machinery the vented disc is an obvious choice and one that I have used with success and reliability.

The final option is the really big discs, seen on some Silhouette cars, of up to 11in diameter. Clearly these will only fit under a 13in wheel, and whilst offering outstanding potential performance they put a hugely increased stress level on the front hubs and ball joints. In simple terms the clamping radius of the pad is so much greater than the ball-joint radius that it has been known for the ball joint to snap under the load, with disastrous results. Certainly, there may have been mitigating circumstances, or even poor maintenance, but I wouldn't take the risk.

The next choice with discs is that of manufacturer. I have used standard Rover-supplied discs with good results, but prefer to use Tar-Ox wherever possible. Tar-Ox discs have radial grooves that take care of the pads better by de-glazing, and they have a larger surface area for heat dissipation by radiation, hence offering improved brake fade characteristics. Finally, improved grip is available by using high-grade and slightly softer disc material.

There are also a multitude of choices in the calliper department. The Cooper S works well, as does the four-pot Metro turbo cast-iron calliper. The serious after-market stuff is where real performance lies, however. The KAD alloy 4-pot version works exceedingly well, even when coping with 180bhp. It is a direct bolt-on item, and the provision of spacer pieces will permit solid or vented discs to be used. Having used these with solid discs in Miglia, and with vented discs in the Silhouette machines, I never expected to be looking for more from the brakes, but things never stand still for long. KAD have now produced a 6-pot calliper, machined from billet and incredibly thin, so that larger disc diameter can be contained within a 10in wheel. The 6-pot calliper has different piston sizes to ensure that the pad pushes evenly and mitigates tapered wear. It works superbly and offers improvement where I least expected to find it.

There are several alternative 4-pot callipers. The Mini Spares Centre produce one which performed well in a test car I have driven, and then there is the older AP Racing solid-backed calliper, used originally in Formula 3 type machinery, which can be used beneath 10in wheels with some grinding down of the casting. This works well, but the modifications are something I haven't tried, and would be reluctant to do so.

In summary, the classic choices are Cooper S disc and calliper, Metro disc and KAD 4-pot calliper or, in classes calling for production parts, Metro turbo discs and iron 4-pot callipers. Take your pick!

Brake pad choice

Pad friction material presents another range of choice, and I have found Carbon Metallic to work best for me. They offer outstanding performance and good life expectancy of up to a season. They are often criticised for being harsh on the disc, but with Tar-Ox 40-groove discs I have never experienced any unexpected rate of wear. Tar-Ox themselves make pads, and in the Cooper S calliper and disc set-up these worked well, although the wear rate of pad was higher, and when first used they smelled of overheating despite not having done so!

The hydraulic pipes must be very carefully routed, clinically clean and totally leak-free. I'm using Aeroquip hosing here – it's aero-specification makes it very strong and it looks good, but it's not an absolute necessity.

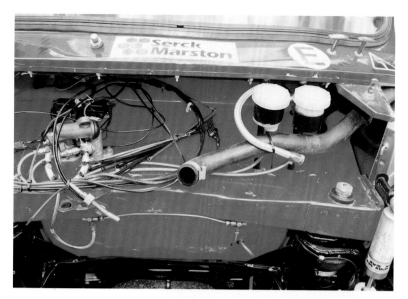

Mintex do a large range of pads in new materials with no asbestos. With pads, more than most things, it's a case of trial and error. The desire is to have the softest pad possible which doesn't overheat and fade. Harder pads take longer to warm up and generally offer less feel to the driver.

Brake fluid

Brake fluid also presents a choice. I have often used simple Dot 4 fluid, it being cheap and available anywhere. Kept in good condition this works well, although regular bleeding is wise, and complete renewal should be undertaken

The hydraulic components have to fit wherever there's room. In my own car, the reservoirs are on the nearside of the bulkhead with the master cylinders being ...

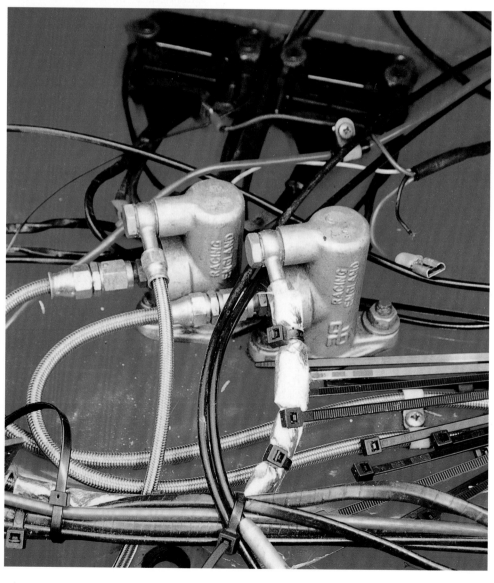

... on the driver's side.

BUILDING, PREPARING AND RACING YOUR MINI

at least once a year. This type of fluid is hygroscopic, meaning that it attracts and absorbs water, lowering its boiling point and hence its suitability for racing. There is a range of race fluids, all offering higher boiling points with proportionately higher price tags! Silicone fluid is non-hygroscopic and claimed to increase the boiling point. It also has lubricating qualities, and for this reason I have used it to assist the pistons in alloy callipers with apparently good results. This, too, is expensive, but looking after the piston to calliper friction levels is certainly worthwhile if the brake drag can be reduced even slightly.

Master cylinder

Having looked thoroughly at the wheel end of things, the master cylinder installation should be considered next. The standard Mini master will work well, but it's relatively small bore (0.7in) means that moving enough fluid to operate 4-pot callipers and standard rear brakes results in a longish brake pedal (too much travel). The solutions are again numerous in number and varied in cost.

If you can find an Austin 1300GT, it had the standard-style master cylinder, with a bore size of ³/₄in. This moves a larger volume of fluid for the same pedal travel and hence gives a shorter pedal throw that will feel better to the driver. In the absence of such a relic, the best option is an AP Racing remote cylinder and separate reservoir. These can be purchased in numerous bore sizes, and will fit directly to the standard mounting and pedal, requiring only the provision of a bracket to support the reservoir in a remote location.

The final choice is to incorporate a true pedal box into the car with two brake master cylinders, one to operate the front brakes and one the rear. This has a balance bar between the two,

permitting adjustment between effort to the front or rear. Tilton make a number of complete assemblies which can simply be bolted to the floor of the car and incorporate the pedals (brake and clutch) master cylinders, reservoirs and adjustment mechanism. This is a one-stop solution, and easy if a little expensive. The alternative is to fabricate around the original pedal, but this is a tricky task which should only be undertaken by those with exceptional skills.

With the hardware installed, set-up and the gaining of confidence in the system is vitally important. RAC regulations state that there should be effort to the rear brakes, but without defining how it should be measured! I set the rear brakes so that with an assistant pressing firmly on the brake pedal it is just possible to turn a rear wheel using maximum physical effort. Bedding-in the pads is important, and the manufacturers instructions should be followed closely. Then it is just a matter of getting confident with the limits, and driving just inside them!

By comparison, on Ian Curley's Miglia the reservoirs are on the offside and the master cylinders are in the floor-mounted pedal box.

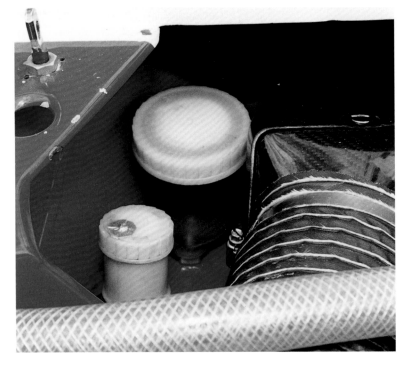

Transmission

A brief history of the Mini transmission

This chapter has to begin with a short history lesson. It is one that most will be aware of, but such is the significance of the event that it is worthy of another airing.

When the Mini first rolled off the production line in August 1959, it was revolutionary in more ways than one. It redefined the family car, and fun motoring, but most significantly it set the future of road car production on a new course. The transverse engine installation with gearbox in the sump and front-wheel drive was a new design, the work of a genius. The critics doubted it would ever work, but now it's the standard layout for family cars.

When dismantled and understood fully, like all great solutions, it is oh so simple. There are no unnecessary complications, and it delivered the 30-odd horsepower of the Mini to the front wheels with ease. There have been evolutionary steps over the years, raising power output on production models to more than 70bhp, but the transmission system can cope with all this and much more. I have pushed 180bhp through Formula 3 tyres to propel the Mini faster than Issigonis would ever have imagined, all on the original concept transmission. Remarkable.

To prepare the Mini for competition always involves some transmission work. Here we will look at the whole system from flywheel and clutch through drop gears, gear kits, differentials and drive shafts, to identify what components and practices are needed, when and where.

When considering the spec for the transmission in a race Mini, remember the fact that the best parts are virtually bomb-proof and, if correctly installed and used, may be expected to outlast the car itself. These components are expensive, however, and if your budget does not stretch, there are alternatives which will serve the purpose at much less expense. Essentially there is a method to suit most budgets.

Though gearbox internals are pretty much like 3D jigsaws and fit together with cool logic, they are complicated, to say the least, and you should consider your personal abilities before you start. If it's something you've never attempted, then either consider bringing in a professional or make sure you know a man who knows, so that you have someone at the other end of a panic phone call! The overriding factor when dealing with gearbox and clutch components is the need to be scrupulously clean; you don't want oil on the clutch or dirt in the oil.

Clutch and flywheel assembly

This assembly comprises the flywheel, backplate, diaphragm (sometimes called the 'cover') and clutch plate. *Without exception*, the use of any

92 BUILDING, PREPARING AND RACING YOUR MINI

of these *standard* parts should be avoided.

Consider first the flywheel and backplate. In competition use these will be called upon to rev to perhaps 8,000rpm or more. The original designer probably never imagined more than 6,000rpm being used. The standard parts are both heavy and made of the wrong material for our intended use. The standard flywheel and backplate are referred to as cast iron. I am quite sure that a metallurgist would frown at the simplicity of this statement, but the intention is correct.

The fact is that cast iron always displays a relative weakness when tested in tension, and the rotation of the parts causes centrifugal force that tests their strength in tension. So the theory is that failure may occur simply by the flywheel or backplate cracking and then disintegrating in use. I would agree that this all sounds a little fanciful, but I have personally witnessed several such incidents, one of which destroyed an entire car, and the lesson is never more clearly understood than when it is seen unfolding. Do *not* take the risk. Quite simply, if you cannot afford a steel flywheel and backplate, you cannot afford to go racing. That's all there is to it!

Some drivers have been fooled into buying iron flywheels and backplates that have been lightened and look like steel items. Perhaps it is difficult for the eye to detect, but the hammer will not lie! It is a simple test, hold the item for test between two fingers, and strike *lightly* with a ball pein hammer. Whilst the iron one will give a dead sound, the steel one will ring. There is no mistaking the difference.

Steel or alloy flywheel?

Having decided to move away from the iron bits, what do you look for as a replacement? The broad choices are steel or alloy, and there are good and bad examples of each. Steel is the

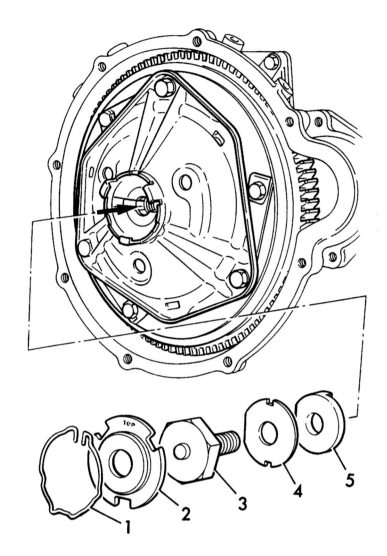

cheaper option of the two, and if price is your major consideration, then look no further because these bits will do the job. Moreover, if they are used well, they will stand the test of time. The steel flywheel is a one-piece item, supplied with drive-strap holes and puller holes all drilled and tapped, but needing the straps to be provided and correctly spaced. The steel back plate has its origins in the Cooper S (AEG 270). Mini Spares have reproduced this and point out that it is actually high-quality cast steel, like the 270. Whatever, I have used this with consistent results – and it passes the hammer test. There are billet backplates around. As usual, check carefully what you are buying – and always do the simple test.

This diagram shows the clutch thrust plate and flywheel securing bolt assemblies for post-1969 cars.

Key
1. Circlip
2. Release bearing thrust plate
3. Flywheel retaining bolt
4. Lockwasher
5. Keyed washer

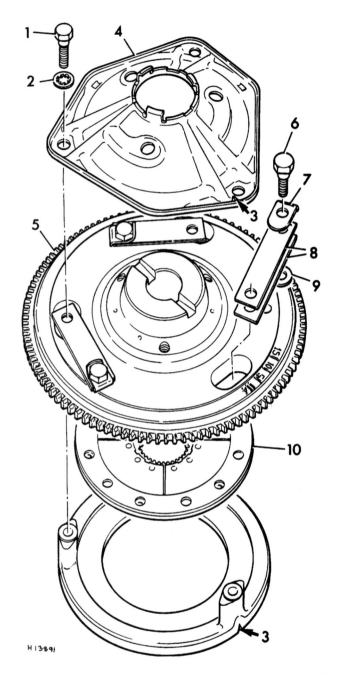

H 13891

Check out what goes where with this exploded diagram of a non-Verto type clutch and flywheel assembly.

Key
  1. Driving bolt
  2. Shakeproof washer
  3. Alignment mark
  4. Diaphragm
  5. Flywheel
  6. Driving bolt
  7. Tab washer
  8. Driving straps
  9. Distance washer
 10. Clutch disc

recall an early alloy flywheel that, it was rumoured, was made from melted down saucepans! This was a derisory comment, and I never used one, but they swiftly disappeared again. The concept remained a good one, and KAD duly produced an alloy flywheel that has stood the test of time. We have used these consistently over the past four seasons with excellent results.

The KAD alloy flywheel uses a centre from the standard Verto flywheel, with an alloy billet disc on to which the friction surface is sprayed. An ordinary ring gear is an interference fit, and although the assembled item weighs only a fraction less than the steel equivalent, if a weld-on takes place the expensive alloy part can be unbolted from the centre which can be cut off and replaced at very modest expense.

If the flywheel offered only a small weight saving, the same cannot be said of the backplate which is much less than its steel equivalent. Again a KAD item, it is machined from billet, with a sprayed on friction surface. I have given these components the sternest tests over a long period of time and find the results to be reliable and consistent.

Having acquired the right bits in either alloy or steel, proper assembly is vital to achieve correct function and reliability. Sourcing new Rover drive straps should not be a problem, and these should be doubled up, using a total of six per flywheel. They are secured using a shouldered bolt that is no longer available new, so good used ones will have to do. Never be tempted to use ordinary bolts, since misalignment will occur. It will be necessary to space the drive straps from the flywheel, so use plain washers to establish the correct amount of spacing. Determine this by laying the friction plate on the backplate with the flywheel on top. With the contact between all three the drive straps should be unstressed, i.e. neither pushed nor

The most common problem suffered by users of steel flywheels is finding that it has welded itself to the nose of the crank, usually condemning both to the skip in the process. This is a problem that I have never actually suffered and, as covered later, it is simply a question of installation method.

The problem of 'welded-on flywheels' was one of the prompts that led to the conception and widespread use of alloy flywheels and, lately, backplates. I can pulled by completion of assembly. Having determined how many washers are necessary, a proper spacer may be prepared.

Friction plate

The friction plate should be chosen according to preference and usage, and the correct diaphragm should be paired with it. Friction material can be either fibre or sintered metal. I always use genuine AP products, and consider the reliability they give me justifies the extra cost. I have used the competition fibre plate (with the friction material bonded as well as riveted to the backing disc) in 1000cc Mini Se7en and Miglia. The AP sintered plate is also reliable and durable and has been first choice for all the 1300cc Miglia stuff.

Diaphragm

Diaphragms are all identical to look at, but are colour coded with a paint mark on the spring itself. Blue, orange and grey are typically referred to as Cooper S, rally and race, although I have used all three in race engines. The blue was preferred in the 850cc Mini Se7en days, as its lesser weight was kinder to the tiny crankshaft thrust washers of that engine, and it coped admirably with the modest torque produced. The larger thrust washers of all other engines means the grey diaphragm can be used with a sintered plate or, if preferred, the orange cover with the fibre plate. The grey diaphragm should be considered a must for engines with more than 100ft/lb torque.

Fitting the flywheel

Now, perhaps the most important task is to fit the flywheel so that it will work without welding itself on, and for it to be possible to remove it when necessary. Probably every successful racer will describe a different 'infallible' method. Mine is a simple one. The tail of the crankshaft should be unblemished. Any

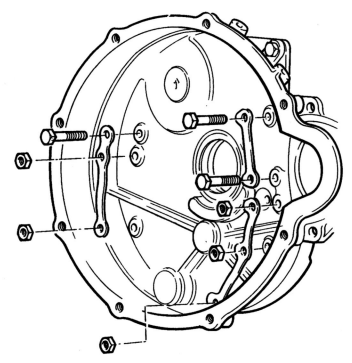

marks caused by fretting are the beginning of a welding-on problem and must be removed. To do this, use an old scrap standard flywheel, and fine lapping paste on the crank and lap the two until the crank is smooth once more. This can take time. If necessary use coarse paste, but always finish with fine. The tail must now be cleaned carefully with a solvent cleaner and be dried. Now inspect the flywheel taper. If this is marked similar remedial action is necessary using a scrap crank with a good tail. Once both mating surfaces are smooth and clean they are ready for assembly.

Slip the flywheel on to the crank and align the offset slot, then with a copper mallet strike the flywheel firmly on to the crank. The standard slotted washer has never failed me in Miglia spec, but for the mega horsepower twin-cams, Kent Automotive Developments produce a hardened steel replacement with tighter tolerances to eliminate any tiny movement there may be, and for the modest cost I prefer to use one of these. Once positioned, and with a standard bolt oiled on the thread and face, the tightening can proceed. The flywheel is

This diagram shows the standard flywheel housing attachments.

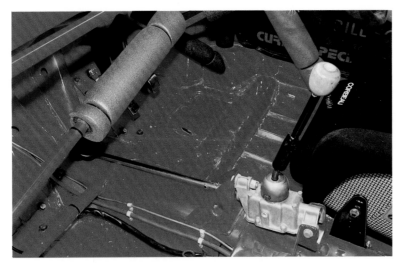

A rod-change gear shift mechanism is used which, like everything else, has to be checked, double-checked and then fastened securely into place. The gear lever itself takes a lot of stick in the heat of battle, and when you move it around, you need to be sure there's a gear there when you let out the clutch!

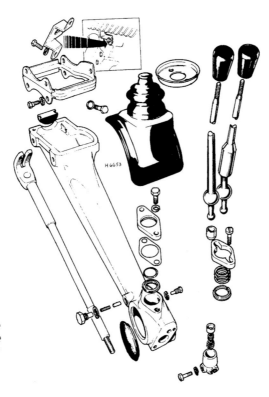

This diagram shows the component parts of the remote control housing used with pre-rod change boxes.

easily locked with a big-end shell bearing in the starter motor aperture, and I tighten as much as is physically possible, using a long arm bar but no further lever extension.

With the flywheel tight, and before bolting the diaphragm on, check that the clutch plate still turns freely. Repeated fitting and removal of the flywheel results in it going on a tiny bit further each time, and eventually this can pinch up the primary gear retaining washer,

binding the gear to the crank and preventing the clutch from disengaging correctly. A good move is to relieve the inside face of the flywheel by 0.030in before the problem occurs, and it should then never arise. Similarly, the tail of the crank can eventually come flush with the end of the flywheel, giving the feeling that the flywheel is correctly tightened up when in fact it is not. This can and will lead to the flywheel fretting on the tail of the crank and becoming heated, causing the welding-on phenomenon. Again, it is worth grinding 0.030in from the end of the crankshaft taper before the problem arises.

A final point on the clutch is not to overlook the function of the release bearing. Repeatedly it is accelerated from stationary to 8,000rpm, almost instantly. This is far beyond its designer's intention. Regular replacement is the answer – it is an inexpensive part that is easily changed.

The gears and ratios required

OK, so the clutch assembly deals with engagement and disengagement of drive. The transfer of motion to the gearbox is by three gears in permanent mesh, collectively known as the drop gears. In production form these are helically cut, and will work in competition cars of modest power. The real solution, however, is to use straight cut drop gears. These offer greater strength, interchangeability of ratio, and eliminate the slight sideways thrust that helical gears cause. The straight-cut gears, of course, do generate the whine which would not be acceptable in a road car, but somehow adds to the charm of a race car!

Jack Knight Developments (JKD) produce the most comprehensive range of race transmission parts. They have been doing this for as long as the Mini has been raced, and they continue to operate at the leading edge of racing, supplying Formula 1 teams as well as American Indy car teams, and so on! They make every transmission part a Mini racer will need, and there are many options available. When choosing drop gears there are several decisions to be made. It is common practice to change the primary gear to alter the final drive ratio.

I have always used the Jack Knight Developments set, which features a 24-tooth primary gear in the 1:1 set with a 23-tooth alternative to give 1:1.04. With a 3.9 crown wheel and pinion, I use the 1:1 set-up for all the faster tracks, such as Castle Combe, Silverstone, Thruxton, Snetterton, Donington, etc. Changing the primary gear gives a nominal 4:1 final drive ratio which is ideal for Brands Hatch and Mallory Park where top speeds are not so great.

The ratio 1:1.08 is also available, but these drop gears must be installed as a set, eliminating the interchangeability feature. Clearly the choice of ratio must be considered in conjunction with the crown wheel and pinion (CWP) to be used. Typically Mini Se7en uses 4.5:1 and Mini Miglia 3.9:1, and if you have this CWP ratio run it with a 1:1 primary gear for fast tracks and a 1:1.04 on the slower ones.

Whilst the intention is to keep the engine working in its optimum power band, it remains important that there is a gear for every corner. There have been occasions, particularly in an old Silverstone Club layout, where second gear caused over-revving and third seemed to let the engine drop off the cam. In these instances, the opportunity to change final drive ratio could be effective. All part of testing – something that must be recorded in your notes, with wind direction if this could have been a factor!

Having settled on ratio, there is the style of idler gear (the middle of the three) bearing. The standard needle roller bearings in the transmission housing and the flywheel housing work OK in modest output set-ups, but the bearings must be maintained in perfect con-

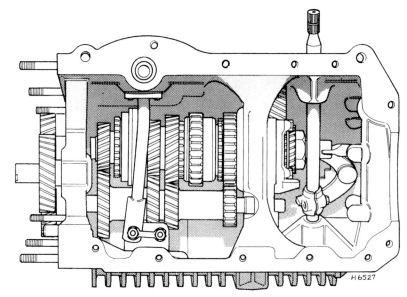

dition. A better option is the A+ casing and housing, since these had large shafted idler gears and bearing housings. Perhaps the best option is the Timkin taper roller conversion of the gear itself, where the gear is machined to receive a bearing through which the shaft is bolted, so that in use the shaft is stationary, with the gear running on it. For ultimate power outputs this is the way to go, but the standard A+ configuration appears to function well with 1300cc Miglia power. Finally, when ordering, remember to specify 1000cc or 1300cc, since the primary gear inner bush is larger on the 1300; and if this is for a three-synchro box, remember that the input gear (the bottom one) will need a spacer to make up the extra depth needed.

When installing the drop gears, take care to see that the manufacturer's specified end-float for the idler and primary gears is met or exceeded. Finally, the

This is what the standard four-speed synchromesh gear set-up looks like and …

… this is the complete mainshaft assembly. As already emphasised, care and cleanliness are the two essentials when stripping and rebuilding a gearbox.

Key
1. Mainshaft
2. Baulk rings
3. 3rd and 4th speed synch-hub
4. Thrust washers
5. Needle roller bearings
6. Third gear
7. Second gear
8. Reverse mainshaft gear and 1st and 2nd speed synch-hub
9. Needle roller bearing journal
10. First gear

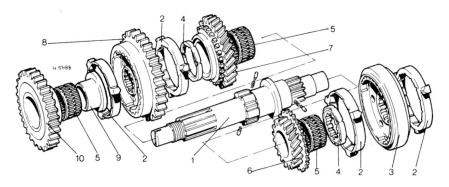

primary gear is bushed front and back. The front bush stands proud of the gear, and it is soft and will damage easily. Prior to installation of a brand new primary gear I leave it overnight submerged in engine oil, in the belief that the bush will soak up a little oil to lubricate it in use. The bush has a tendency to spin in the gear at high rpm and many engine builders tack weld it to the gear.

Next consideration is the gear set to be used. Price will be a major factor, since there is considerable difference between the options. In four-speed, there is straight cut synchromesh and the dog engagement kit, both of which are close ratio, and again are made by Jack Knight Developments. These are the choices to be considered for the Mini Challenges, but beyond that there are further options. If you are racing in the FIA Historic Challenges, then three-synchro is mandatory as it was the homologated equipment of the day. JKD still produce the gears, although the selectors, forks and some of the synchro hubs are unavailable new and will have to be sourced from used gearboxes.

For championships where more gears are allowed, there are five-speed and even six-speed kits available. At the time of writing, I have yet to try a sequential shift 'A' series 'box, although I have seen the basis of several mock-ups, so presumably it is only a matter of time!

Whatever your decision, and it will be based on regulations first and cost second, remember that gearbox maintenance is time-consuming, since the engine has to come out and the 'box separated from it, and this can quickly become a drag. If you choose the synchro option it necessarily involves some regular maintenance of the baulk rings, which wear in use. The dog box is much more the 'fit and forget' option.

Gear assembly

When assembling the gear kit, choose a good casing and make sure that the idler gear bearing size matches that of the flywheel housing. There is the choice between rod and remote change, and having used both extensively I would always choose the rod change version. It offers much more precision and reliability of change and is in current production, meaning that the selector forks and, for that matter, every component is available new. Again, if regulations call for the remote change, hang on to all your old 'boxes, since some of the bits are no longer available new.

Before beginning the build, inspect the casing thoroughly, and in particular the drain plug thread. This can easily be helicoiled now, but not when it's all built up and installed! For synchro boxes the choice of baulk ring is a little tricky. I have used new ones and suffered rapid failure. This results in crunching of gears and rapid deterioration of the tiny dog teeth. Failure is caused by the ring binding on to the gear too tightly, and effectively bursting. It will then do nothing to equalise gear speed.

There are two further options. Mini Spares produce a bronze baulk ring for competition use. This is based on the Cooper S design and grips less tightly to avoid the bursting tendency. It does, however, wear fairly rapidly depending on your driving style, but it is a working solution to the problem. The final choice is my favoured option, but finding the right baulk rings is difficult. The Cooper S had a steel ring, as opposed to the standard sintered type, and this was susceptible to neither bursting nor accelerated wear. They are identified by a series of M-shaped machine marks around the outside that you will recognise when you see them! They can occasionally be found in non-S three-synchro 'boxes, so good luck hunting – it does teach you the skills of disassembly!

BUILDING, PREPARING AND RACING YOUR MINI

Engine

This chapter could form a whole book in its own right. However, rather than detail every option for every conceivable engine build, we will look in more general terms at the task of engine building, and at broad considerations and methods for producing an engine which will function correctly and have acceptable life. Good workshop practice is an essential element of success with engine building, so we will look at that too.

Rules and regulations

As always, the first step with the construction of a competition engine is to consult the regulations laid down in your chosen formula. If these state that all modifications are free – or, indeed, if you wish simply to build a fast road engine – then your hands are not tied. The reality in '90s motorsport is that the regulations will be carefully written and will follow one of two basic concepts. Older formulae with greater freedoms will list permitted and prohibited modifications, and within these bounds there is liberty to build as you wish. In order to counter expensive development work, conducted in the search for advantage, it has become more common to simply describe an engine spec, including part numbers where applicable, so that every engine is, in theory, identical. Mini Miglia and Mini Se7en fall into the first category, and the 1.3i Mini Challenge into the latter.

The organisers hope that your reading of the regulations will enable you to understand exactly what can and cannot be done, but it is wise to seek inside information by attending races to gather information. Competitors are normally happy to talk about how they have done it, and such guidance can help you avoid expensive misinterpretation or misunderstanding of the rules.

With an understanding of what is required, the first decision can be taken. This is whether to enlist the services of an acknowledged engine builder to produce a complete lump, or take the plunge and attempt a self-build project.

The professional engine build

Provided you choose an established engineer with a proven track record in your formula, route one will very likely provide you with a reliable, legal and reasonably competitive engine. The guarantee of these qualities comes at a price, however, and for many participants, myself included, the cost is prohibitive. It may be that the message here is simply that the whole project will be financially impossible, and is best abandoned before any expense is incurred. If, however, your personal skills include engine building, either potentially or established, it is possible to succeed with a much-reduced outlay. It is crucial to be objective at this stage – most of us like a challenge, but if you struggled with Meccano as a kid, then

Working on your own engine is tremendously satisfying, especially when you win with it. However, because the down season is the winter months, you'll be literally working in the dark for many lonely hours, and you'll need some anti-freeze in your blood – check out the rally jacket! (Courtesy Norman Hodson, CCC magazine)

you'd probably be taking on too much. I learned all my technical skills from watching and reading – so it can be done!

If you plump for route one, the professionally-built engine, go about it in the right way. You should use somebody with experience in the formula, with their engines out there being seen to do well. The success you observe will be

the fruits of development work (at someone else's expense!), knowledge and skill. You should obtain a quotation for the work required. If you so desire, a fixed price which cannot be exceeded should be agreed. Remember to find out if there are any championship assistance schemes, making the purchase of parts cheaper, either through the manufacturer or trade support. These offers are sometimes open only to the private competitor, so purchase of some or all of the components before being passed to the engine builder may be cost-saving. You should agree this with the builder, of course, to ensure that you do not obtain parts other than those he uses in the build. Finally, once you have made your choice, let the guy do his job. His advice should be followed, and if things go well and to your liking, nurture the relationship; demonstrate loyalty and allegiance and it is likely to be reciprocated.

The self-build engine

If self-build is the plan, there is every opportunity to produce a competitive engine – both in terms of performance

This photo shows the basic underbonnet components of a standard 1000 (998cc) saloon.

Key
1. Brake master cylinder reservoir
2. Clutch master cylinder reservoir
3. Fuse block
4. Carburettor piston damper
5. Air cleaner
6. Windscreen wiper motor
7. Radiator pressure cap
8. Engine/transmission oil filler cap
9. Alternator
10. Engine/transmission oil dipstick
11. Distributor
12. Ignition coil
13. Vehicle identification plate
14. Clutch slave cylinder
15. Windscreen washer reservoir

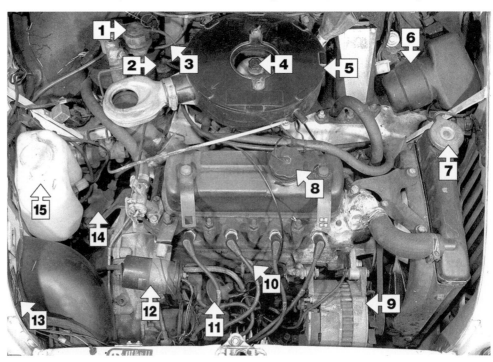

This is the underbonnet layout of a late Mini Cooper with a 1275cc engine complete with single throttle body fuel injection. In both cases the radiator is mounted to the side – not the best position for a race car where cooling is very important. Though these bays look quite well-ordered, they are distinctly disorganised when compared with a top-notch race engine ...

Key
1. Alternator
2. Ignition coil
3. Engine/transmission dipstick
4. Engine management ECU
5. Radiator pressure cap
6. Brake fluid reservoir cap
7. Brake system vacuum servo unit
8. Relay module
9. Fuel cut-off inertia switch
10. Manifold absolute pressure sensor fuel trap
11. Fuel return pipe
12. Fuel feed pipe
13. Accelerator cable
14. Throttle body assembly
15. Heater coolant valve
16. Charcoal canister purge valve

and price! In actual fact, the self-builder is really only an assembler of parts. The machining and balancing work should be entrusted to an established machine shop (unless you've got some serious workshop facilities!). Use the criteria set out above to identify an appropriate place.

By reading the regulations and canvassing opinion, you should be able to decide which components to use. Refer to *Example engine re-build* for illustration of the process and practices to be followed in the build process.

Throughout operations, each measurement and decision taken should be

... like this one, a superb example of a well-prepared 1293cc post-1993 Miglia unit. It's clean, with everything neatly routed or plumbed, and with no expense spared when it comes to choice of equipment. A glance back to the previous photos shows the extent to which all unnecessary clutter (wiring, pipes, etc.) has been removed. From 1994 all engines had to run on unleaded fuel.

This particular unit is based on an A+ block, as can be seen here by the ribs on the front of the block and the smaller core plugs. This has a standard stroke crankshaft (the choice being either a Cooper S or A+) and con rods to match the crank. The pistons are free, and in this case are of the Omega forged variety. The cylinder head is a 12G 940 head casting which has been the most popular one for many years. Modified to race spec (in this case by Swiftune Racing) the head is probably the single most important element of building a successful (i.e. powerful!) racing engine. The level of skill and knowledge required for effective polishing, porting, etc., is such that, although I build the rest of the engine myself, I always entrust the head to a specialist.

In this shot you can see how great attention has been paid to creating a really compact engine bay layout, despite the addition of a massive Formula 1 radiator, an oil cooler and a large ram air scoop at the offside.

Not absolutely necessary, but very nice all the same, is the use of Goodridge aircraft style hoses and fittings, especially when they're colour-coded, as here. They add a truly professional look to your car – at a price, of course.

noted. I keep a book dedicated to the purpose, and it is essential for looking back over what was done before. The workshop surroundings need not be elaborate at all. I worked for many seasons on a single timber bench. Cleanliness and organisation are the essential qualities, these cost nothing and are more a matter of self-discipline than skill.

Example engine rebuild

I have built Mini Miglia engines over the past six seasons. The formula is almost 30 years old, and although the 1300cc era only began in 1994, I do not believe that there are any secrets or that there is any black magic involved in building a competitive engine. On the contrary, I think of it as a straightfor-

Attention has to be paid to the oil, and where it's going to go from the breather pipe (the thick reinforced pipe at the rear in this photo). In this case, it leads ...

... to a fabricated alloy catch tank at the rear of the offside wing. It pays to check and empty this on a regular basis.

Because space is so tight in the engine bay, many drivers remove the original oil filter head from the front of the cylinder block (usually to make more room for a front-mounted radiator) and reposition it elsewhere. In this case it's fitted on a mounting just inboard of the offside damper.

No-one gets it right all the time, and this is what can happen when valve and piston make contact! Apart from ruining this particular race ...

Cylinder block

The regulations call for a standard 1275cc A-series item; hence they permit the builder to chose between Cooper S, 1300GT, and A+. The first is ruled out by rarity and value! The second, although used by some drivers is reckoned to lack the rigidity of the later block, which is the most favoured choice. Identification is a subject of its own, but the 'S' block has removable tappet chest covers, the 1300GT has cast-in tappet covers, but no ribbing to the front and rear of the block. This ribbing, along with the cast-in tappet covers clearly distinguishes the A+ block. At the time of writing, A+ blocks are available new at moderate cost. I have used these with good results, but still prefer a good used version. There is additional cleaning and inspection time, but this is offset by reduced cost.

ward matter of decision-taking and implementation. An engine stand can be obtained at reasonable cost from tool specialists such as Clarke, and this should be viewed as essential for the home builder. Bolt the block to it, and prepare for action.

First, gather together the principal engine components, as follows:

Crankshaft

The regulations state that a Rover Cars crankshaft with standard stroke is mandatory, and identical EN40B

... it did the owner's wallet a power of no good, having to replace this little lot. As you can see, the valve heads have come off their stems and caused massive damage to the piston and combustion chamber.

replacements are permitted, whilst billet crankshafts are prohibited. There are false economies to be made here, so choose with care. The A+ crank is still in production and available new. It has rolled fillet radii (effectively the right angle where the journals meet the webs), is relatively inexpensive and has proved to be reliable and competitive in use. I would advise against the earlier 1300GT (pre A+) cranks as these had ground fillet radii as opposed to rolled. A used A+ crank should be OK if it has never been distressed, but I would suggest it best to seek a new one. The alternative is an 'S' crank. These were forged in EN40B, a top quality steel and nitrided (a heat treatment to provide a hardened skin approximately 0.020in thick). The A+ and GT cranks are EN16T forgings. This is a cheaper alternative steel without any hardening heat treatment, but, as stated, it has proved effective and reliable if prepared properly. The 'S' crank may be purchased second-hand, although it remains available new at considerable cost.

Crankshaft preparation may necessitate only balancing, but there are plenty of options. The crank may be lightened on the webs by wedging and general polishing of all rough surfaces. Later 'S' cranks were all cross-drilled, but A+ are not, and this can and should

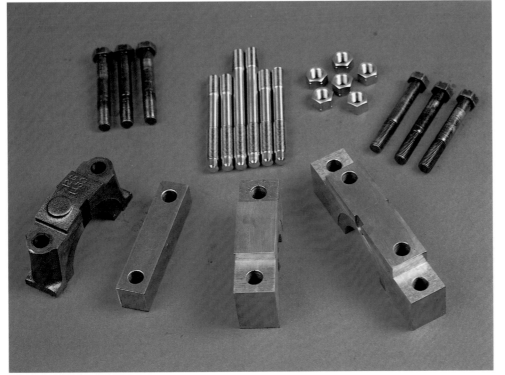

The heart of the engine is the crank. Seen here are a pair of Mini 7 cranks; at the top is the standard item and below it is the same but wedged, shaped, balanced and tuftrided. Guess which one you need to go for? (Courtesy Norman Hodson, CCC magazine)

Yet more engine options, this time it's main caps, bolts and studs. On the left is the standard cap next to which is a steel strap to reinforce it. Alongside this is an aftermarket steel centre main cap, and on the far right is a four-bolt cap for ultimate long-stroke motors. The studs at top centre are Selby rolled thread studs and nuts with the equivalent standard bolts at either side. (Courtesy Norman Hodson, CCC magazine) be done. The original oil feed from the main journals to the big ends is a single drilling, and the use of high revs for extended periods can lead to the oil being centrifuged away from the mains and to the outside only of the big-ends, resulting in bearing damage and ultimately failure. This drilling is, therefore, blanked just below the surface of the big-end journal, and the journal is drilled right through at right angles to, and passing through, the original drilling. The size of the hole is controlled to ensure that the main journal cannot be run dry, and the two feed holes to the big-end take care of that bearing. Once these operations are complete the crank must be balanced, and finally any heat-treatment applied. Tuftriding is the most common and available treatment, giving surface hardness to the material.

Connecting (con) rods

Regulations for 1997 were that con rods were free but that they must maintain original distance between centres (5.75in). This permitted any produc-

tion rod except the 970S version which was slightly longer. Also permitted were the bespoke steel con rods, manufactured most famously by Carrillo, with similar products available from Richard Longman & Co and Farndon Engineering. These are 'fit and forget' components that will last a lifetime, but they have been voted out of the Mini Se7en and Mini Miglia regulations for 1998. Although they are unparalleled for light weight and strength, they are not an essential element of a competitive engine. Rod selection should be dictated by the crank. For A+ crankshafts (which have larger big-end journals) the A+ rod is an obvious choice, and it remains available new at minimal cost. For an 'S' crank, with its smaller big-end journals an 'S' rod must be used. These also have been remanufactured; hence they are still available new, whilst originals must be sought in the second-hand market.

Con rods may be lightened, polished and balanced, before being shot peened. None of these operations, except balancing, is essential, but I consider it worthwhile. No short cuts should be taken with the nuts and bolts. Having suffered a bolt failure, I can assure you that you lose virtually the entire engine and gearbox, so under no circumstances economise in this area. ARP bolts and nuts are available to suit both A+ and 'S' rods and, although not cheap, they simply must be used. The flywheel assembly complete should be dynamically balanced, as should the front pulley, before the dry (or dummy) build is undertaken.

Pistons

These are free of restriction, although for '98 magnesium alloy is a prohibited material, not that it will affect the build plans of anybody, professional or otherwise, that I am aware of. The regulations permit a +0.020in rebore and, whether using a new block or not, the

The con-rod at the top is an AEG 177, early S-type which has been lightened, balanced, polished and shot-peened. Not quite so pleasant on the eye is the rusty standard rod below, taken from a scrap engine. Both are 1300-type rods but are not interchangeable because of different sized big-ends. (Courtesy Norman Hodson, CCC magazine)

extra 18cc capacity should be used – every little helps. Naturally, a +0.020in piston should be selected. Rover produce a nice looking three-ring piston at minimal cost and, although I have used these with perfect reliability, best results have been obtained from engines fitted with Omega-forged pistons. These are lighter, and theoretically stronger, and feature race style rings. Cost is considerable, but justifiable.

Camshaft

Mini Miglia has a mandatory camshaft. Profile, timing and lift must conform to Rover Cars STR0930. There is little to debate, really. The cam is available new through Rover, at reasonable cost.

Reprofiled versions are permitted, and I have obtained good results using Myk Cable Developments (MCD) supplied cams based on a good STR0930 and reprofiled and hardened. This amounts to a blueprinting lick-over of each lobe and, most importantly, a heat treatment that virtually assures the user of a season's use given correct installation.

Cylinder head

Here lies the critical component. In very simple terms, if the bottom end is correctly built, the performance of the engine will be as good or bad as the cylinder head modifications. A production Rover A Series five-port head casting must be used, and may be modified

Choose your weapons; at the top are Mini Spares Keith Dodd, 1.5 ratio high-lift rockers, which are cheap and effective. In the centre are Mini Spares roller-tipped rockers, again in 1.5 ratio. But for the ultimate in performance and reliability, go for the Titan roller rockers (standard or 1.5 ratio), seen at the bottom in this photo.
(Courtesy Norman Hodson, CCC magazine)

The basic Mini head is a complex piece of equipment, even before it undergoes the treatment from a specialist head tuner.

Key
1. Cylinder head
2. Valve guide
3. Plug
4. Water outlet elbow stud
5.. Rocker bracket stud – short
6. Rocker bracket stud – long
7. Manifold stud
8. Stud
9. Cover plate
10. Cover joint
11. Washer
12. Nut
13. Inlet valve
14. Exhaust valve
15. Outer spring
16. Guide shroud
17. Packing ring
18. Spring cup
19. Valve cotter
20. Circlip
21. Rocker shaft
22. Rocker shaft plug
23. Rocker shaft plug – screwed
24. Rocker bracket – tapped
25. Rocker bracket
26. Spacing spring
27. Valve rocker – pressed type
28. Valve rocker – forged type
29. Rocker bush – forged type
30. Tappet adjusting screw
31. Lockout
32. Locating screw
33. Bracket plate
34. Double coil washer
35. Washer
36. Washer
37. Nut
38. Valve rocker cover
39. Oil filler cap
40. Rubber bush
41. Distance piece
42. Cup washer
43. Nut
44. Cover joint
45. Cylinder head joint
46. Washer
47. Nut
48. Water outlet elbow
49. Elbow joint
50. Washer
51. Nut
52. Thermostat
53. Thermal transmitter
54. Bypass adaptor
55. Bypass hose
56. Clip
57. Sparking plug
58. Gasket
59. Inner spring (twin-carb application)

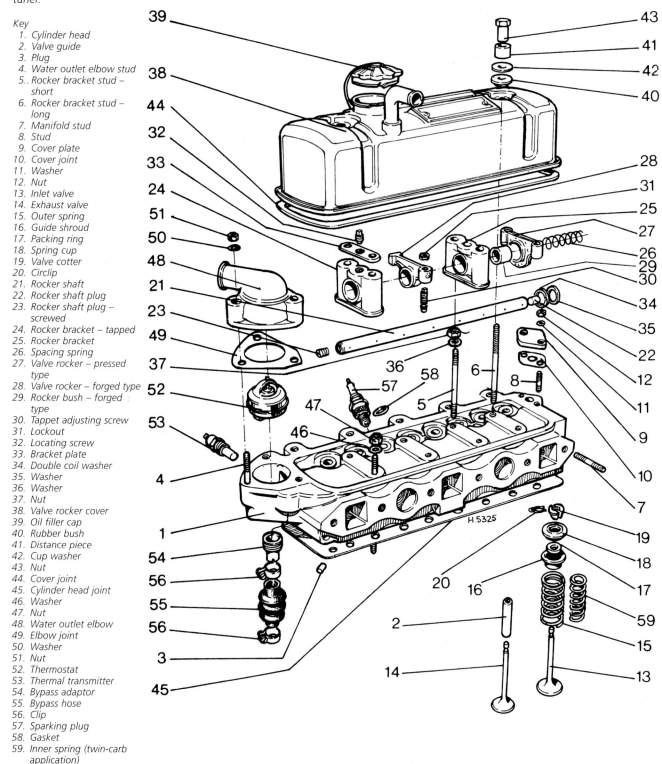

H.5325

by polishing and machining to combustion chambers, ports and machined faces. It is not permissible to exceed 35.7mm inlet valve diameter, neither may the valves or ports be inclined. These regulations mean that a race cylinder head, produced by one of the experts in the field, is the best part of a week's work from a bare casting to the finished job ready to bolt-on. It is of, course, one of the most expensive single items. In my opinion, you can take the budget option on all the components listed previously, put them together correctly and add a top specification cylinder head, and finish up with a very respectable engine.

Machining operations

The block, crank, rods, flywheel, backplate, diaphragm and front pulley/damper should all be taken on the first visit to the machine shop. The block must be bored +0.020in and the block face should be drilled and tapped for the two extra stud holes (as per Cooper S). The centre main bearing cap is best reinforced using a steel strap, and for this the existing cap will have to be machined flat to take the strap. I have had blocks with complete steel caps fitted, but feel the strap to be more than sufficient. Indeed, in Japan I raced a KAD twin-cam-headed 1300 with the standard centre main cap, and that was fine! I like to have the oil gallery brass blank plugs replaced with threaded steel plugs, and the machine shop will be able to tap the block and supply the plugs. Similarly, for 1300cc engines I have always used $^5/_{16}$in UNF cap screws for the gearbox-to-block flange, and it requires the block to be drilled and tapped accordingly at this stage. If the cam bearings need renewal because of wear, get that done too. I like to have the block mains housings line honed to ensure that they are both correctly sized and perfectly in line. Not all machine shops are equipped for

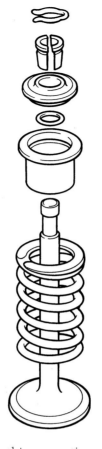

Over the years, different valve assemblies were used. Seen here from left to right are the early type, the later type and the type used in the Cooper and Cooper S.

this operation, so you may have to shop around. For me, Rob Walker Performance Engineering in Enstone do this and all my other machining requirements.

The dry build

The object here is to assemble the parts, only for the purpose of measuring piston height in bore. Accordingly, the piston rings can be removed from the piston, the bearings should be only lightly oiled and the full torque figures need not be applied to the main and big-end bolts and nuts. Turning the crankshaft over by hand, each of the pistons should be raised to top dead centre, using a dial gauge to determine the exact point, and their height in the bore measured using a depth micrometer. It is wise to take readings either side of the piston, above the gudgeon pin. These should be within a thou ($^1/_{1000}$ of an inch) or two. Make sure that the piston isn't canted or tipped in the bore, and if there is excessive disparity between the two measurements it indicates that the rod is slightly bent; something that the machine shop should be able to rectify. Number each piston, and record the measurements taken. Next, determine the lowest piston, this one will not be machined. For each of the other three, calculate the amount of material that needs to be machined from the crown in order to leave it at the same height as that established as the lowest. Once machined accordingly, all pistons should come to the same height in the block when at top dead centre. The pistons chosen will probably have a 6cc dish in the crown, and this will have been slightly reduced, and must be enlarged again as necessary. The next consideration is how much to machine from the face of the block. This must be considered in conjunction with the wider issue of compression ratio and, for the Mini Miglia formula, the minimum stated unswept volume.

Compression ratio

As an explanation, the compression ratio is that of swept volume to unswept volume, and is usually of the order of 10:1 or thereabouts. Swept volume is that covered by the piston as it travels from bottom dead centre to top dead centre. This is a simple calculation based on bore and stroke dimensions, and is usually expressed in cc (cubic centimetres). The swept volume of one cylinder is equal to a quarter of the engine capacity (because it is a 4-cylinder engine). Unswept volume is more tricky to determine, but it should not be over difficult, given a little patience. There are lots of elements to it, the largest being the volume of the combustion chamber in the cylinder head. If you have purchased a new modified head, this figure may well be stamped on it, something in the order of 16cc to 24cc. Take the precaution of verifying this figure with the supplier, and ensure that all the chambers are balanced, i.e. have the same volume! If, for whatever reason, you cannot immediately determine the chamber volumes beyond doubt, then measurement is the only solution.

Prepare yourself with good light and patience. First, all the valves must be lapped in absolutely perfectly. With your race spark plug (NGK–B8 EGV) tightly screwed in, a piece of Perspex 4mm or 5mm thick is required. This should be placed across the combustion chamber, and sealed with a thin smear of grease. A small hole drilled in the Perspex will allow you to fill the chamber with paraffin from a burette calibrated in cubic centimetres. By subtracting the volume of liquid left in the burette, after filling the chamber, from the volume you started with, the volume of the chamber can be determined. This is a procedure that can be perfected after a few trial efforts. This is the same method used by eligibility scrutineers, so it is certainly worth doing for peace of mind, even if your head is already marked.

Having determined the combustion chamber volume, add to this the volume of a compressed head gasket – the one that you will use. Mini Miglia regulations give agreed figures for this. I use the copper/asbestos AF460 which is quoted at 3.4cc. Next, add the volume in the dish of the piston, normally about 6cc, but check using the head chamber method if machining has been carried out. Then there is the matter of the volume known as the ring land – this is the space above the top ring up to the piston face, and this is calculated using the difference of the bore diameter (and thus volume) and the piston diameter (and thus volume). There are some people who choose to ignore this volume and see it as the safety margin against error.

The final remaining element of the unswept volume is that between the very top of the piston and the face of the block. Simple mathematics will calculate this amount, and adding it all up will give the total unswept volume. This may have to be juggled. The regulations for Mini Miglia call for 32cc and there is no allowance so, for safety, aim for 32.5cc as it will make little if any difference in performance. So, one volume will have to be varied to get the total right. It may be that you will order the head to suit the piston being flush with the block, or you will have to juggle the piston height to tally with an existing head. There is a school of thought that places the piston at top dead centre slightly above the top of the block, in which case the piston height will amount to a negative volume. Whatever, my preference is to run the piston flush to the top of the block and have a head chamber volume to suit.

Cleaning up

Now that machining has been concluded it's time for the big clean up. Every component should be washed and dried in a recommended cleaning solvent. If you're really into your building, investment in a purpose-made parts washer, complete with electric pump, will pay dividends.

Remember to protect your hands, and ensure that every last piece of swarf is removed. The block is the biggest challenge. Remove every fitting, and the threaded gallery plugs. Run cleaner down every oilway and passage and blow through with an airline. Bottle brushes and pipe cleaners are also use-ful. When clean and dry the block can be painted, and stood aside for assembly. The same applies to each component; use pipe cleaners through all the crank drillings, and take special care with shot peened rods, since the tiny steel balls used can get trapped, and if left in the system will eat shell bearings and crank journals in no time at all. It is worth cleaning everything and laying it all out ready to assemble, prior to a change of overalls before assembly begins.

The final build

For basic assembly procedures and torque setting, refer to the Haynes Workshop Manual. All torque figures should be adhered to; where proprietary components such as big-end nuts are tightened, follow explicitly the manufacturer's directions.

If you started with a scrap 1275cc A+ engine and 'box, you should have retained and cleaned all the nuts, bolts and minor parts that will be used in the build. The bench and all of the tools to be used should be clean, as should the floor and the assembler!

This should be the home run. Take time and care, rush nothing, and never take a chance; the failure of a single component can put the entire engine at risk. I have lost a block, crank, two rods, two pistons, the cylinder head, gearbox casing and two gears all for one ill-chosen big-end bolt. That turned out to be the most expensive bolt I have ever come across!

As you build, each component should be lubricated. Some people prefer specific compounds for this purpose, I use the same oil in which the engine will be run.

Chapter 8

Cooling

Cooling is a simple matter of equilibrium. The standard road-going Mini is equipped with a system to suit the requirements of the car over the complete range of environmental conditions that it will meet in normal use.

Basic description

The cooling system comprises a volume of water – with anti-freeze additive – in a water jacket cast in the block and head. The water absorbs heat from the engine, and a pump circulates it through a radiator to dissipate that heat to the atmosphere, either by direct airflow, a fan or a combination of the two. A header tank is usually incorporated, with a filler cap of the pressurised type so that the whole system works at a pressure generated by the expansion of water when heated. The pressure, usually a maximum of 15psi, increases the boiling point of water, so that it will not boil-up in normal circumstances. A thermostat is included to ensure a more rapid warm up by closing the part of the system that goes to the radiator until normal temperature is reached. The system is completed by the rubber hoses that join the components together.

The standard system fitted to the Mini works perfectly for a road car, but as power output is increased so it begins to struggle. The effectiveness of the whole system is essential to power output and, indeed, ultimately the survival of the engine.

FIA Touring Car cooling

The first point to note is that the FIA Historic Touring Car Challenge, in which the pre-'65 Cooper S competes, calls for the homologated spec of the day; hence modern alternatives are not permitted. These cars run at approximately 130bhp with the side radiator installation, and for one-hour duration races, too; so, given sufficient incentive, it can be made to work. The methods employed carefully exploit the loopholes in the regulations and, although the radiator respects standard height and depth dimensions, one-off double thickness versions are made which still incorporate the original specification top and bottom radiator tanks. Clever stuff. Further advantages are gained from the regulations that state plumbing is free. Various cars appear with all manner of lengthy pipework runs, all in the interest of increasing the water capacity, and hence reducing the rate of temperature rise.

The front radiator

The above are extreme measures to stay within specific regulations, but most competition Minis are not so restrained, and the average circuit racer will be equipped with a front radiator at the very least. This alone is a huge step forward. There is, of course, a great choice. The majority of Mini Se7en and Miglia cars use the 'A' series-engined Metro radiator. This appeared in two basic designs: thick and thin. For easy identification, the thick radiator (alloy and plastic initially and lately copper and brass) has the water inlet and outlet connectors at the same end. The thin version, which was only ever alloy and plastic, has those connectors at opposite ends of the radiator. I have used both types with satisfactory results, but prefer the thick version for ease of plumbing and its larger capacity. A number of other options exist; other Rover products are widely used along with rather more exotic alloy bespoke radiators and even some derived from obsolete Formula 1 cars!

The front radiator needs to be installed with a header tank to provide the filling point, and a head of water to ensure no pockets of air are trapped in the upper parts of the head. The matter of plumbing will involve a mix and match approach using a selection of Mini and Metro top and bottom hoses.

In its simplest form little else is required. It is common practice to remove the thermostat from its housing in the cylinder head. It is essential that this is replaced with a blanking sleeve to ensure correct circulation to the far end of the block. With a standard pump this set-up can be ready to run, and will adequately serve Mini Se7en and Miglia cars. Development has not stopped there, however.

Adding a side radiator

In search of still further cooling capacity, many cars run the front Metro radiator with a side Mini radiator in series, and contain water temperature at 60 degrees or less. The side radiator is usually turned at an angle to get a better flow of cold air, and the plumbing routes water out of the cylinder head, into the top of the front radiator, out the bottom of the front radiator into the top of the side radiator, and then back

A really cool installation in all ways! To the right is a huge alloy-cored water radiator taken from a Formula 1 car, and it is extremely efficient. On the left is an oil cooler, neatly packaged so it doesn't impinge on the room required for the giant air scoop. This particular car is running a standard alloy water pump, belt driven from ...

... a non-standard front pulley. This has the effect of slowing the pump down slightly, which is useful because you're less likely to get cavitation in the water system. And the toothed belt (quite wide) is reliable and not likely to break. The water temperature gets up to 70 degrees but rarely any more, which is absolutely ideal from a racing point of view. Note the use of Samco silicone hoses – very nice and unlikely ever to burst, but not exactly cheap.

radiators, with plumbing from front to rear. The installation was certainly made to work, but Mini Challenge regulations call for engine-bay-mounted cooling only, so there has been little development in this area, and the solutions achieved by the individual are a matter of trial and error. The final one-off installation of twin Mini side radiators appeared to work in a Mini Miglia, offered the advantage of an exit airflow to the side, presumably keeping air intake temperatures a little lower.

Whichever radiator solution you choose, ensure that the matrix is fully in the air flow and, most important, remember to consider other installations requiring grille aperture space such as oil coolers or air intakes for brake ducts or cold air for the engine to breathe. Once the choice and location are decided, the mounts will usually have to be fabricated. The best bet is to take a look in the paddock for ideas. I favour locating the bottom pegs of a front radiator in fairly tight rubber grommets, and then allowing a measure of movement at the top, effectively locating the radiator only by the hoses attached to it. It is essential to ensure that nothing can strike against or chafe the radiator – and allow for engine movement, which inevitably will occur in hard use.

Water pump and header tank

The next decision to make is that of water pump and header tank. If a standard belt-driven pump is the choice progress is simple, but if you wish to use an electric pump, as has become fashionable, you will be faced with further packaging, wiring and plumbing challenges. The header tank selected must be positioned so that, when filled to the correct level, the water will be above the highest point of the whole cooling installation, preferably by at least an inch. The 'A' series Metro header tank in a post '76 body shell will sit perfectly on the offside tower bolt, and

into the water pump using a normal Mini bottom hose. Slightly less extreme measures have been taken, using either a heater matrix or an oil cooler between the heater outlet on the cylinder head and the bottom hose. Currently I use the heater outlet simply as an escape for hot water, piping it directly into the front radiator so that the water is cooled before being re-introduced to the block.

Alternative radiator positions

There are a small number of unique solutions to the problem. Minis have been known to sport boot-mounted

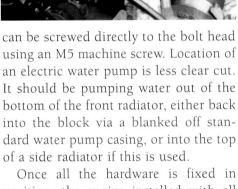

Hoses

When preparing the hoses, look for generous sweeping bends as they promote smoother, less turbulent flow. Never be tempted to tighten a bend artificially, for when hot there is a risk it may collapse, closing off the flow. Finding the correct hoses can be very time consuming, but when you get it right, note down the part numbers and

The header tank can be positioned wherever there's room, as can ...

... the catch tank, in this case an alloy fabrication which sits snugly behind the nearside wing.

can be screwed directly to the bolt head using an M5 machine screw. Location of an electric water pump is less clear cut. It should be pumping water out of the bottom of the front radiator, either back into the block via a blanked off standard water pump casing, or into the top of a side radiator if this is used.

Once all the hardware is fixed in position, the engine installed with all ancillaries and the bodywork and grille all fitted, it's time to start juggling with the plumbing. The header tank feeds the system via a ⅝in pipe, and this should be fed into the hose between the water pump (electric or mechanical) and the front radiator. If a side radiator is used, its filler should be retained, obviating the need for a header tank. If you do this, make sure the water level in the side radiator is high enough to meet the criteria stated earlier. If not, the side radiator will need a blank (non-pressurised type) cap, and a pressured header tank, but space will be getting tighter and tighter.

keep them. Where it is necessary to join hoses, take great care. Remember that the system runs under pressure, and many a race has been lost because of a blown hose. Worse still, such a failure can lead to major engine damage if not noticed immediately. This is a classic area which can easily be overlooked at great expense. I usually choose copper plumber's fittings to make hose joins. Because they are non-ferrous there is no corrosion, and they're available in a multitude of sizes, bends and T-pieces, etc. If the solder ring type are used, the raised ring gives a guarantee of good anchorage using a hose clip.

Finally, consider obtaining maximum reliability from the water pump, whichever type you use. The mechanical pump has been blighted by belt turning and jumping. If the belt breaks and the pump stops you have about ten seconds to kill the engine before the water boils – even at pressure – blowing the cap and letting the water out of the system, with the certainty of major engine damage. If the same belt serves the alternator, then the charging light should give instant warning of belt failure. If not, I have used the temperature switch that should operate an electric fan to switch on a dash warning light, but this will be a late warning, and disaster will already be on its way.

Water pump belt failure

So how do we stop belt failure? There are many options, and I have tried most of them. There are any number of toothed belt kits, and these are generally reliable, though they rely on frequent belt changes. My favourite solution is to stick with a standard V belt and fine tune the set-up. That means ensuring that the three pulleys are perfectly in line. Usually only the alternator requires adjustment, and this can be achieved by simple spacing. Always choose the shortest possible belt. This will reduce the distance between the alternator and bottom pulleys, and pulling the alternator in will maximise clearance to the front radiator. If you consider that the bottom pulley turns clockwise, it is clear that any slack will be in the run between crank pulley and alternator pulley. This is also the longest run, so I use a Ford cam belt tensioner here to stop any whip (which I believe is the only cause of belt jumping) once the pulleys are correctly aligned. For the record, I prefer the S-type bottom pulley since it is solid, as opposed to the later type which incorporates a damper.

Electric water pumps

If you intend to use an electric pump, as is my current preference, some simple rules of installation should enhance reliability. The main reason for choosing an electric pump is not the belief that huge power savings are available. Plenty of figures are claimed, ranging from 0 to 6bhp. I expect the figure is somewhere between these two. The real advantage comes after a race when the whole engine is thoroughly hot. When it is turned off, a pulley-driven pump stops, too, but the water temperature in the head continues to climb for some while, peaking 30 or 40 degrees above the running temperature, as the heat held in the head casting is conducted into the water that sits in the head. I couldn't quantify the effect of this, but it's not likely to be good! On the other hand, an electric pump can be kept running for twenty minutes or so after the engine has worked, and there is no localised increase in temperature. That is why I run this type of pump.

In order to avoid an accidental switch off of the pump, wire it through the battery master switch only, and take great care to protect the wires in the engine bay. They should be protected by a PVC protective sleeve and routed away from moving parts and excess heat. Use a plug/socket connector so that the pump can easily be removed from the chassis, and ensure that this cannot be separated accidentally. The pump should be installed as low as possible, and be vertical. It should never be allowed to run dry, and is best mounted to permit some degree of movement, ideally using small rubber mountings.

Cooling system maintenance

Finally, take good care of the system. The radiator should be kept clean externally. Any oil contamination will

collect dust and dirt, blocking the cooling fins and reducing efficiency. Make sure that the anti-freeze is added to the water, for its anti-corrosion properties as much as anything. Watch for small water leaks, remember that the gaskets can weep when subjected to the vibration that high revs generate. The 'A' series engine was never designed with this degree of tuning in mind! The use of anti-freeze, which is usually coloured, makes leaks easier to spot, as they usually show up as dried-up green or blue rivulets along the hoses, etc. And while you are driving, watch the instruments, in particular the water temperature gauge – a capillary type is most reliable. And make sure the charging light (and, for that matter, the oil

pressure light) are bright enough to gain your attention.

Oil coolers

The oil needs cooling, too, but here the system is much simpler. In a standard car, the oil is cooled not by a specific system but along with the water. Engine tuning demands more of the oil by putting more heat into it, and in order not to exceed the manufacturer's temperature limit a dedicated radiator is introduced. The term 'oil cooler' is used to describe purpose-built radiators for cooling oil. They are stronger in construction to withstand internal pressures in excess of 100psi, and they are usually made with threaded fittings for the attachment of fittings swaged to armoured hose.

Fuel Systems

At the rear of the car, this is my boot-mounted alloy fuel tank, complete with Facet electric fuel pump mounted above it. Note the use of top-quality Goodridge hose – not a necessity, but nice to have, if only for peace of mind.

Petroleum spirit; where would we be without it? The entire motoring history of the twentieth century has been built on it, and for as long as we can extract it from the ground the story will continue. Thereafter new fuels will become common; solar, nuclear, hydro-power – who knows?

Whatever, whilst we have petrol, how should its supply and calibration system be built for use in the racing Mini?

The fuel tank

The first consideration with regard to fuel tanks is one of the RAC 'Blue Book' requirements; if the tank compartment (i.e. boot) has a sealed floor, then the tank filler neck *must* have a splash tray around it to drain any spilt fuel. With an open boot floor this is unnecessary.

There are two problems with the factory-fitted tank, and these are (a) fuel surge and (b) the design of the filler

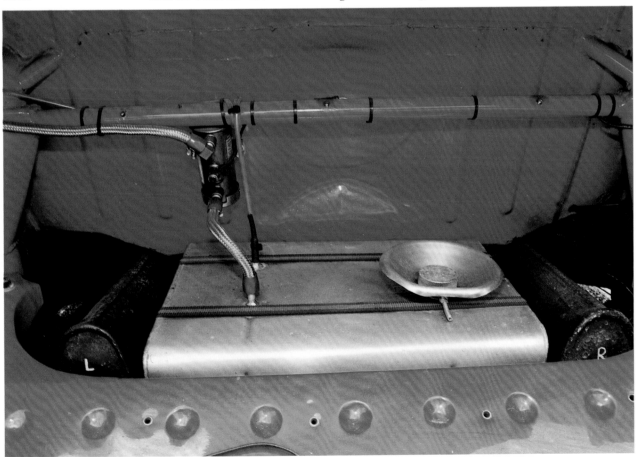

A more upmarket (i.e. expensive) solution is to use a professional fuel cell like this one from ATL.

neck causing it to stand proud of the bodywork where it may be damaged in an accident or when racing close to other cars.

European historic regulations demand that the tank is unaltered. The dangers associated with the filler neck cannot be addressed by modification to the tank. Instead, alternative caps are used, the most common being the Monza-style quick-release alloy version, and competitors use stainless steel lock wire to prevent accidental opening.

The matter of surge is addressed by 'foam filling' the tank. The material used is a petrol resistant light density

Note how the cell can sit low down below the boot floor because it is protected by a carbon-fibre moulding. This means that the centre of gravity is slightly lower and the handling is improved accordingly.

foam, widely used in bespoke alloy tanks. To fill a standard tank it must be cut into shapes that can be forced through the neck, the intention being to fill the whole tank. The foam readily absorbs petrol, so tank capacity is not reduced. The petrol is unable to flow so easily, hence the likelihood of surge is greatly reduced. It is essential that the correct foam is used; the sort that will not degrade in petrol.

Where regulations do not require the use of the original tank, then the installation of an alloy replacement, much lower in the boot (for better weight distribution and improved handling), is common practice. If you take this route, choose the capacity carefully, thinking of the longest race you are likely to contest. For Mini Challenge, eight racing laps at Spa-Francorchamps plus a warm-up and slow-down lap is unrivalled at 43 miles. My own Miglia car is equipped with a 20-litre tank (approximately 4.4 gallons), and the Spa circuit consumes the lot! There are various options on tank design. I have always used the rectangular foam-filled type, these being relatively inexpensive, although they do require specially fabricated mountings.

Other options include the circular type which will fit perfectly in the spare wheel well if you retain the standard boot floor. The ultimate choice for safety is the bag-type tank. Manufactured in high-tech fabric material, the tank is deformable (with reduced risk of rupture) and fitted in the car in an alloy housing.

Whichever tank you choose, it is only as good as the mountings provided for it. If, as is usually the case, you have to make your own brackets to retain the tank, remember that it will be full of petrol when in use, and considerably heavier than when it is empty. If you are retaining the boot floor and the spare wheel boss is in good order, you will need to do little, but you will need a filler splash tray. If the boot floor is

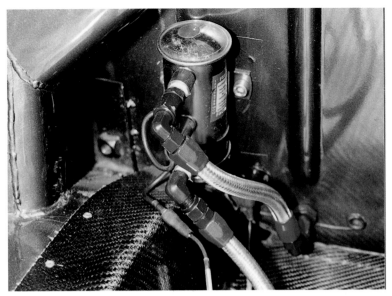

This car also uses the ubiquitous Facet fuel pump.

coming out, then there is no better option than a Curley Specialised Moulding carbon fibre Mini boot floor which includes location for a 20-litre rectangular tank. Fixings can be made using webbing straps, and this is a hassle-free and neat solution. If you make an alloy boot floor, you'll have to devise your own tank mounts. Try to avoid bolt-down lug type fixings, and choose instead the strap-over-the-whole-tank approach.

The tank is lower still in my '96-built Miglia, sitting in the void between the subframe legs on a fabricated platform. This installation was the work of Peter Vickers and Tony Baskerville, and is not one for the faint hearted, since the exhaust system required some elaborate tube work to fit it all in. The reasoning was to position the tank so that it was best protected in case of accident. Side or rear impact would not harm it in this location. Added to this are the benefits of a lower centre of gravity and the use of the mounting platform to further stiffen the subframe

The fuel pump

Next selection is that of the fuel pump. It is unwise to economise in this area. I have always had perfect reliability from the Facet Interrupter Pumps. These are identified by colour; we used Silver Top Competition for Mini Se7en, and Red Top Works for Mini Miglia. Though outwardly identical they are distinguishable by fitting size; the Silver Top has ¹/₄in fittings and fuel hose, the Red Top needs ⁵/₁₆in fittings and hose. The pump should be mounted vertically, as close to the tank as possible, on rubber bushes to avoid transmission of resonance from the vehicle body into the pump. When installing, ensure that the pump body is earthed to the vehicle, bridging the rubber mounts if necessary.

Pressure regulator

The next item of hardware in the fuel delivery line is a pressure regulator, which may also incorporate a filter. Generally this would be located in the engine bay, and needs to be afforded a degree of protection from accidental damage, since the filter bowl full of fuel represents a substantial fire risk if ruptured.

The pump would typically deliver fuel at 6psi or 7psi. Although the Weber DCOE family of carburettors can deal with this at the float chamber valve, SU carbs have proved to be more sensitive. Accordingly, I consider the use of a regulator as optional on a Weber installation and compulsory on an SU set-up. The output fuel pressure should be adjusted to 3psi.

Hoses and fittings

Completion of the delivery system now only requires hose and fittings. The fuel line should be routed away from the underside of the car, since it can be flattened by grounding out either over kerbs or when off the track. Wherever the line passes through the driver compartment, it must be either metal pipe (Kunifer or Copper) or metal braided hose. Any joins should be metal screw type within that compartment. The expense of stainless braided fuel hose is fully justified, and a single length can be run from boot to engine bay. In the driver's compartment the hose must be protected, and the deep ribs of the latest floorpan pressings are ideal for this. Alternatively, the inner sill line is sufficiently out of the way to afford protection from accidental damage. Plastic 'P' clips are perfect to secure the pipe, and the ends can be finished with proclamps. These are anodised alloy housings for stainless hose clips and, although costing a few pounds each, complete the job neatly.

Carburation

So that is the delivery system. Now the calibration of the air/fuel mixture and its passage into the engine is achieved

The heart of the matter – this is the 45DCOE Weber on a short manifold, pretty much de rigueur for Miglia cars at the time of writing.

using a carburettor and inlet manifold. These are simple items to acquire, but their set up is more difficult and is essential to the performance and survival of the engine.

The 'A' series engine started life with an SU carburettor. In its own right, the SU carburettor is a masterpiece of design – simple in function and easy to maintain and tune; there can be little criticism. But then came the side-draught Weber DCOE family, and for motorsport and tuning use these proved highly successful. Both still play a large role in the racing 'A' series scene.

The first production Mini Cooper appeared in 1961, and with it came twin 1¼in SUs. These worked well, and the Cooper S was similarly equipped. When homologated for International Competition, larger SUs were specified, and these are to be found today in the European Historic Touring Car Championship Minis.

The Mini Se7en challenge began in 1966 with a single SU, but this was quickly cast aside in favour of the Reece Fish carburettor. Eventually this, too, was superseded by a Weber 45DCOE, modified so that only one of its two barrels worked, and bolted to a special manifold. The reason for the Weber is simply that it flows more air than its rivals.

There are those who rightly point out the plus-points of the SU, and indeed Nick Cole has spent hours of dyno time in a search for progress with SU-equipped Miglia engines. The clear advantage of this installation is that, since the carbs are separate items, the manifold can be made with straight inlet tracts, giving identical flow characteristics to both of the Siamesed ports. The Weber in contrast uses a swan-necked manifold that gives different flow characteristics to each of the ports.

The choice of carburettor will likely be dictated by regulations. Where there is a choice to be made, I recommend

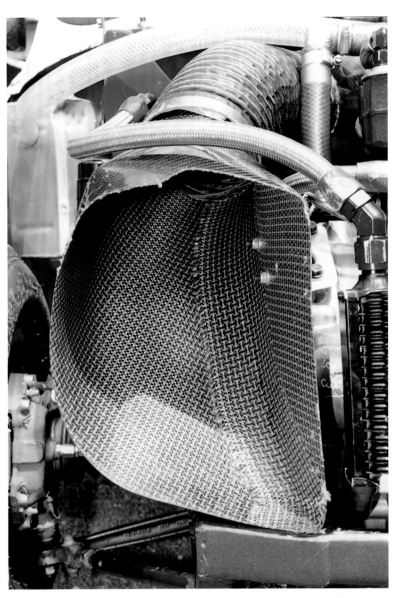

Getting cool air forced into the carb at a rate of knots is the current holy grail, and using a huge duct like this to shovel in the rushing wind is one way to go about it.

selection of that most commonly used by other competitors. As always, have a look around the paddock and ask some questions. If you want to be adventurous and spend dyno time evaluating the options, prepare to take considerable time looking for advantage. Remember, time costs money in this instance!

The home-builder should be primarily concerned with installation. As far as the manifold goes, take advice from the producer of the cylinder head. He will identify the most suitable manifold, and match it to the head face. This involves correcting the head-to-manifold flange alignment, and then inserting split dowels into the head, and drilling holes for them in the manifold flange. This guarantees perfect alignment at each assembly.

The matter of throttle linkage should not be overlooked. All sorts of home-made devices are in evidence in the paddocks, and many work really well. However, underestimate the importance of this assembly at your peril. Many a race retirement has been caused by a broken throttle cable, and these failures can usually be blamed on the linkage or installation. I recommend use of that supplied by the carburettor manufacturer. Twin-cable systems are commonplace, but I dislike the extra mechanical drag that accompanies them, and if installed and maintained correctly I can see little likelihood of a cable failure on a single cable set-up.

Air supply

The final consideration for the carburettor is that of air supply. It has been common practice in Mini Se7en and Miglia to create an air box in the front bulkhead to allow the carburettor a reasonable space from which to draw its air. The Weber relies heavily on such a box, since its intake trumpets would be perilously close to the standard bulkhead and speedometer opening. Such airboxes, constructed when the car is built, should have some sort of trunking to bring cold air in from the front of the car. The matter of carburettor intake temperature is an important one, since the colder the air, the greater efficiency and power. Mini Challenge has followed the Touring Car lead, and most Miglia cars now feature a ram air system. Supplied by Myk Cable Developments, a large air collector with K&N filter is fitted just inside the grille. This is plumbed with 5in flexible trunking to a sealed intake box on the carburettor, and the forward motion of the car is believed to generate a positive pressure to the carburettor.

Linking the front scoop to the carb air box requires some flexible ducting. This is 5in diameter, typical of the size used in the paddock, although because of the overall design it's about half as long as most, thus there is less turbulence. Though the pressure advantage has yet to be fully proven, there's no doubt that a carb which gets a healthy diet of cool air will help the engine produce more power – without such a system, it can only draw hot air from the engine bay.

BUILDING, PREPARING AND RACING YOUR MINI

In my opinion the ram effect is difficult to quantify; the car is forever changing speed, there is the effect of head, tail and side winds, and the factor of surrounding cars to consider. Moreover, there is little hard evidence or qualified research to show that quantifiable ram effect is obtained. The unquestionable benefit, however, is that of intake temperature, which is held at ambient. The position of the exhaust manifold must increase the under-bonnet temperature dramatically, and knowing that this is undesirable there can be little disputing the effectiveness of a ram air system (or perhaps we should call it a cold air system!). The Cable version is the only commercially available kit, but the careful home builder could certainly produce something similar at a considerable saving.

Fuel injection

Despite its only relatively recent arrival on production Minis, fuel injection is nothing new in Mini Tuning. Peter Baldwin's BDA-engined Wardspeed Mini, a giant-killer in the '70s and '80s was fitted with Lucas mechanical fuel injection. It was effective, even if somewhat rudimentary by today's standards.

The current production Mini is fuel-injected, a move necessitated by the need for ever-lower exhaust emissions. As a by-product, economy was enhanced and a greater control over all engine running conditions was permitted. There was no great power hike, just a refining of the existing engine. There are all sorts of commercial upgrade packages available, but the injection and ignition side of the modifications are generally outside the scope of the home tuner.

For serious competition, with little restriction on tuning, such as is permitted by Special GT/Silhouette regulations, the 'A' series engine has run with the Webcon Alpha programmable system which can control both fuel injection and ignition. The KAD twin-cam

This is a combined fuel regulator and filter. It's not necessary and, while some drivers swear by them, I haven't found driving without one does me great harm.

Special Saloons were thus equipped, and I can speak from first-hand experience of the stunning performance of these cars. For on-the-edge tuning there is no better way to go.

The installation of injection has wider implications than simply what hangs on the manifold. Injection requires fuel pressure in the order of 40psi. Accordingly, the fuel pump is different, as is the plumbing. The injection bodies have a fuel return circuit and this must be piped back to the tank, in high pressure braided hose, too. The tank must have an additional spigot for that return line. Once installed, expect to spend time on the dyno/rolling road if you wish to extract all that the system has to offer.

Whether fuelled by carbs or injection, set-up time is essential but, providing that nothing changes to settings achieved, it can be considered a worthwhile long-term investment.

Chapter 10 Ignition systems

Standard ignition system

The Mini began life with an uncomplicated ignition system; a distributor (housing points and capacitor), a coil, high tension leads and four spark plugs – and that was it. Add 12v DC to the coil, maintain the correct clearances for the plugs and points, and there was little to go wrong.

I was once advised that if you suspect fuel starvation, the problem is certain to be electrical, and on numerous occasions these wise words have been borne out. Usually the capacitor has given up, and a couple of quid has the problem solved. The other likely difficulty, characterised by intermittent misfires and breaking down, is loose connections, usually the low tension connection to the coil; again, easily fixed. To quote Nick Cole of KAD fame, 'If I were setting off across the Sahara desert in a Mini, I'd choose to equip it with an SU carburettor and points ignition!' This is certainly an interesting view in the light of all the modern technology that now surrounds us, but the back to basics option always has virtues.

I have raced and won, albeit some years ago, in Mini Se7en racing using a standard distributor equipped with Cooper S points. This set-up was reliable, easily maintained and cheap. I suffered absolutely no points bounce, even at 8,500rpm, and only the presence of some prize money burning a whole in my pocket persuaded me to consider electronic ignition. I chose Lumenition Optronic, which was and still is very popular in Mini Se7en, and commissioned the system on the Rolling Road at Marshalls of Cambridge. Peter Baldwin noted the power figures using our existing dizzy, and then swung in the newly equipped Lumenition version. The results were pleasing. An engine that had been considered excellent (producing 87bhp at 8,400rpm) was now the best 850 ever seen on these well-used rollers, showing 89.5bhp! Peter felt that the (inevitable) scatter was reduced using the Optronic system, and for the modest outlay the 2.5bhp was an ample return. I have to say there was nothing to feel in the way the car drove, or indeed with the

The system is linked to a crankshaft sensor, seen here alongside the water pump belt.

BUILDING, PREPARING AND RACING YOUR MINI

results gained, but I never again used points.

Programmable ignition

Mini Se7en regulations permit nothing more elaborate, but Miglia cars are allowed programmable systems that take ignition technology on to a new plane. When I considered the move to Mini Miglia, most (not all) of the competitive cars used the Zytek programmable system. This had front pulley mounted triggering, dedicated coil and amplifier, and relied on the distributor body to do nothing other than route the sparks down the correct HT lead. It offered zero scatter and the ability to tack the advance curve up and down as the revs climbed – something that a conventional dizzy controlled advance curve could not be made to do. The down side was that initial cost was relatively high, and tuners with the expertise and equipment to programme the kit were few and far between.

Eventually I bought a car complete with the system. The engine had been built by Eurotech, who had dyno'd it and installed the Zytek system. It was the best move for me because all these expensive moves had been made already. The downside of such exotic equipment was that I certainly could not afford to carry spares, and if anything was damaged or stopped working we were in big trouble. The previous owner of my new car, Gerald Dale, had thought along similar lines, and his solution was to use the empty dizzy body to house a Lumenition Optronic kit, so that if necessary he could swap systems. We took this a step further, and wired it up through a dashboard switch so that simultaneously one kit could be switched on as the other went off. This could be done with the engine running and driving. It turned out never to be necessary, because of experiments on the rolling road.

Again in the hands of Peter Baldwin, 101bhp was well on the pace for top

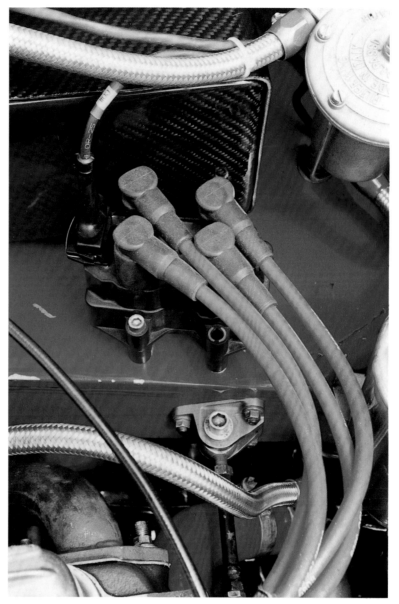

Miglia engines. This was set using the Zytek. To ensure that the Lumenition would be safe should it become necessary to use, this was run and a dizzy swing completed. Imagine our surprise to see 107bhp, rock steady. We rechecked and there was no doubting the conclusion. Clearly the programmed advance curve did not get the best from the engine, and for the following four seasons the Optronic did a sterling job. It would have been the logical step to have the engine dyno'd back at Eurotech, and the programme optimised, but cost was prohibitive, and we

You've got to pay attention to the simpler aspects of your ignition system, too; use top quality leads that will make sure your engine gets the spark, the whole spark and nothing but the spark and ...

So, which way to go? There were cars running Polestar, with good results. There were a few still running Zytek, although the difficulties associated with programming were now eased by Swiftune who supply, install and programme the package. There was also a Lumenition kit, although details on this were sketchy. My preferred choice was the Webcon Alpha kit. The KAD Works machines which I had driven in Silhouette Formulae, with considerable success, all used this system. Also it was well proven in all fields of saloon car racing, and its development has been exhaustive. There were also several Miglias already running the system. But perhaps the single most important factor was that Southern Carburettors and Injection were not only suppliers of the system, but their rolling road man, and Alpha expert, Ross Buckingham, was a Miglia racer himself. I reasoned that time invested in development would be beneficial to both of us, and progress would lead to further motivation.

So, then, the Alpha system has everything permitted for Miglia and plenty more which cannot be utilised, indeed it is also capable of running fuel injection. Remember, when purchasing this system, such is its wide acclaim, it will always have a second-hand value should you decide to go in another direction.

The kit is supplied with everything necessary to run the car. This includes the programmable module (the ECU, also known as the black box or the brain) and its own mounting bracket, full wiring harness, amplifiers, coil unit, trigger disc (to be mounted on front pulley), trigger switch and its mounting bracket. Installation is uncomplicated and straightforward, since the loom is fully made up and bound with labels and a fully colour-coded scheme with illustrated diagram. For standard 1.3i Minis the trigger disc will bolt straight on to the existing front

were still showing the best figures ever for a 1000cc Miglia at Marshalls, and winning some races, so why worry?

Inevitably there is the thought that the overall package could be improved. Certainly I have never felt that any car I have raced is beyond improvement, and perhaps this is another reason for such a lengthy affection for one formula. When we built an all-new car for the '96 season, the ignition system was one of the areas earmarked for improvement. Every other competitive car was running a programmable system of one sort or another, and we were well overdue to catch up.

pulley, although race cars with steel pulleys will require some modifications. Southern Carburettors and Injection completed this for my car and made an excellent job of it. There remains the task of fixing the trigger switch bracket to either the front plate or timing cover. This we completed with ease using a MIG welder. With the wiring harness connected as directed, live feed is required to the module and coil, and the engine is a runner.

There is a start-up programme already installed, and in search of the ultimate the engine can deliver we spent our time on the rollers at SC&I. Within half an hour the engine is carefully run in, and after an oil change the serious business of horsepower chasing begins. The effectiveness of any rolling road is dependent solely on the expertise and experience of the operator. Ross is technically well qualified and has spent countless hours playing with the 'A' series in all forms. Hence swift progress is made (*see* Chapter 12).

A fully objective view can be built up over a longer period of time. In a year's use we suffered no problems whatsoever with this ignition system. The car has never failed to start, and indeed never missed a single beat. An early difficulty with a small flat-spot at around 5,000rpm was sorted in half an hour on the rolling road, and there has been no need to return, even after a full strip and rebuild. The scatter is zero, and such is the control we have run 39 degrees advance, which would normally be perilously close to detonation.

If there is a down side, it is cost. The Webcon system is not cheap, but nothing is for nothing and you do get the proven quality and reliability. The Mini packages from SC&I include those which retain the distributor, purely for spark distribution, and these offer an associated saving in cost.

To summarise, you can get pretty close to optimum performance using the most rudimentary components, providing that they are in perfect condition and are maintained as such. There is considerably less risk with a crank triggered programmable system, but the costs are clearly greater. Going a step further, the Webcon system has a data-logging facility, which can take testing on to an altogether higher plane – but time costs, of course. As always, you get what you pay for.

Webcon's Alpha electronic fuel/ignition management system costs a bob or two, but it really does the business. This is the brain mounted safely out of harm's way behind the driver's seat. Other systems currently in use include Polestar and Zytek.

Electrical installation

The current regulations state that the lights must work, although there's obviously no MoT-style beam setting to go through. Because they're relatively unimportant, most drivers opt for standard units – they have to be taped over for a race, of course, to prevent glass flying everywhere in the event of a bump.

Over the course of the last decade the electrical installation on new cars has become incredibly complicated, and there's been a tendency for owners to believe that anything involving wires and watts is unapproachable. This simply is not true – wiring a racing car is an uncomplicated task. As long as it is undertaken in the right frame of mind, it simply requires patience and a basic understanding of electricity. The racing car will not be needing the fripperies that complicate road-going versions – electric windows, sunroof, seats and mirrors; front and rear screen heating; mirror and seat heating; automatic load-levelling lights; central locking and alarms and immobilisers are all things that can be left in the garage!

Regulations and necessities

As always, consult the regulations. The Mini Challenges require that the charg-

ing system be fully operational, with working lights (headlights, tail and stop). The scrutineers will expect the wipers to work, and they will also require a battery isolator to be fitted. These are the official requirements, and everything else should be there purely for functional purposes. The ignition system will require a switched live supply, as will the fuel pump, and if you're running an electric water pump that will need a supply (and one that cannot be inadvertently switched off!). Get a power supply to the starter motor, and the car should now be a runner.

The remaining electrical items are those which relate to information you need to gather while driving. The rev counter (tachometer) will need a switched live supply, and its trigger wire, and ignition and low oil pressure warning lights are essential in practical terms. Those are the bare essentials but, if you're feeling flush, you may wish to add an on-board timing system or even a data-logging system.

Making the right connection

It's wise to solder any connections you make, but remember that soldering is only used to make an *electrical* connection – there should always be at least one *physical* connection where a terminal is fastened to a wire. This is achieved by using a crimping tool. It is also possible to crimp the electrical join and, in truth, a well crimped join is better than a badly soldered join. It's generally better to find someone who *can* solder if you find it difficult.

It is specifically *not* recommended that you use the self-stripping type of connector (usually known as a 'Scotchlok') on a race car. Whilst these connectors have their place, it is very easy to strip too much wire (in which case the cable may overheat) or too little (in which case there could be an intermittent contact).

The cunning plan

So the idea is to plan it out first. Without going near the car all this can be written down. The Haynes Mini Workshop Manual is an essential aid whilst planning the wiring, and it will show you how the alternator is wired and how the ignition light fits in with it. Essentially, a schematic diagram is drawn showing which wires are going where – very simple, really. The diagram needs to be drawn with colour coding identifying each wire. The Workshop Manual diagram will show the convention for each colour/function. It is vital to follow this so that

On the outside of the car, there must be a clearly marked (with a 'lightning' symbol) electrical cut-off T-handle that can be operated by a marshal in a dire emergency. This should cut all electrical power except that to the fire extinguisher system. (The T-handle alongside, marked 'E', is for the marshal-operated fire extinguisher.)

repair (especially panic repairs on race afternoon) are simple to effect.

Current calculations

Next, you must assess the maximum current that may be drawn by any individual circuit, and establish the correctly colour-coded wire with sufficient current rating. This is easily calculated using the equation: A = W/V (where the slash '/' is the mathematical symbol meaning 'divided by').

A = current in amps
W = power in watts
V = voltage in volts

For example, to calculate the current in amps drawn by two brake-light bulbs each rated at 21 watts, working in a 12 volt car, we apply the equation thus:

A = W/V
therefore A = (2 x 21W)/12V

From this we can see that the current in amps is 3.5A, and the brake lights in this case should be wired using a cable with a rating in excess of 3.5A.

The battery

Having assessed the wire requirements for the whole installation, you need to decide on which battery to use, and the most appropriate location for it. Mini Challenge regulations state that battery and location are free, and an ordinary lead acid battery, which is cheap and will provide reliable starting, is a wise choice – its weight is the only disadvantage. Any battery located in the driver's compartment *must* be within a sealed, non-conductive box, and this includes the dry-type racing batteries which are lighter but considerably more expensive. It's a matter of personal choice, and until the regulations were changed I always used a race battery in the cockpit. Nowadays, it must be boxed, and the consequent increase in bulk makes repositioning in the boot a more realistic possibility, although

Curley Specialised Mouldings can produce a lightweight but incredibly strong carbon-fibre case to suit any size and shape of battery.

The car must be fitted with a battery master switch that kills all circuits (except those to power electrical extinguisher systems). It is common practice to locate this within reach of the belted-in driver, and to have a remote pull handle on the front scuttle (below the windscreen) to be used by marshals or fire crews, etc. I use an alloy box bolted to the floor next to the driver, and place within it the master switch and fuse box. The screw-down lid carries the switches for ignition, starter and fuel pump, lights and wipers. The water pump is controlled only by the master switch to avoid accidental isolation when groping for the wiper switch mid-race! Having spent many wet races not using the wipers because it was inconvenient to look down to the right switch, I have now started fitting a small switch on the steering wheel in addition to the conventional one. This has proved well worthwhile, making a single wipe at a time easy. There are some who retain the conventional column controls. These are somewhat bulky, and require adequate protection so that the driver does not receive knee injuries in the case of a severe accident.

Fuses

There is much contention over the use of a fuse box in a racing car. I consider this an essential item, and always wire each circuit through a separate fuse. Few would disagree with this practice for the lights and even wipers, but many contend that the functions on which the running of the car depends should not be fused. My view is that this risks damage to the whole loom in the event of overload, and, even worse, the possibility of fire. I run all the vital circuits – ignition, fuel and water pumps – through individual fuses.

The loom

Having planned the whole system, building up the loom should be uncomplicated. Lay out the wires that will travel common paths and tape them together; using electrician's tape or, even better, electrician's looming tape, which is designed to stick to itself but doesn't go sticky and gooey when you need to open it up again. You can also use heat-shrink tubing, where the individual wires are threaded through a rubber-like tube and then when heat is applied (from a hairdryer, say) the tubing shrinks around the wires, making a neat and generally waterproof loom.

The loom should be installed away from danger. It should be fully bound and secured to the floor with 'P' clips or similar. Where wires pass through a hole (whether in metal or even plastic) there should ALWAYS be a rubber grommet; this is to prevent the possibility of the wires chafing and causing a short circuit. At best, this could cause a problem to put you out of a race; at worst, it could fire the car – with you in it!

The engine bay

Under-bonnet wiring is where the most attention should be paid. Nothing should be left loose, and tape binding should be thorough to afford protection. Given that water ingress is likely to be a problem, this is a place where heat shrink tubing can be used effectively. There will be parts of the loom that must be detachable, i.e. the headlight wiring if you have a removable front. These joins should be made using multiblock connectors, which have a male and female plug designed to make connection and unplugging simple and quick. Because these will often be unplugged in a hurry, it is essential to make absolutely sure that these connections are really solid.

The charging circuit

The charging circuit should be based on an alternator. The ordinary Mini type is

When underbonnet space is tight (i.e. all the time!) a smaller than usual alternator can be manna from heaven. In this case, a large radiator had been fitted which limited the space behind it. The answer was to use a tiny alternator from a Kubota mini excavator – neat or what?

perfectly adequate, and will push out a high charge when necessary. However, this results in a heavier drag, and power to drive the alternator is robbing that shown at the wheels. The easiest solution to this problem is to ensure that the battery is always fully charged, it will then present little load to the alternator. It has become popular to substitute the standard item with a small alternator, apparently sourced from a Kubota mini-excavator! This has only a very small output, resulting in little

Starter motors

The standard Mini starter motor is both durable and reliable. The pre-engaged version, standard fitment since about 1986, is generally more persistent with an engine reluctant to start, and it is my preferred choice. A further advantage is that there is no protrusion beyond the flywheel housing and allows maximum space for the collection of air. That said, the earlier inertia starter will do the job and is considerably cheaper.

Instrumentation

The range of instrumentation available runs from simple to Space Shuttle. It's down to personal choice, but any driver should have a tachometer (rev counter), oil pressure and water temperature

Inside the car, you'll need a simple and clearly-marked set of switches for operating the vital functions. I've used a simple alloy box with large red/white labels for fuel, ignition, lights, wipers and starter motor. Note the battery, mounted in the cross-member and enclosed (as per the regulations) in a carbon-fibre box. It could be mounted in the boot without the box, though the weight-saving would be negligible.

mechanical drag. These are available from Myk Cable Developments, and offer the extra benefit of allowing increased space for the front radiator and oil cooler.

Switch positioning is paramount – switching off the fuel pump as you grope around for the wiper switch is not a happy situation to be in! To this end I fitted a second wiper switch on the steering wheel, which makes it easy to opt for a single wipe when required.

gauges (with two warning lights), with an oil temperature gauge and gear shift light being highly recommended. Personally, I can find little to justify the expense of memory tachometers, but accuracy and effective needle damping are essential, and the Elliot LC80 provides this at realistic cost. It requires only feed and trigger wires, and is simple to install and use. The oil temperature and pressure and

water temperature gauges are available with capillary tube action, requiring no wiring. These can be relied upon provided they are handled with care.

Oil pressure and no charge warning lights should be powered by ignition-controlled feeds which use the oil pressure switch and alternator terminal to switch to earth when in alarm mode. Mini side repeater lights are perfect and inexpensive as warning lights.

Maintenance

Once installed and working, the electrical system needs little maintenance, although a thorough inspection after every race will not go amiss, especially if you find a wire partly chafed through because it's come loose, or a connector block full of water. All electrics should be kept dry, and it pays to spray regularly with WD40 and/or silicone spray to keep moisture at bay and prevent the onset of corrosion on electrical terminals.

Carbon king, Ian Curley's futuristic dashboard has a suitably hi-tech digital dashboard display which takes information from the GP-style data logging system. Thunderbirds, eat your heart out! Is it necessary? Well, Ian has won the Miglia title with it, and I've won it with my much simpler set-up, so it's purely a matter of personal choice – and the size of your wallet.

By comparison, my own layout looks stark, but it still gives everything I need to know at a glance, with a large tachometer in the centre flanked by a water temperature gauge on the left and a combined oil pressure/temperature gauge on the right. Note the use of Mini indicator repeater lights as emergency warning lights to give a bright and instantly noticeable advance warning of impending engine disaster.

Chapter 12 # Tuning and set-up

This is the big arena. On every grid there will be plenty of cars built to a high standard, with all the right bits, but not all will be winners. True, some may not be driven sufficiently well, but there are countless examples of cars being lacklustre performers until someone takes the time and trouble to set them up properly, at which point they become fully competitive.

Indeed, there are cars that are technically inferior but are successful as a result of effective tuning and set-up. In short: never mind the pretty bits; a few hours spent on set-up will pay rich rewards and compensate for the frustratingly slow progress that is often part and parcel of the set-up process. Problem-solving can only be done effectively by altering one component/adjustment at a time and then trying it out.

Suspension geometry

To consider chassis set-up first, the car must be complete and ready to race. It should be full of oil and water, and with a mid-race fuel load. The

tyres should be inflated to race pressures. The tyre manufacturer will advise starting point on pressure if you enquire.

The equipment needed to measure the suspension geometry is not cheap, although there are various options on the market to limit costs. It may be possible to borrow some of it, and there are certain devices that can be made up at little cost. One thing is absolutely vital, and that is the surface on which the car stands. It must be level, and fairly smooth. Near enough, or almost there, *will not* do. If your floor is not even, you will have to make provision to ensure all four wheels are on the same level. Steel plate, or even plywood, fixed

Getting the car to corner well is essential. When power outputs are so very similar, you can make up a lot of ground in the twisty bits.

However much you try, it seems that keeping all four wheels on the ground in tight corners ...

where needed to bring the four tyres all to the same level will suffice. Use a long straight edge and spirit level to check front to rear and side to side as well as diagonally. Once established and fixed, mark the floor – black felt marker on

'gaffa' tape is effective. This is an essential investment and one that will reap rewards.

To carry out the setting-up process you will need a note pad and pencil, a tape measure, corner weight gauge,

... is pretty much impossible!

castor and camber gauges, and a means of measuring the tracking.

Ride height

It will help to define two terms that are frequently used when talking of suspension dynamics – 'bump travel' and 'rebound travel'. These describe the movement of a wheel, damper, spring, etc. 'Bump' is the direction as the wheel moves up inside the wheel arch, lowering ride height, compressing the spring and closing the damper. 'Rebound' is the opposite, when the wheel drops from the wheel arch, with an increase in ride height as the spring extends and the damper opens.

You need your car to be on your side, not fighting against you. Leaping about on the kerbs isn't the best way to win, and is likely to give you some mechanical headaches back in the paddock.

Getting it right isn't pure fluke – it requires time, patience and, ideally, the right tools for the job. I use Dunlop equipment, which is of superb quality and staggeringly accurate. This is an optical alignment gauge for setting up the tracking.

Looking like a giant tyre pressure gauge, this is the all-important corner weight gauge.

*CORNER WEIGHTS
Setting up the suspension as a whole demands patience, logic and a willingness to work through a set of procedures one at a time. Remember that, in most cases, changing one aspect of the car's suspension will affect at least one other. To set up corner weights, the car must be 'settled'; if it's just come down off the jacks, any adjustments won't work properly. It should also be in race condition, with fuel. You'll need a thin piece of plastic, or similar, to use as a 'feeler gauge' – I usually use a small pit-board marker.*

The ride height of the car is important. Established in conjunction with corner weight measurement, the aim is to lower the car as much as is practically possible. The limiting factor for ride height is set by the front, and specifically the angle which the ball joints can achieve. As the car is lowered, the top ball joint pin increases in angle, and eventually it can tip no further. If pushed to this point or beyond, the joint will break with loss of steering and major damage to the whole of the suspension. A failure of this nature at any speed at all could easily write off the car!

Measure the ride height from the sill line (where the outer sill is welded to the lower body flange) at the front and rear of the sills. The minimum safe height at the front is 7¼in (184mm), and I like to set the car with a half inch rake, so the rear measurement should be 7¾in minimum (197mm). To ensure

the safety of your car before commencing set-up, it is essential to remove the rubber doughnut and trumpet, then reassemble the rest of the suspension and lower the car, using a trolley jack, to discover the exact sill height at which the front suspension goes solid (the point beyond which the top ball joint will not go). There must be at least 1in (25mm) of bump travel available between normal ride height and going solid.

Corner weights

This is simply the measured weight carried by each wheel of the car. It is essential that the car is on the known flat level surface to carry out the process. There are two principal methods of measurement. Traditionally a lever type gauge is used to lift the wheel just clear of the floor, and a reading is taken from the gauge. Now increasing

Roll the car (don't lift it!) on to the centre of the 'feeler gauge', and then …

… (inset) use the corner weight gauge to raise the wheel slightly until …

… (below left) the 'feeler gauge' can just be slid from under the tyre. The fit of the gauge can be likened to setting up contact-breaker points, in that there should be the slightest amount of friction rather than having no contact at all with the tyre. It's something to practise – the rewards are worth it. Note the pressure reading here of just under 300lb. Checking the other three wheels will clue you in as to what needs doing, but remember, all these readings have to be correlated with …

… (below right) the ride height, the measuring of which requires nothing more high-tech than a steel rule. I always reckon that you don't actually select the correct ride height/corner weights – rather, you sneak up on them, a bit at a time, until eventually they come just right.

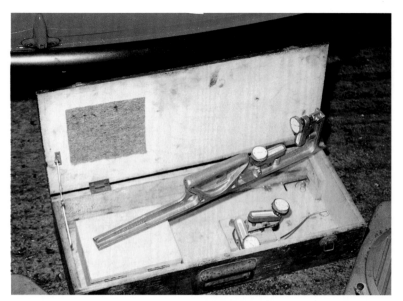

Anyone who appreciates build quality would be impressed by my camber/castor gauge. Despite being older than me, its accuracy is spot-on and it is a joy to use.

little shorter than the other three – when you sit on it, the chair will rock. The car that you begin working on will be the same, so it will rock as it moves, resulting in weight transfer and imbalance. In extreme cases it is possible to feel this by attempting to lift a rear wheel rim. I have been able in the past to lift the 'lazy' wheel clear of the ground with one hand, whilst the other was immovable!

So, what should you look for? In theory, the driver should be in the seat (or an equivalent weight placed there). With this done the readings will clearly be higher on the offside (RHD car), and then there are a series of calculations to determine the percentage of weight carried on each side and front and rear. These result in the ideal weights, and adjustments are made in their pursuit. I have used this method and obtained excellent results. However, I was aware that some drivers left the weight out of the seat during set-up and simply worked on a symmetrical basis. I employed this method as an experiment, and could not detect any difference in the end result. Accordingly, this

in popularity, but considerably more expensive, is the Intercomp type system which has four load pads so that all wheels can be measured at once and adjustments made in situ. Whilst the latter method is clearly superior, I have always relied upon the single mechanical gauge and obtained satisfactory results from it.

To gain a basic understanding of the principles behind corner weights, consider the case of a chair with one leg a

The camber/castor gauge is used with a pair of turntables. Again, far from cheap, but you're certainly getting what you pay for.

is the method I have adopted. It means there is no need to calculate the correct setting, it is merely a case of equalising side to side.

Camber measurement

Camber is a measurement of the angle (expressed in degrees) of the wheel compared to an imaginary vertical line. It is measured with the wheels pointing straight ahead, and termed as positive if the top of the tyre leans outward, and negative if the top of the tyre leans in. Most commonly used for this is the Dunlop gauge, which is simple to use with a spirit-level type bubble that is

WHEEL GEOMETRY

When you're happy the car is running four-square, you can progress to wheel geometry and sort out the camber and (front wheels only) castor. Here, the front wheels have been rolled on to the turntables and the rear wheels raised by the same amount (an important point). The gauge is held as shown, and a reading taken, but no adjustments should be made until the castor has also been checked – as ever, one affects the other.

The castor gauge is fixed on to any one of the road wheel nuts, and then ...

... the wheel is turned to give a reading of 20 degrees toe-in (i.e. front of the wheel pointing inwards).

centred using a degree calibrated wheel. Take care to avoid the bulge where the tyre sits on the road, and place the gauge slightly to the side but still vertical. The variation is the ADA Camber/Castor gauge that uses a plum line and calibrated plate. This is cheap in comparison and, although I cannot comment on its use, plenty of people have achieved good results with it.

The castor angle is that between the vertical and a line drawn through the top and bottom ball joints, when viewed from the side. Minis leave the factory with a typical castor angle of three degrees positive (meaning the lower ball joint is forward of the top). Measurement is rather complicated since there is no single line against which a camber type gauge can be placed to take a reading (some single seaters have a flat machined surface on the front upright for this type of simple measurement). Instead there is a

method which involves turning the steering first 20 degrees in and setting a bubble type gauge at zero. The steering is then centred and turned, in addition, 20 degrees out. The bubble is then re-centred and a reading is taken from the calibrated thumb wheel used to centre the bubble. The ADA camber gauge referred to above has a facility to measure castor, and is the cheapest method of doing so. The traditional equipment, made by Dunlop and utilising the spirit-level method is more expensive. Both methods rely on the steering movement. Dunlop also make front wheel turntables to facilitate accurate measurement of steering angles. These are expensive, but are occasionally advertised second-hand as professional teams move on to optical and electronic equipment. The turntables make application of the steering angles and operation of the equipment a one-man job, and also prevent the tyre from dragging against the surface and giving inconsistent measurements.

Having achieved a measurement which should be in positive degrees, adjustment is a simple matter, the tie bar is shortened to increase castor and lengthened to reduce castor. It is entirely logical, since adjusting the length of the tie bar pulls or pushes the position of the bottom ball joint relative to the top.

Tracking

The best-known of all suspension variables, this is the relationship between any pair of wheels in terms of their direction. Parallel tracking describes a pair of wheels that are both pointing directly ahead, i.e. both wheels are 'steering' directly ahead. To measure the tracking, various equipment is available, but it all relies on checking the distance between the outer faces of the leading edge of the wheel, and comparing them to the outer faces of the trailing edge of the same wheel. If the pair of wheels are steering in towards each other, the track would be deemed 'toe in'. If they were effectively steering out the track would be deemed 'toe out'. This is not particularly easily explained without the use of hands, but if you accept that the front part of the tyre is the toe, the two principal terms are self-explanatory.

Adjustment of the front tracking is achieved simply by screwing the track rods in and out of their jointed ends. Care should be taken to keep both sides even, and usually the steering wheel will need to be straightened. If the steering wheel is suddenly not pointing as straight as it did, this is a fair indication that the tracking has altered, and should be checked.

The rear track of the standard Mini is not adjustable and does not need to be. It will only be out in the event of damage to the major components of the rear suspension, and would under such cir-cumstances be rectified by replacement of the damaged parts.

For the race car, things are different. The rear track can be used to influence handling quite dramatically, and will therefore need adjustment. The standard set-up gives a fair measure of toe in, which aids straight line stability, and is the safe and logical set-up for a road car. There is a need to reduce this to nil, and sometimes, if you prefer, to set the rear track to toe out. Adjustment is achieved by shimming the rear camber plates that carry the outer ends of the radius arms. To space the plates away from the subframe, shims will need to be specifically prepared.

Having got this far, the big question is what settings should be sought, and how to progress the process of moving all things in the right direction? Adjustment of camber affects castor, for example, and so the whole process is one of 'sneaking up on the ideal'.

Start with a clear head and a pencil and note book. I maintain a book dedicated to chassis set-up that can be referred back to easily. For a new car, or if you are inexperienced, think upon the task as a whole day's work. Experience and practice will see this time halved or quartered, but it is a job that should not be hurried. Before starting, set all the dampers fully soft, remove all bump stops, and disconnect or remove any anti-roll bars.

Step one is to bring the ride height and corner weights close to the desired settings. Working first with the tape measure and looking for 7.5in at the front and 8in at the back, adjust the Hilo trumpets a little at a time. Remember to roll the car forward and backward to de-stress the tyres, and if necessary bounce the suspension to settle it down. If possible, avoid jacking the car up, since the suspension will not immediately resettle to the running level. With the height set, next measure

TRACKING
Sorting out the tracking is relatively easy when you've got this sort of equipment. However, it still needs to be set up correctly to be of any use at all. Rest the arms of the device against the wheel rim and adjust height and width to suit. Having done that on both sides, it is vital that ...

the corner weights. I use the traditional gauge, and work round all four wheels in no particular order. To take consistent readings I use a plastic lap board number, and roll the tyre on to it. Do not be tempted to lift the car with the gauge to position the 'feeler'. Now use the gauge and gently increase the lift until the plastic can be moved backward and forward, just like a feeler gauge. At this point, maintain constant pressure and read the gauge, noting the results as you go. Once all four corners have been assessed, you must decide if it is necessary to make alterations and if so, how?

I generally see figures of 450lb at the front and 250lb at the rear, and I expect to equalise them side to side within 5lb. On a good day it is possible to get them

identical. Provided the car is at ride height, as explained above, then the corner weights will be related on a diagonal basis. There will be one diagonal pair light and one diagonal pair heavy.

To picture the diagonals relationship, think back to the chair with one short leg! The pair of diagonal wheels carrying excess weight should be lowered slightly, that is to say the Hilos should be wound anti-clockwise to drop the car and hence allow the previously light diagonal to carry more of the weight of the car. The amount of adjustment should be small and a reading taken at each step, so that you can build an understanding of the reaction to your changes. Having dropped that diagonal, taken readings and measured the ride height again,

... the gauges read zero and are perfectly aligned with each other.

record it all on paper and consider the next move. The decision to lower one diagonal pair should have dropped the car evenly on all wheels if you got the ratio of adjustment right, re-membering, of course, that there is a 3:1 ratio at the front and 5:1 at the rear, the new corner weights should have moved closer to balance. When getting closer to the correct weights, the choice

It's then just a question of placing them back on the wheel rims, taking a reading and adjusting accordingly.

of corner to adjust becomes more important. The decision is guided by ride height, and the juggling act is one that improves with practice. As the desired balance is neared, consider the next factor.

Rear camber

Set rear camber next. This is a simple task, winding the outer end of the radius arm up or down as required. Remember that there is an effect on ride height, albeit only marginal, but this can alter the corner weights. When racing Mini Se7en, I always set rear camber at zero, i.e. vertical. In Mini Miglia the wear on the outer edge of the tyre was rapid, and for this reason we experimented with some negative camber, purely to control tyre wear. This worked well and we settled at $^3/_4$ degree negative. There is another side to that change. Clearly, when working in corners, the tyre was only placing a small section of its width on the road. The increased width we were now working with should have offered more grip and less slip angle. This change should have increased understeer, since the back was less likely to move out now it had greater grip. This wasn't the case and I conclude that the grip afforded the car at zero camber was enough to control it, and the additional grip did not enhance rear end grip. The conclusion is that we run $^3/_4$ degree negative camber at the rear to look after the rear tyres, which will now last for a whole season.

Rear tracking

Having set the camber, now consider rear tracking. The factory spec is a good safe start for an inexperienced driver, or one who requires a very stable rear end. Once experienced with car control, that driver should consider running parallel rear track. This was my initial Mini Se7en spec, having the rear straight up and straight ahead, for best straight line speed. Latterly the desire for sharper turn in led me to use the increasingly fashionable rear anti-roll bar, and to match it with toe out rear track! The theory was that, upon turning in, the Mini would raise its inside rear wheel clear of the ground. This happened readily enough without an anti-roll bar, so its addition served only to enhance the characteristic. At the point when the inside rear wheel lifts, the outer will steer the back of the car out, so assisting the turn in! This could rightly be called 'bastard engineering' since it uses a component for a function other than that intended, but for an under-powered car which slows down in direct proportion to the amount of steering lock applied, it proved a worthy asset, and kept the pilot busy at the wheel. This tactic is one to be used with due regard for the wider implications, for the car will be inherently less stable generally, and will require regular control with discrete use of opposite lock!

The latter technique I continue to employ with Mini Miglia, but stress the need for caution in an inexperienced driver. Placement of shims under the camber bracket to space it away from the subframe is the simplest method. Use the thickest shims possible, since the bracket needs support from the subframe, and thin shims can squash and give. Use steel instead of alloy for the same reason.

Many people have a slotted hole in the subframe through which the inner end of the radius arm passes, and use various methods of supporting the selected position. This method is fundamentally flawed because moving the inner end of the radius arm has a drastic effect on ride height and hence corner weights, since the trumpet knuckle joint sits in a cup at the inner end of the arm. Furthermore, many cars have then broken the securing device allowing the rear track to move drastically and without warning. I consider the shimming method altogether superior.

Front castor and camber

With rear end adjustments complete, for the time being at least, the real fun and games begin at the front. Castor and camber will be addressed together, but before taking initial readings, set the front track to parallel. This is important since the function of castor is to add camber to the turning in front wheel as the steering is applied, and so if the track is toe in any significant amount, then the camber readings will be artificially high.

Two things make the adjustment of camber/castor significantly easier, these are front wheel turntables and bottom arms that are adjustable in situ. If you are without the turntables, great care must be taken to ensure that the tyres are de-stressed before each reading is taken – the car must be pushed back and forth, at least a complete rotation of the wheel each time. The measurement of castor is more difficult, since accurate wheel angle is not easy to assess. In addition, a second person will be needed to turn and then hold the steering wheel. It must also be remembered that the rear wheel must be raised by the same amount as the front to keep the car level, and ramps are available to match the turntables for the purpose.

If the cost of turntables cannot be justified, the bottom arms really can be. Without the in situ adjustable version, the car must be jacked up for each change, and the matter of resettling it to the normal height is not easy. I have used the Selby Engineering lower arms for some time and they are worth the additional cost. Not only do they have all the adjustment virtues, but they are stronger with a larger bush that is welded all round.

With the assets set out above, roll the car on to the turntables, and rear ramps, then apply the hand brake, and the foot brake by wedging the pedal down. The centring lock pins can now be released from each of the turntables. An initial reading of castor and camber should be taken. Look for figures in the range of 1 to 1½ degrees negative camber and 5 to 7 degrees castor. It has been fashionable to run castor in double figures, and twice the amount of camber. I have tried these options and returned within the parameters set out above.

The adjustments themselves are relatively simple. Negative camber is increased by lengthening the bottom arm. Positive castor is increased by shortening the tie bar. The factor that complicates the matter is that the two interact. Increasing (negative) camber reduces castor, and vice versa. Working on the turntables, move one step at a time, measuring the effect on both fronts. If a large (a degree or more) change is made to camber it may be necessary to roll the car off and back on to the turntables to allow the tyre to de-stress and place a revised footprint on the turntable. Continue to check the tracking, and eventually, with everything within range, roll off the turntable and start the process back at the corner weights.

The most difficult element of the whole job is balancing the corner weights and ride height. This requires both patience and manipulation which can really only be based on experience. With a good car with a square shell and sound subframes it should be possible to get the weight and heights spot on. Occasionally, with less than perfect cars, I have been unable to get the two dead right, and under these circumstances compromise is necessary. When push comes to shove, I prefer to see the ride height slightly odd but the corner weights right, rather than vice versa.

Now, continue all round the car, fine tuning any straying variable and rechecking the effect on the whole.

Eventually it will all be right. It is possible to convince yourself that it's near enough when things aren't going well. That is time for a coffee break before getting it spot on! When you are finally content that everything is right, stand back and admire your efforts. It is the cheapest significant progress you will ever make with a racing car.

The final move is to tighten all the lock nuts, and realign the steering wheel. The dampers can now be clicked up with suggested settings of mid to upper range at the front and mid to lower range at the rear. Fine tuning must be done in testing at a circuit. The rear anti-roll bar (if fitted) should now be reconnected. The links from radius arm to anti-roll bar will be adjustable in length, and this facility should be utilised to ensure that there is no tension in the bar with the car still on the known flat surface. The adjustment in the link length is sometimes confused with adjusting the roll stiffness which is, of course, wrong. The roll stiffness is altered by changing the leverage that the force applied to the bar works through. A long leverage makes the bar twist more, and hence reduces the roll stiffness. The same force applied through a short leverage does not twist the bar as much and there is greater roll stiffness.

The car can now be considered ready for the track, and the serious development work which will hone the technically sound car into a proven winner.

Engine set-up

There are some people who believe they can tune a car by ear, and to a lesser extent this is possible for an ordinary road car. However, if you wish to extract the best performance, reliability and long-term life from your car, time must be spent in the hands of an expert equipped with state-of-the-art equipment. The investment you make in the right components will only be ful-filled if the ignition and fuel requirements of the engine are optimised. Finally, there is the perfect environment to run-in an engine, a process that will ensure greater efficiency and life once in use.

There are many considerations before choosing which facility to use – rolling road or engine dynamometer. The rollers do test the whole car and are convenient, in that the car will be ready to race immediately after. An engine dyno is tailored for engine development work rather than tuning but can perform the latter task perfectly well. I have used both, but if I had to make a choice, I'd have to take the rolling road. But which one? As always, asking regular competitors where they go will be a good starting point. Location and cost are usually the principal concerns. It is likely that a competitive car will visit the rollers at least twice a season, some more often than they race! So, a local facility will save time, but only if the operator knows his job and your breed of car. A better equipped facility with an operator who knows the formula and sees other examples, but charges a higher hourly rate may well work out cheaper thanks to his expertise.

I use Southern Carburettors and Injection in Wimbledon, not least because the technician there, Ross Buckingham, knows Mini Miglia inside out. The succession of similar cars on there also gives me a comparison with power figures. For some years I trekked to Cambridge to see Peter Baldwin at Marshalls, it was a long way, but justified by the expertise on arrival.

Whatever you choose, never omit this as a final step before driving the car in competition. The engine is unlikely to be set-up perfectly by chance and, worse still, it may be dangerously high on advance or low on fuelling, spelling a rapid demise for a potentially competitive engine.

Driver comfort and safety

Chapter 13

Seating

It stands to reason that a driver must be seated comfortably, and this is absolutely essential if he, or she, wishes to perform to the highest standard. To this end, the seating position should be one of the criteria included in roll cage design. Quite simply, the seat position must not be compromised by any other concern, the rest of the car should be built around it!

The first decision is to select the seat itself. It is wise to buy the very best you can afford. In an accident the seat will protect your back, and its effectiveness and fit will determine the extent of your injuries (or in many cases, prevent you from getting any). I have had one large accident, and my Corbeau Pro-Race seat protected me perfectly. I stepped from a 100mph impact, with no pain – except for the obligatory stiff neck! I chose this seat because it fitted my body shape, sat me fairly upright and fitted in the relatively narrow Mini without difficulty. It is important to get a good fit, just like shoes, because when racing hard the driver should be seated comfortably, and with the belts tight there should be no effort put into remaining comfortable. The days of bracing yourself for a corner are gone!

Having selected the seat, its mountings are equally important. I have always used the manufacturers' own brackets made for the seat. There are those who build their own, but great skill is required to ensure that the seat's original safety parameters are not compromised.

It is actually very difficult to position a seat in a bare shell, since the lack of pedals, steering and even bonnet and wings, prevents the driver from gaining a realistic assessment. If necessary, it is worth dummy fitting these items to give normal perspective. Over the years, I have systematically lowered the seat nearer the floor. It now virtually touches the floor, the main reason being to give maximum headroom in the event of an accident. A secondary benefit is the lowering of the overall centre of gravity of the car, which is a

Good racing seats are not cheap, even at the lower end of the scale and ... (Courtesy Demon Tweeks)

... (below) for this little beauty you'd pay around three times as much. Once more, this is both a comfort and a safety item, so don't skimp! (Courtesy Demon Tweeks)

This is the seat in my last Miglia car, bolted in an unusual way to suit my preferences (see text).

Ian Curley has (by coincidence) the same style of seat, but prefers different belts (we both have 4-point harnesses) and different fixings.

theoretical handling advantage. It would be unwise to put the seat straight on the floor, especially for a novice, as judging distances for close dicing is more difficult. The Corbeau mounting brackets which I have used make it easy to progressively lower your position.

Over recent years the radical advances in standards of saloon car preparations have seen much development on seat mounts. It was once expressly forbidden to attach any part of the seat mount to the roll cage. Current thinking makes it very much the intention. Originally, the seats were mounted straight on the floor pan. This has become unfashionable in the belief that a side impact could rupture the floor, moving the seat or even breaking it, and hence loosening the

belts. It was felt that if the seat were actually mounted on a transverse roll cage element, in a severe impact the seat would be part of the strongest structure, the cage itself, as would be the belt mountings.

The theory is fine, but in practice this would raise the driver in a Mini by at least 40mm, and probably considerably more. My own solution places the right-hand seat mounting rail on a wide alloy plate independently bolted to the floor. The rail is bolted through the alloy and floor pan, and on the underside a one-inch wide steel strip that spreads the load across all four bolts. The left-hand rail is cut and turned inside out, so that the angle of the rail matches that of the transmission tunnel. The tunnel is reinforced with steel plate during the build and before paint, and is able to support the rail in sheer. There are again four bolt holes and these are plated similarly on the underside. With the rails fixed, the seat height can be altered within the range of bolt holes front and rear, and for maintenance the seat is easily and quickly removed. I really cannot overemphasise how important this part of the whole car is, so get it right.

Safety harnesses

Note: The RAC 'Blue Book' has illustrations of installation recommendations and requirements which must be adhered to. It's important to read and understand this before getting carried away with your installation.

Seat harnesses (or belts) are another safety essential. Motorsport inevitably involves accidents that you must accept and prepare for. The harness will save your life – try crashing at 100mph without one! Over the last five years or so 3in wide webbing has become popular for shoulder and waist straps. Prior to this 2in was almost universal, but 50 per cent extra support from the wider webbing in event of impact is clearly going to lessen the bruising to shoulders, and in my experience there is little practical difference in driving terms. There are numerous manufacturers, and choice is a matter of personal preference. I like the TRS Magnum harness for its buckle design, and have crash tested one myself! If you do have a serious impact the harness must be discarded, as it will have stretched, and in another accident would go immediately to that

again and then stretch further still. It is always difficult to do, especially when there is the cost of repairing the car, but do not economise on safety. It is now recommended that your seat, too, should be returned to the manufacturer for inspection after a major shunt, especially so in the case of a rear impact.

Most harnesses are supplied with latch type fastenings, which attach to eye bolts. The eye bolts are supplied with

One of the cheaper harness options is something like this 2in webbing, 3-point Clubman version, but if you can run to it ... (Courtesy Demon Tweeks)

threaded plates, and these can be welded to the roll cage during its installation in the appropriate position. To achieve the correct angle on the shoulder straps it may be necessary to weld a transverse tube into the cage for this purpose alone. This should be included at the design stage of the cage. Some of the harness manufacturers include padded shoulder pads. I feel these add to my comfort when the belts are properly tight, but there are those who prefer the plain strap. A matter once again of personal taste – try before you buy is the motto.

Attention to your race harness does not begin and end with its purchase and wearing – far from it. Make a point of checking its condition, all the way along the length of the webbing, on a regular basis. You're looking for any sign of fraying or other damage; at the first sign, throw it away and buy another. Equally, **never** be tempted to buy a used harness – all seat belts are designed to work by stretching themselves internally in the event of an accident and once used in

... opt for the full monty 4-point professional style harness, like this one, with quick release. It'll hold you in better and let you out quicker! (Courtesy Demon Tweeks)

(Right). A fireproof racing suit is essential. (Courtesy John Colley)

The suit is seen to better effect on this young lady, though I must admit I can't recall seeing her down in the Miglia paddock! (Courtesy Demon Tweeks)

Apart from the fire safety angle, racing boots allow lots more feel for the pedals – an essential when racing. (Courtesy Demon Tweeks)

Racing gloves are essential and, of course, so is ... (Courtesy Demon Tweeks)

... a decent quality helmet made to a suitable safety standard – such as the BS (British Standard) Kite mark BS6658-85A. It must carry an RACMSA sticker of approval. (Courtesy Demon Tweeks)

Style and colouring is up to you – try a few different styles to get the one you like best. If you need to paint a helmet with a sponsor's logo (lucky you!), then always go to an expert, as certain paint finishes and preparations can have a disastrous effect on the composite material. Although the price of a top helmet is anything from £150 to £400, do NOT skimp here, and remember the good old Americanism: 'If you've got a ten dollar head, wear a ten dollar helmet.' (Courtesy Demon Tweeks)

a serious bump, cannot safely be reused.

Dressing the part

Having obtained your licence, there are various safety items of attire that are essential – naturally enough, the authorities are rather keen that motorsport is no more dangerous than it need be. Protection against fire is a key issue here and, though it does nothing to make it cheaper, it has often been said that fire is the racing driver's worst enemy, and just because you're not racing a Ferrari or McLaren, doesn't make it any less so.

It is a racing requirement that you have a fully-approved fireproof racing overall. They're not cheap, but neither is your life, and many racing drivers have literally had their skin saved by the incredible efficiency of a good overall. There are many names, styles and colours to choose from, so it's up to you – just check that it meets the RACM-SA requirements before you buy. Many retailers can arrange to have sponsors' logos attached before you buy, which may be a consideration. It's important that you are

totally comfortable in the suit – one which is sloppy or too tight will lead to you thinking about personal comfort and not the racing line while you're on the track. You'll also need fireproof gloves, which again should be a perfect fit to enable easy operation of controls while racing.

You can't go racing in your Adidas trainers – even if the rules allowed it, you wouldn't want to after having tried a pair of pukka racing boots. As ever, it is vital to buy exactly the right size and style of boots so that you are totally comfortable – lifting off mid-corner because your boots are pinching your toes is not a good scenario! Sparco, OMP and Momo are just a few of the major players in racing overalls, gloves and footwear.

The purpose of a racing hel-

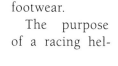

BUILDING, PREPARING AND RACING YOUR MINI

met is to absorb the energy of an impact that would otherwise be absorbed by your skull and, by definition, if you have a bump where the helmet takes even the smallest shock, it is wise to replace it. In any case, the race officials will inspect it after the incident.

Your helmet MUST be an exact fit. If it's tight, it will be painfully uncomfortable and will distract your attention from the job in hand. Too loose, and as well as being a distraction, it will be downright dangerous in the event of a shunt. Buy from a professional race supply company who will be able to advise you what to look for. Take particular care if you wear spectacles, as these can make a real difference.

Sound reasoning

As part of helmet comfort, you are well-advised to consider some form of ear plugs – the racket created by a pack of racing minis (not least your own) is loud, to say the least. The simplest form is to use scrunch-up foam ear plugs, which are relatively cheap but, by being universal, aren't always too effective. At the other end of the scale, there are made-to-measure earplugs from companies such as Elcea UK, which offer a massive reduction in noise levels and,

by definition, are very comfortable to wear (the company has links with several GP bike racing teams as well as the Williams, Benetton and Jordan Formula 1 GP teams). Don't underestimate the effects of loud noise on your concentration or your long-term hearing. The figures shown here are the recommended MAXIMUM safe listening times, the figures being in decibels (dB). The important factor is that sound levels increase logarithmically – i.e. the sound level doubles for every 3dB increase. Note that the no protection figures relate to the amount of time in ANY eight-hour period. The noise level inside a typical racing Mini is likely to be well over 100dB.

Average safe listening times

Noise level (dB)	No protection
85	8 hours
88	4 hours
91	2 hours
94	1 hour
97	30 minutes
100	15 minutes

Is that all?

You may think that the seat/seat belts, helmet and overalls are all there is to

The rules strongly recommend a fireproof balaclava underneath the helmet, but I think they're wrong; it is an essential item. Even though it can get mighty hot inside a racing Mini on a hot day, it would get a darn sight hotter in the event of a roll-over and fire! Again, try various styles with your helmet to find one that's really comfortable. (Courtesy Demon Tweeks)

Don't imagine that a full-face helmet will offer hearing protection – in fact, this type of helmet tends to amplify any exterior noise. And if you think that wearing earplugs isn't quite the image for a macho racing driver, check out the after-race footage at the next GP, and see what Messrs Villeneuve & Co pull from their ears.

Note that, unlike sporty road cars, it is not good practice to go for a trendy small steering wheel – you'll need as much help as you can to turn those wide, slick-shod wheels.

driver comfort – not so! Many things can be tailored *exactly* to the driver's liking and with very real results. The biggest single step I ever made in this area was right at the beginning of my career when I replaced the Perspex windscreen that the car had come with, with a laminated one. The difference was unbelievable – all of a sudden I could see *everything*; as a result, placement of the car became more precise and I began to practise the art of race-craft, simply by being able to see more of what was going on!

Pedal position

In pursuit of comfort, attend to the pedals. Seek the most comfortable height and use pads to give the foot easier purchase. The throttle pedal in particular should be extended and can be bent to make 'heel and toe' easier. The steering column should be lowered to the most desirable angle for comfort and then adequately braced to stop flexure.

Steering wheel

The steering wheel is another example. The contoured wheels made by manufacturers such as Momo, Sparco, Personal and Nardi, provide an easy shape to grasp, allowing the hands to relax a little. Precision of placement of the car counts, and every little bit helps, and though a good wheel will be far from cheap, it should be seen as an investment which will definitely pay dividends.

Gear lever position

The position of the gear lever should be comfortable for the driver. If the seat is moved significantly backward it could be a big stretch to reach it. The current trend is to bring the lever and its housing inside the car and fabricate mountings for it. My latest car features this arrangement. The operating rod is over sleeved with an extended length of steel tube, and to the end of this a universal joint (UJ) is welded. The UJ bolts on to the gearbox spigot, and the housing is mounted at an angle to mate directly with the 'box. With the housing in the right place, only a short lever is necessary, and this is shortened and oversleeved with steel tube.

If you opt to leave the housing in its original location and alter the gear lever, this will provide an adequate solution. Many a race has been lost to a broken gear lever – do not be the next victim! I have suffered two such failures (unforgivable), but experience enables me to highlight the causes. You will notice that Rover include in the lever a rubber joint. It was once accepted practice to either remove this or weld it up. I now leave this as standard, as the shock absorbing qualities are useful to counter the very deliberate and sometimes rough treatment the lever receives. If any welded joints are to be made, do not underestimate the stress these will be subjected to. Any join should be over sleeved and welded top and bottom, and made the subject of pre-event checks.

OK, so now you are comfortable and secure and can see what is happening, there is every chance that you will be able to devote maximum concentration to the task of driving and, through the process of understanding and analysing the performance, real progress will result.

Track tuning the handling

This chapter should perhaps include in the title 'learning to drive', because this is what most people do when they go testing. Indeed, it's a worthwhile pursuit because only when a driver has reached a plateau of understanding will he be capable of developing the car. The idea is that operating at a consistent level, say 95 per cent of pace, changes in set-up can be assessed by the driver, and then alterations made to the car to address its shortcomings. It is no easy task, and for some it is impossible. The great drivers of our era demonstrate that.

Nigel Mansell is said to have been a poor tester, fuelled only by desire to be quickest, however achieved. In comparison, Alain Prost was outstanding, prepared to work patiently for days and weeks, unconcerned by lap times, and interested only in the progress he facilitated and felt. It may be that every time you test it will be to drag that bit more pace from yourself, but try to move up a plane because that's where the big steps are to be found.

Keeping a track

Every time the car runs, notes should be made – date, weather, track and ambient conditions, set-up spec, tyre compound and condition, lap times of your own and other relevant cars. All this information should be recorded uniformly and kept for future reference. I use a hardback A4 book dedicated to this alone. Quickly it becomes an invaluable reference to 'How quick were we here?', 'What gear ratio did we run there?', and 'What tyre compounds did we use somewhere else?' This book will clearly not be the work of the driver. I have been fortunate enough to have one

Check your tyres regularly and make a note of wear patterns. Learning what they mean and how to correct things when they're wrong is all part of modern racing driving.

person with me from the very start of my racing days – Bob Cooper – who has maintained my book, and worked with me as we tested in the role of engineer. The engineer working on a car will decide, in conjunction with the driver, on the best way to alter the car for a given set of circumstances that a driver describes. The driver can engineer his own car, but it is easy to lose the plot and get bogged down. Someone standing slightly aside can look more objectively at all the information and usually reach a sound decision on the direction to pursue.

Suspension geometry and tyre wear

Starting at the beginning there are a million avenues to explore. The geometry chosen for the front can best be

assessed by looking at the tyres. Wear alone will indicate a great deal. Do bear in mind that the 10in Dunlop tyres used by both Mini Se7en and Miglia both tend to wear the centre of the tyre more quickly than the outsides, but beyond this expect to see even wear to the inside and outside if the camber setting is correct. The most scientific method is to use a tyre pyrometer, a temperature measuring device with a probe particularly for tyres. A hot tyre, driven properly and well set-up should show uniform temperature across the tread. Take three points to assess – inside, outside and middle – and record the results. Disparity between inside and outside shows which is working harder and this can be sorted by a change in camber to work the lazy edge harder. If the centre is different from

Shaking down a brand new car during a Silverstone test day. (Courtesy Chris Harvey)

the edges, tyre pressure should be increased to raise temperature and dropped to lower it.

Castor

Castor is more an assessment by the driver. Increase it to address turn-in understeer, but heading to double figures only makes the steering heavy and almost violently self-centring. If you make changes in the course of testing to either castor or camber, remember to recheck the tracking, since it will be affected.

When considering turn-in understeer there are a myriad of possible causes and effects. Insufficient camber or castor at the front are obvious things to consider first. Do not overlook the fact that excessively worn or overheated tyres will produce understeer in a car that is otherwise perfect. It should always be remembered that even a perfect car will understeer straight off the circuit if the driver doesn't ever lift off the throttle!

The rear suspension is often the cause of dramatic oversteer, or even understeer – but it's less likely. Rear camber has been mentioned in Chapter 11, and if you want the back to step out at the slightest hint of a corner then a whole bundle of positive camber on the rear wheels should do the job for you. This will not be a quick car, but it sure will be spectacular!

Sometimes it helps to consider the extreme, to understand the effect an adjustment will make. A car that's all understeer may be loosened at the rear by a tad of positive, but take care not to mask one error, by introducing another to make up for the first. An example of this is the use of toe out rear track to make the car turn in. This is more subtle than the positive camber route, but you must ensure that the apparent gain does not affect other things detrimentally. As an example, the toe out rear must have an effect on straight line speed since the rear tyre will scrub ever so slightly. I have been unable to quantify this effect and am confident that it is not a significant problem.

Springs, dampers and anti-roll bars

When the fundamental chassis characteristics are sorted to your liking, fine tuning is the next priority.

This is a function of spring rate in purest terms, and since the springs on a Mini are rubber doughnuts there is much less that can be done than with a car on coil springs.

State-of-the-art dampers will not alone transform a mid-field car into a winner, but if you are right on the pace and looking for an edge over other front-runners, this is an area where progress can be made. There's a lot to consider with dampers, particularly with the top-notch (i.e. very expensive) double-adjustable units. This requires great patience and testing skills. The stiffness of bump and rebound should be set to complement the springs, for it is their oscillation that is to be controlled. In the case of the Mini damper rates higher than those necessary for the doughnut/trumpet set-up have the effect of increasing the overall suspension stiffness, and the car will work better on the limits, if you are brave enough! This sort of set-up should be approached with caution since the car will be a handful. Experience with the car is essential, and the settings should be gradually advanced to bring on the characteristics progressively. On bumpy surfaces the car will hop and jump, and this can become dangerous if you've gone too stiff; so, approach with caution and respect.

The use of rear anti-roll bars is a contentious area – some front-runners don't have one, but most cars are so-fitted. There are even a few cars with front bars, too, although they're very much the exception. As a starting point, set a

The importance of testing cannot be over-emphasised. (Courtesy Mary Harvey)

rear bar up on the softest setting, and get a feel for it, moving up towards full stiffness until you find the setting that you like and, of course, results in good lap times. But don't make the car so lively that your energy is consumed simply living with it!

So, then, with stiff doughnuts and Hilos or Adjusta-rides you have the maximum practical spring rate, and with properly set-up dampers and rear anti-roll bar, the Mini will handle extremely well; it will have excellent grip, perfect traction and minimal body roll.

Development

Finally, enjoy the development process. It is an ongoing and integral part of Mini Se7en and Mini Miglia. Much development can be conducted by watching what people achieve. Don't forget that espionage is alive and well in motorsport, and learning from the mis-

takes of others saves time and money. Keep your ears and eyes open, go about it discretely and you'll make some rapid progress; but remember, when *you're* the quickest, everyone will be looking at you!

Track time

Thankfully, you don't have to book the entire circuit for yourself! Check out the ads in the motorsport mags (such as *Autosport* and *Motoring News*) for dates when circuits across the country have open testing days when anyone – suitably qualified and with a safe car – can test. The cost varies with the circuit, typically being £85 a morning for the larger ones to £100 a day for the lesser circuits. Whatever, this is small beer and, anyway, is one of the best investments you can make. After all, if you've a major handling problem, it's best to find out *before* the race!

Race car maintenance

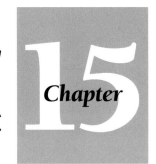

Chapter 15

Maintenance and why you need it

Every machine known to man requires maintenance of some form or another to keep it at peak efficiency. It may mean simply keeping it clean, or changing the lubricant, or it could be much more complex, but the rule stands. Ignore it at your peril.

Modern road cars require service at regular, but ever-longer intervals. Racing cars are similar machines, but the stress levels at which they work constantly demand much greater attention. It is always necessary to caution someone considering Mini racing as to the nature of what they are taking on. It is not all glory. The time spent in the driving seat is a tiny percentage of the overall input required. If you don't like evenings and weekends working on the car, hours towing to and from circuits and days spent in the paddocks, then you ain't going to enjoy it much!

When you get to the circuit, short of polishing the car, everything *should* be done. If it's been done well, there is every chance of a successful day. People often comment that the front runners don't seem to bother with their cars at all. On the contrary, they have bothered to such an extent away from the circuit, that race weekends run smoothly.

There is a crude saying – 'you can't polish a turd' – and there has never been a better analogy for racing. Before you can maintain something it must be fit for the job. So, maintenance is a follow-on from thorough preparation.

At the race track

Assuming you have built a good car, what's to be done to keep it at its best? If you've done all your homework, the following checklist is all you should have to do before qualifying AND the race, regardless of how many or how few laps have been completed.

Item	Check
Oil level	☐
Coolant level	☐
Fuel level	☐
Tyre pressures	☐
Tyre condition (no cuts, etc.)	☐
Wheel nuts ('clicked' with torque wrench)	☐

Check for security:

Boot	☐
Bonnet	☐
Wheel arches	☐
Mirrors (and correct adjustment)	☐

As long as all goes well (nothing falls off on the track, least of all you!), then that should leave you plenty of time for gossiping, eating, dozing in the sun and even watching a few races. We can all dream …

In the workshop

In the workshop after every race the car should be up on axle stands with all the wheels off. Complete a full tightness check of *every* nut and bolt using the torque wrench. Once accustomed to the routine, this will take little more than half an hour. Take care not to further tighten every time this is done – this is why the torque wrench is used, and the 'click' confirms torque.

Provided that no accidental contact has been made with either the scenery or other cars, rechecking of the suspension geometry is unnecessary, although the ball joints and rose joints can be checked for play by attempting to rock the tyre top to bottom. Swift visual checks of the seat and belts, and heavy items such as battery and extinguisher are next. If the car has been exposed to rain, either on the track or trailer, any under-bonnet electrical connections that could harbour moisture should be separated, purged with WD40 and reassembled.

Check the security of the fuel tank and the fuel pump and hose lines all the way to the carburettor. All the brake lines and clutch hoses should be inspected for damage and cracks, and the brake pads for wear. So that's all the easy stuff done, and if the car was well built initially, and has been driven sensibly, there is little likelihood that anything will be found amiss.

Engine

Here I would agree that there is an element of luck. I have had engines that literally never needed to be dismantled, and when they were eventually stripped there was nothing to see and nothing needing replacement; all an exercise of self-satisfaction. Other engines are always needing care, despite the fact they're running well. The minimum engine maintenance between races is to check tappet clearances, fan belt tension and general security (drive couplings, engine mounts, etc.). For many years I left it at that, and nothing prompted me to change until I used a leak tester. This is an excellent piece of kit that, within the confines of your own workshop, without any noise, tells all about the condition of some of the major components. An air supply is fed through a pressure regulator and into each cylinder via the spark plug hole.

When it comes to cars and budgets, the paddock sees all extremes, from parking the Mini and servicing from the tow car to ...

... a professional two-car set-up, with rows of Snap-On Tool boxes and support truck alongside.

The piston is placed at TDC, with both valves shut, and obviously a perfect engine would show no leakage at all. In reality anything less then 10 per cent is considered good but nearing the time to look at it, whilst the motor trade would only investigate leaks in excess of 20 per cent. That's clever enough, but the real coup is that the escaping air can be detected by ear or touch, and the source of the problem is thus highlighted. Whether it's going past the piston rings, head gasket or either valve is easy to determine. I have been in the habit of removing the head for valve lapping every second or third race. The leak tester removes the guesswork. The one I have used is a Snap-On item, and cost around £150. I have yet to use this over the course of a season, but will look forward to doing so, confident that it will tell me what I need to know. For those of us more cost conscious, an adapted spark plug and air line would give an indication of any source of leak and, although the percentage would not be indicated, the small leaks we should accept are quiet in comparison to those of the order of 20 per cent. So, if the leak test checks out OK, the engine is more or less ready to go.

It is wise to change the oil every third outing – some say even more often, but I have always had excellent protection from Duckhams QXR and, now, QS. The later type oil filter housing (as shown in the photo) has always been a source of oil leakage, because it is only secured by two fasteners at the top, with nothing at the lower section. The oil pressure is high, and if the joint is not absolutely perfect, leakage is inevitable. It is possible to swap this type of housing for the earlier type where the design gives a much more useful gasket area with less likelihood of leaks. If you stick with the later type, it is important that the surface of both the block and housing are perfectly true and that there is nothing other than the gasket between them – gasket goo makes leaks a 'racing' certainty. Whichever type you choose, always keep a weather eye on the condition of

If you have the 'wrong type' of oil filter housing, it can cause you endless grief. This is the infamous later type. See text for how to tell which is which and what to do about it.

the gasket and replace at the merest hint of a leak. Balance the cost of a gasket and five minutes to fit it, against the cost of a rebuild and lost track time.

To strip – or not

If all the indications are good I delay a strip/rebuild to the sixth race, or even longer if forced by circumstance. Maintaining oil pressure at 60+psi, water temp below 65 degrees, and revs below 8500 should ensure nothing unexpected within this rebuild frequency.

When you decide on a engine strip and rebuild, schedule it with a couple of weeks in hand in case any major works prove necessary. If you are removing an apparently healthy engine as a matter of routine, it's likely that all will be well, but the oil pump and timing chain should be replaced regardless of wear. Shell bearings should be inspected and only replaced if there is sign of wear. In general you may expect a season from bearings that are lubricated with good quality synthetic oil. If the big-end bearings are in good order, I usually pull off the mains caps and, if they too are OK, I refit the caps and leave the rods and pistons alone. The leak tester will have shown the rings not to be leaking, and are therefore best left undisturbed.

If the pistons are removed from the bore, the rings should be replaced, and the bores glaze-busted to allow the new rings a surface on which to bed in. Anytime that new rings are fitted in new, or glaze-busted, bores, the engine should be run-in on a rolling road or engine dyno on ordinary mineral oil. I use the Unipart Blue for this purpose. The reason is that it has been found that engines run initially on high spec synthetic oil never bed the rings in properly at all.

At yearly intervals it is wise to replace the big-end nuts and bolts, as a failure of either is catastrophic, with damage to all the major components. The camshaft will usually last a year, although it must be inspected carefully at every opportunity. Look particularly at the ramps, as well as the peaks of each lobe. Every time the cam is changed, followers too must be renewed, or their wear pattern will be transferred straight to your new cam! Other items on the yearly list are valve springs and seals, clutch release bearing and rocker shaft.

Items such as clutch plate and diaphragm, pistons and bores themselves, crankshaft journals and ancillary items should be inspected thoroughly at each rebuild and serviced/replaced only when wear becomes pronounced.

Transmission

The gearbox has to be the subject of strict maintenance. Dog engagement type boxes require little attention. The selector forks should be renewed annually, along with the differential pin and planet wheels. Provided that the oil is kept fresh, there is little else to worry about. Synchromesh gearboxes are much more dependent on maintenance. The gear speeds quickly wear or break baulk rings, and renewal of these involves a full strip-down. If they are neglected, the tiny dog teeth rapidly deteriorate, leading to missed changes and jumping gears. I have managed with this type of box for many seasons in the past with success and reliability, but that was based on a strip down at least three times a year.

Oh, lucky man!

Whatever you choose, and however you maintain it, remember the famous loser's adage: '*The unlucky cars always break down and the lucky ones always finish.*' Those who claim this the loudest do least to assure themselves of good luck. It really has nothing to do with luck – but to an onlooker at the circuit it appears that way because the hours were put in behind closed doors.

Race car transportation

It doesn't matter how good a driver you are and how good a car you've got if you don't get there on time! Transportation is a major part of the financial and logistical commitment to going racing.

It is worth reflecting on the sentiments of the, then new, Jordan Grand Prix team upon its entry to top level motor racing. 'You won't be seeing flash trucks and equipment until the cars are competitive,' said Eddie Jordan. His idea that getting the cars right was more important than presenting a flashy image was valid, and he now has both!

You can be assured that even in the early days, however, the modest transporters and the equipment they carried were capable of doing the job. So, too, should the new Mini competitor. It takes little time or money to think ahead and carry a small quantity of all the workshop consumables you normally need. Items like a foot pump, battery charger and tyre pressure gauge are essential.

Vans, trailers and boxes

I have always been fortunate enough to have the use of a van, borrowed at first

This is a pretty basic trailer, no frills, but it does the job, and cheaply, too.

A similar set-up – still a single axle, but this time with a front tyre rack and ...

and later my own. This was a tremendous asset, since considerable spares can be carried, along with a whole crowd of people (provided there are fitted seats and belts for them, officer!). Furthermore, when you arrive there is somewhere for everyone to congregate if (when) it rains. We towed a two wheel trailer, and the whole lot could cruise on the motorway at the speed limit of 60mph, and it would have done considerably more had we been the sort to flout the law.

Later we added a tent style awning to the van, which was a simple but effective way of providing a little more privacy and cover from the elements. Next there was a bigger van, diesel-engined

for better economy, and surprisingly super quick.

The biggest step was to buy an enclosed box trailer. These are becoming increasingly popular. Since the car is enclosed, it is more secure and arrives at the meeting clean and ready to go. Furthermore, there is a multitude of carrying capacity for tools, spares, wheels and tyres, paddock transportation and toys! However, do not overlook the weight of the whole assembly or the fact that it has the aerodynamic qualities of a small bungalow! Whilst the manufacturer stated that a large family saloon would tow such a trailer, my Transit and later a Volvo 850 estate were simply not up to the job. Whilst they could pull it along, it was hard and depressingly slow work for both car and driver, leaving both weary even before the racing started. My answer was to invest in a large 4WD vehicle – a Land Rover Discovery, though there are plenty of alternatives – and would be reluctant to ever try it again with anything less. It does end up being a rather expensive package, however.

A better option for some would be a 7.5 tonne lorry. Equipped with a tail lift to get the car inside this would be cost-effective since purchase prices seem remarkably low. With a twenty foot box, there is space for the race car and living accommodation. The downside is storage, and vulnerability to theft. One advantage of the box trailer/lorry solution is the fact that if it is parked in a secure space there is not a need to unload immediately on return, it can be left safe and dry whilst you rediscover enthusiasm and/or energy!

Whatever you choose, make sure it's well serviced and tyred (as opposed to tired!). For long trips, especially into Europe, breakdown assistance is essential to prevent irritating problems becoming a financial disaster. And if you do book a ferry crossing for your lorry, make sure that you do not have to pay commercial rates; the dockside is not the best place to argue your point on this one!

Of the kit you take with you, ensure it includes your race licence, final instructions and passes, race-wear and waterproofs. I have yet to carry a spare engine worthy of the name, but have often had a load of bits bolted together that looked the part, but would not have been a suitable alternative motor. The cost of a whole spare is considerable, and I have always got away without it, but it pays to carry as many spares and tools as you can. Mini Se7en and Miglia drivers as a group are

... at the rear, the ramps have become part of the trailer assembly.

renowned for their willingness to help anyone in need, but don't rely on it. Better that you be the one doing the lending!

Towing and trailer rules and regulations

There are many rules and regulations relating to towing, the main points of which are shown here. Where you are unsure, refer to the vehicle/trailer manufacturer or directly to Indespension, who can supply detailed information for most set-ups.

1997 licence changes

It is worth noting that a new driving licence towing restriction came into force in January 1997 whereby anyone passing the driving test after that date has to take a specific trailer towing test, where the weight of car/trailer exceeds 3,500kg. Though most standard car and caravan combinations will not be affected, with the larger vehicles and trailers used for

race car transportation, it is possible that you may be affected – check before you drive! If you do need to take the extra test, you can practise on public roads as long as 'L' plates are displayed and you are accompanied by someone 21 years or over and who has passed the relevant test at least three years ago.

Towing speeds

These apply where the tow vehicle and trailer/race car gross weight is no more than 7.5 tonnes.

Motorways/dual carriageways   60mph
All other non-restricted roads   50mph

Towing Weights

Note: Gross weight is the weight of the trailer PLUS its load.

Max gross weight/Max load

Unbraked trailers: 750kg *or* half the kerb weight of the towing vehicle, whichever is less.

Overrun braked trailers: As long as it does not exceed 3,500kg there is no official limit, rather the practical limitation of the towing vehicle's ability to tow it. The vehicle manufacturers will usually quote a maximum figure. 3,500kg *unless* the trailer was manufactured before March 1977, in which case the limit is 3,560kg.

Dimensions

Maximum trailer length: 7m *unless* the trailer has four wheels and is towed by a commercial vehicle with a GVW of more than 3,500kg, when it is 12m.

Maximum trailer width: 2.3m *unless* the trailer is being towed by a commercial vehicle with a GVW of more than 3,500kg, when it is 2.5m.

Maximum trailer height: There is no official ruling with regard to trailer height.

Common sense should prevail here, bearing in mind that the higher the trailer, the more vulnerable it is to crosswinds.

Maximum length overhang: 1–2m. The end must be clearly visible. 2–3.05m. An end marker board must be fitted and be illuminated in the hours of darkness. No load should project more than 3.05m from the rear of the vehicle.

Maximum width overhang: No load should project more than 3.05m from the sides of the vehicle. If you need to carry a load which is over 2.9m wide, the police must be informed.

MoT and trailer maintenance

MoT certificates are not required for trailers of less than 3,500kg gross weight. However, you should treat the maintenance of your trailer as seriously

(Thanks to Indespension for their help in preparing this section.)

Transporting your race car in the back of a truck like this isn't as expensive as you may think. Backing down off those ramps can test your nerves, though!

as that of your race car – imagine the total disaster of a wheel coming off a trailer on the motorway! After every trip, check the security of all fasteners (using a torque wrench) and lubricate all moving fittings and cables as required. When loading your car on to a trailer, you cannot check too often that it is securely mounted. If you interrupt a long journey for a food break, check once more that all is well with the trailer and its precious load.

Brakes

Where brakes are fitted (whether compulsory or not) it is a legal requirement that they are in full working order.

Braked trailers manufactured after 1982 should have a system complying to EC directives. Since 1989, only reversing brakes apply. Where brakes are fitted, the linings must be asbestos-free.

Couplings

Trailers manufactured after 1982 must be fitted with a coupling which includes a hydraulic damper. Spring overrun couplings can be retro-fitted to pre-1982 trailers.

Suspension

All road-going trailers must have a suspension system fitted between the wheels and chassis frame.

Tyres

They must be capable of carrying the gross load of the trailer. DO NOT mix radial and crossply tyres at ANY point on a trailer (i.e. even on a twin axle trailer, it is illegal to have one radial-tyres axle and one fitted with cross-plies). Current car tyre legislation applies equally to trailers. Retread tyres must be marked as such and comply with the British Standard BSAU 1446. All radial tyres must be 'E' marked for EC approval. Tyres should always be kept at a suitable pressure for the load in question.

Mudguards

All trailers must be fitted with mud-guards UNLESS adequate protection is offered by the body of the trailer.

Markings

All trailers must be marked on the near-side of the drawbar with the maximum gross weight the trailer's designed for. In addition, the plate should also show: the manufacturer's name, the chassis/serial number, the number of axles, the max. weight for each axle, the max. load imposed on the drawing vehicle and the year of manufacture. The trailer must, of course, be fitted with a number plate showing the same number as the drawing vehicle.

Lights

All lights should be 'E' marked. This table shows the basic requirements:

Item	Number required	Colour
Rear reflecting triangles	2	Red
Rear marker lights	2	Red
Stop lights	2	Red
Direction indicators	2	Amber
Number plate light	1	White
Rear fog light*	1	Red
Front reflectors†	2	White

* Not required if the trailer is less than 1.3m wide.

† Required on trailers more than 1.6m wide but not those less than 2.3m long and manufactured before October 1985.

Insurance

Most insurers cover the use of a standard trailer with a car. However, towing a race car to and from meetings may be classed as a different kettle of fish, so it is essential that you check beforehand.

Action!

After all those months of hard work, preparation and late nights, the reward comes when you get out there on the track. A combination of adrenalin and fear is a heady mixture and far better than any class A substances – so I'm told! Here, Steve Bell, 1997 Mini Se7en champion, puts in some serious lappery whilst …

… '97 third placed man, Dave Braggins, snaps at his heels in an attempt to move up two places for '98. Note the heavy sponsorship on both these cars and compare with …

... the distinctly bare car of Steven Hopper. The more sponsorship you can get, whether in terms of products or cash, the more chance you have of getting nearer the front of the grid. However, many sponsors want to see you nearer the front of the grid before they'll stump up the readies – a Catch 22 situation which requires almost as much persuasive talent as driving ability.

The great thing about this kind of racing is that it is always close all the way down the field – the guys hustling for 12th place are charging just as hard as the guys at the front, which is good for the spectators as well as the drivers.

BUILDING, PREPARING AND RACING YOUR MINI

Apologies for embarrassing Ian Fraser, but we happened to be there at the wrong time, as he demonstrates how easy it is to get Thruxton's chicane all wrong. At this point he's deliberately unsettled the car coming into the corner rally style, in order to get through it quicker, but alas ...

... a little too much which ...

... requires some hasty application of opposite lock but again ...

... too much of a good thing sees the car heading off in the wrong direction and ...

BUILDING, PREPARING AND RACING YOUR MINI

... up on to the kerb and ...

... beyond it, doing a little lawn-mowing before ...

... eventually getting it all sorted for the start/finish straight. Don't make the mistake of thinking that only beginners can do this – even the best of us can get it wrong under pressure.

Useful names and addresses

The following addresses and telephone numbers were believed to be correct at the time of going to press. However, as these are subject to change, particularly telephone area codes, no guarantee can be given for their continued accuracy.

In line with the latest in technology, the electronic contact details have also been included where known and/or available. These are E-mail (an electronic address for writing to the company) and the Web site (effectively an electronic catalogue for the company, enabling them to give you up-to-date details of products and services). In many cases, products can be ordered electronically – if so, it is important to recognise the importance of having a **secure** connection to prevent your credit card details falling into nefarious hands. It is important that the address is entered exactly, otherwise the connection will not be made.

SUPPLIES AND SERVICES

Aero Tec Laboratories Inc. (ATL)
37 Clarke Road, Mount Farm
Industrial Estate
Bletchley, Milton Keynes,
Bucks MK1 1LG
01908 270590

Aluminium fuel tanks, filler hoses, internal safety foam, surge tanks, fuel cell suppliers.

Autocar Electrical Equipment
49–51 Tiverton Street,
London SE1 6NZ
0171 403 4334
autocar@denaploy.co.uk
http://www.denaploy.co.uk/autocar

Lumenition electronic ignition conversion systems.

Burlen Fuel Systems Limited
Spitfire House,
Castle Road
Salisbury,
Wilts SP1 3SA
01722 412500

SU/Zenith carburettors, fuel pumps and all spares and accessories.

Elcea UK Limited
129 Southdown Road,
Harpenden,
Herts AL5 1PU
01582 767007

Specialists in hearing protection and distributors of Elacin custom-fit ear plugs.

Corbeau Seats Ltd
17 Wainwright Close,
Churchfields Industrial Estate,
St Leonards on Sea, Sussex
01424 854499

Specialist seat manufacturer.

Cobra Limited
Units DS & D2,
Halesfield 23,
Telford,
Shropshire TF7 4NY
01952 784020

Specialist seat manufacturer.

Cole, Nick
Race Car/Engine Preparation,
Ruckinge, Kent
Fax: 01233 731057

Curley Specialised Mouldings
The Square, Yalding,
Nr Maidstone, Kent ME18 6HB
01622 814159

Headed by Miglia racer, Ian Curley, a company specialising in producing carbon fibre mouldings, notably complete front ends, door trim panels and boot lids.

Demon Tweeks
75 Ash Road South, Wrexham
Industrial Estate, Wrexham,
Clwyd LL13 9UG
01978 664466

All manner of Mini racing accessories, including roll-bars, overalls, racing seats, harnesses, fire extinguishers and helmets.

Dent Publications
Newbarn Court, Ditchley Park,
Oxon OX7 4EX
01993 891000

Publishers of the Autosport Circuit Guide (see Appendix 2).

Facet
180 Hersham Road, Hersham,
Walton-on-Thames, Surrey KT12 5QE
01932 231973

Electric fuel pumps.

Farndon Engineering
Bayton Road, Exhall, Coventry CV7 9EJ
01203 366910

Manufacturer of crankshafts, con rods, flywheels and other engine components.

Formula One Racewear
Main Road, West Kingsdown,
Sevenoaks, Kent TN15 6EU
01474 852271

GGB Engineering Spares Limited
98 White Hart Lane, Wood Green,
London N22 5SG
0181 888 2354

Importers of Tar-Ox high performance brake discs and pads.

Goodridge (UK) Limited
Exeter Airport
Exeter, Devon EX5 2UP
01392 369090

The world's leading supplier of aircraft standard race hoses and fittings.

Grand Prix Racewear
Power Road, Chiswick,
London, W4 5PY
0181 987 5500
racewear@grandpri.demon.co.uk
http://www.grandpri.co.uk

All kinds of safety racewear, stopwatches, pit boards, data-logging, etc.

Indespension
Belmont Road, Bolton, Lancs BL1 7AQ
0800 720720 (for nearest stockist)

Complete and kit-form trailers, all manner of parts, accessories and security items for towing and trailers generally, trailer rental.

Jack Knight, Developments Ltd
Butts Road Industrial Estate, Woking,
Surrey GU21 1JU
01483 764326

Design and manufacture of specialist steering and transmissions for racing cars.

KAD (Kent Automotive Developments)
Brooker Farm, Newchurch,
Romney Marsh, Kent
01303 874082

K & N Filters (Europe) Ltd
John Street, Warrington,
Cheshire WA2 7UB
01925 636950

Less-restrictive air filters with a million mile warranty, ideal for tuned engines.

Longman, Richard, & Co
5 Airfield Road, Airfield Industrial
Estate, Christchurch, Dorset BH23 3TG
01202 486569

Race preparation, race engines and Mini specialists.

Lumenition
(See *Autocar Electrical*)

Mini Machine
Darlington
01325 381300

Manufacter of Mini panels. Mk1 specialist.

Mini Spares Centre
29–31 Friern Barnet Road,
New Southgate,
London N11 1NE
0181 368 6292

All kinds of Mini spares and uprates.

Moss International Limited
Hampton Farm Industrial Estate,
Hampton Road West,
Hanworth, Middx, TW13 6DB
0181 867 2000

Major manufacturer and distributor of Mini spares and accessories for road-going and racing Minis.

Northern Ireland Sports Council
Upper Malone Road,
Belfast BT9 5LA
01232 381222

Rollcentre
Somersham Road, St Ives,
Cambridge PE17 4LY
01480 464052

Manufacturers of standard and made-to-measure roll cages.

Serck-Marston
2100 The Crescent,
Solihull Parkway,
Birmingham Business Park,
Birmingham B37 7YE
0121 717 0007

Radiator specialists, with branches across the UK, offering all types of radiator off the shelf with free testing service. Also anti-freeze, water pumps, intercoolers and exchange turbochargers.

Society of Motor Manufacturers & Traders
(SMMT) Forbes House, Halkin Street
London SW1X 7DS
0171 235 7000

Southern Carburettors & Injection
Unit 6, Nelson Trading Estate
Morden Road, Wimbledon SW19 3BL
0181 540 2732

Sparco UK
52 Tanners Drive
Blakelands, Milton Keynes MK14 5BW
01908 216916

Motor racing equipment, including overalls, racing shoes, seats, belts, etc.

Spax Limited
Telford Road Industrial Estate, Bicester,
Oxon OX6 0VV
01869 244771

Manufacturers of all kinds of racing dampers and springs.

Sports Council – England HQ
16 Upper Woburn Place, London
WC1H 0QP
0171 388 1277

Scottish Sports Council
Caledonia House, South Gyle,
Edinburgh EH12 9DQ
0131 317 7200

Sports Council for Wales
Sophia Gardens, Cardiff CF1 9SW
01222 397571

SU Carburettors
(See *Southern Carburettors and Injection*)

Tar-Ox:
(See *GGB Engineering Spares*)

Vickers, Peter
Altered Image Coachworks,
Rochester, Kent
01634 721011

Weber Concessionaires
Dolphin Road, Sunbury,
Middx TW16 7HE
01932 788805

Weber carburation and fuel injection.

Zytek Automotive Limited
London Road, Bassettes Pole
Sutton Coldfield, West
Midlands B75 5SA
0121 323 2323

Automotive electronics, design and manufacture of engine management systems.

Tyres

Avon Tyres
Cooper-Avon Tyres Limited,
Bath Road,
Melksham, Wilts SN12 8AA
01225 703101

Colway Competition Tyres
Ainsley Street, Durham DH1 4BJ
0191 384 6319
http://www.dialspace.dial.pipex.com/pdpr/colway.htm

Dunlop Tyres Limited
Fort Dunlop,
Birmingham B24 9QT
0121 384 4444

Pirelli Ltd
Dalton Road, Carlisle,
Cumbria
01228 281666

Toyo Tyre (UK)
Toyo House, Shipton Way,
Rushden,
Northants NN10 6GL
01933 411144

Yokohama Motorsport Division
Unit 7, Humphreys Road,
Dunstable, Beds LU5 4TP
01582 471471

Tools

Britool Ltd
Churchbridge Works,
Walsall Road, Cannock,
Staffs WS11 3JR
01922 419977

Clarke International
Hemnal Street
Epping, Essex CM16 4LG
01992 565300

Draper Tools Limited
Hursley Road, Chandlers Ford
Eastleigh, Hants SO53 1YF
01703 266355

Halfords
0345 626625 (for nearest store)

Jack Sealey Limited
East Lea Road,
Moreton Hall Industrial Estate,
Bury St Edmunds,
Suffolk IP32 7BJ
01284 757500

Sykes-Pickavant Limited
Warwick Works, Kilnhouse Lane,
Lytham St Annes, Lancs FY8 3DU
01253 721291

Snap-On Tools Limited
Telford Way
Kettering, Northants NN16 8UN
01536 413800

Teng Tools
Unit 5, Flitwick Industrial Estate,
Maulden Road, Flitwick,
Beds MK45 1UF
01525 718080

Racing clubs and official bodies

BRSCC (British Racing and Sports Car Club)
Brands Hatch Circuit, Longfield
Dartford, Kent DA3 8NH
01474 874445

BARC (British Automobile Racing Club)
Thruxton Circuit,
Andover,
Hants SP11 8PN
01264 772607/772696

BRDC (British Racing Drivers Club Ltd)
Silverstone Circuit,
Towcester,
Northants NN12 8TN
01327 857271
info@brdc.co.uk
http://www.silverstone-circuit.co.uk

Mini Se7en Racing Club
Membership secretary,
Mike Jackson, 345 Clay Lane,
Birmingham B26 1ES
www.mini7.co.uk

RACMSA (Royal Automobile Club Motor Sports Association)
Motor Sports House,
Riverside Park
Colnbrook, Slough, Berks SL3 0HG

The UK motorsport governing body and the starting-point for all would-be Mini racers. RAC membership discounts for RACMSA members (0345 414151). 01753 681736 (Phone enquiries 10am–5pm Monday–Friday) racmsa@compuserve.com http://www.rac.co.uk

Magazines

Autosport
Haymarket Magazines Limited
38–42 Hampton Road
Teddington, Middx TW11 0JE
0181 943 5998

Cars & Car Conversions
Link House Magazines Ltd
Link House, Dingwall Avenue
Croydon, Surrey CR9 2TA
0181 686 2599

Mini Magazine
A & S Publishing Co Ltd
35 St Michael's Square
Gloucester GL1 1HX
01452 307181

MiniWorld
Link House Magazines Ltd
Link House, Dingwall Avenue
Croydon CR9 2TA
0181 686 2599

Motoring News
Haymarket Magazines Limited
38–42 Hampton Road
Teddington, Middx TW11 0JE
0181 943 5998

Race & Rally Scotland
72 Carfin Street
New Stevenson, Lanarkshire ML1 4JN
01698 833949

Racing rules and regulations

Unfortunately, nowadays you can't just roll up at the circuit with your car and join the fun. There are plenty of items on the check-list to consider. Apart from obtaining a racing licence, the most important recent development is the requirement to take a training course before you are allowed out on the track to race against other competitors. In the past, it was possible to take to the circuit with absolutely no prior experience, which, as well as being nerve-racking for the novice competitor, was doubly so for the more experienced drivers trying to avoid him!

How to get your racing licence

The UK's motor sports governing body is RACMSA (Royal Automobile Club Motor Sports Association) and it implements rules and regulations made by the RAC Motor Sports Council. It covers all forms of motorsport in the UK, with the exceptions of stock car racing, grass track racing and motorcycle sport, all of which have their own governing bodies. For many motorsport disciplines a racing licence is not necessary, just membership of a motoring club. However, racing your Mini does require a racing licence, and this is how you go about getting it.

To apply you must be at least 17 years old and hold a valid Road Traffic Act driving licence OR be 16 years old with at least one year's experience in karting. In order to race, you have to be a member of a suitable racing club, which can be regional or national just as long as it is affiliated to the RACMSA – a list is supplied with your licence application pack. Club membership should not be seen merely as a technicality to fulfil. By definition, club members are enthusiasts and will have a wealth of experience to share if you care to ask.

1. You should apply to the RACMSA for a 'Go Racing' starter pack which includes a useful video, a copy of the *Competitors' Yearbook* and the various application forms and full details of what is required. The cost of the pack is currently £37.
2. If you are over 18 you will need to obtain a medical certificate – the form is part of the 'Go Racing' pack. Most GPs will make a charge for performing a medical for this purpose. You should be aware that there are some 'disabilities' that would not prevent you getting an ordinary driving licence but which could prevent the granting of a racing licence, such as some eyesight problems, diabetes and epilepsy.
3. You MUST complete a one-day RACMSA driver training course at an ARDS-approved racing school (*see* list at the end of this appendix). The current cost (1998) is £140.

There are four grades of competition licence; the Clubman, National B, National A and International. The Clubman allows you to take part in events all over the UK. The National A licence is valid through the European Union (as well as Andorra, Iceland, Monaco, Norway, San Marino and Switzerland) and the RACMSA International licence is recognised all over the world.

Each race carries a licence classification and the requirements are as follows:

Licence type

Discipline Club National 'B' National 'A' International

Car race Race National 'B' Race National 'B' Race National 'A' Race International

Historic car race Race National 'B' Race National 'B' Race National 'A' or Race International Historic Race International or Race International Historic

Racing licence fees for 1998 were as follows:

International 'A' £530
International 'B' £174
International 'C' £100
International Historic £100
National 'A' £54
National 'B' £37

Everything you wanted to know about racing but were afraid to ask! The RACMSA 'Blue Book' and other publications are what you need to start your racing career.

On receipt of a licence, the successful applicant will also receive the RACMSA Competitors' Yearbook, more commonly known as 'The Blue Book', which contains a wealth of useful information, such as various regulations and lists of scrutineers. This can be obtained separately by applying direct to the RACMSA.

Every time you race, you'll get a signature on your licence from the steward. The more you get, the more experience you log up and the closer you get to being able to upgrade your licence to full nation-al status and, ultimately, to international racing.

Another useful publication is the *Autosport Circuit Guide* (available from Dent Publications), which gives details of all major UK circuits and some European ones. It has a location map, diagrammatic representation and explanatory text for the line to take through each corner.

Disabled drivers

Many disabled drivers compete in motor sport, though each case is individually assessed by the RACMSA. For further details, contact the British Motor Sports Association for the Disabled, Tony Reynolds, PO Box 120, Aldershot, Hants GU11 3TF (Tel: 01252 319070).

Women drivers

Women drivers are increasingly becoming involved in motorsport and the rules apply equally to both sexes. There are two organisations that may be of interest to any ladies wanting to race their Minis:

British Women Racing Driver's Club

Linda Drew, 3 Dugdales, Croxley Green, Rickmansworth, Herts WD3 3JW (Tel: 01923 775673).

Motorsport for Women

Marianne Walford
Tel: 01323 899958

Training

Once upon a time you could just roll up with a suitable car and, if it passed scrutineering, you joined the others on the track. I know from experience what a terrifying experience it can be for the novice driver, and it's probably much more so for the experienced pilot coming across a new-boy in the middle of the track and wondering which way he's going to go!

It's no bad thing, therefore, that it is now compulsory to successfully complete a one-day RACMSA driver-training course before you take to the track proper. It does add to the cost, but £140 is not the end of the world, and it can easily be lost in the season's budget. Moreover, it is a safety item, and price is irrelevant. The course must be taken at an ARDS-approved racing school, selected from the current listing shown here:

ARDS-approved racing driver schools.

School Circuit Telephone
Aintree Racing Drivers' School, Three
Sisters Circuit, Wigan 01928 712877

Anglesey Motor Racing School,
  Ty Cores, Anglesey and Kirkistown
  Northern Ireland
  0800 376 0033
Castle Combe Racing School,
  Castle Combe Circuit, Wilts
  01249 782417
Everyman Motor Racing,
  Mallory Park, Leics
  01455 841670
Ian Taylor Motor Racing School,
  Thruxton Circuit, Hants
Jim Russell Racing Drivers' School,
  Donington Park Circuit
  01332 811430
Knockhill Racing Drivers' School,
  Knockhill Circuit, Fife
  01383 723337
Nigel Mansell Racing Schools, Brands
  Hatch Circuit, Kent;
  and Oulton Park Circuit, Cheshire;
  and Snetterton Circuit, Norfolk
  0990 125250
Peter Gethin Driving Courses,
  Goodwood Circuit, W. Sussex
  01243 778118
Silverstone Driving Centre, Silverstone
  Circuit, Northants;
  and Croft Circuit,
  County Durham
  01327 857177
Tom Brown Racing Drivers' School,
  East Fortune Circuit,
  Midlothian; Jurby Circuit,
  Isle of Man
  0141 641 2553

Which competition for you?

In 1998, there were many ways to compete in your Mini, including:

BRDC/Mini Se7en Racing Club
Mini Miglia Challenge (1300cc)
Mini Se7en Challenge (1000cc)
Winter Mini Challenge

BRSCC
Mighty Minis Championship
(Road-going 1.3i)
(Telephone: 0181 981 2055)

BARC
Classic Saloon Car & Historic Touring
Car Championship
Classic Touring Cars Championship
Post Historic Touring Car
Championships

FIA
European Historic Touring Car
Championship

Rallycross
MDA Minicross Rallycross
BRDA Compomotive Wheels Rallycross

Stock Cars
Ministox

Non-racing Formulae

Speed Challenge
Speed Challenge organised by The
Mini Cooper register is a nationwide
sprint/hill climb challenge for Cooper
or Cooper S cars, 997cc–1400 cc. One
of the less dangerous forms of Mini
Sport (for the car at least) as the club
claim that none was damaged during
the 1997 season!
(Telephone: 01423 860407)
m&dfoster@netmatters.co.uk

Rallying

Mini Cooper Register Road Rally
  Championship
Demon Tweeks/Classic & Sportscar
  Historic Championship
Safety Devices Historic Rally
  Challenge

(More details of all the above formulae
can be obtained from the RACMSA.)

Workshop procedures and safety first

Creating your Mini racer will give you immense satisfaction, even if you don't win! However, it's important to take a leaf or two from the professional mechanic's book of safety, with a logical approach, correct procedures and the use of the right tools for the job.

Preparations

When you're working on your car, always make sure that someone knows where you are and ask them to check up on you on a regular basis, especially if you are some distance away in a lock-up – it could be your life-saver.

- Wear overalls, not least because there are less likely to be loose items of clothing to get caught in moving parts.
- Impose a NO SMOKING rule in your workshop at all times.
- Remove watches and jewellery where possible.
- Keep things tidy – a workshop with cables and pipes running all over the floor is a recipe for disaster.

- When cleaning components DON'T use petrol (gasoline). Use white (mineral) spirit, paraffin (kerosene) or purpose-made industrial cleaners.
- When using any power tools, or even hand tools where there is the danger of flying detritus (chiselling a seized nut, for example), wear goggles to protect your eyes, especially when using grinders, etc.

The camera never lies

If you're working on particularly complex items, make notes and diagrams as to where the various component parts should go. Alternatively, use a camera or even a video camera to show a dismantling procedure and replacement order.

First things first – it's always wise to protect your hands, not least from the unpleasant effects of oil and grease, which are now known to be carcinogenic. Use a quality barrier cream before you dirty your hands, so that any dirt/oil you get on them will simply wash off. Better still, wear vinyl or latex gloves to keep dirt and oil off your skin altogether. When you wash your hands, use a purpose-made cleaner which will pull off the dirt without removing the skin's natural oils.

Use high quality tools all the time – many Sunday-market specials are simply manufacturers' rejects and likely to break under load. If you can afford a compressor, it's an investment you won't regret, as it opens the way for using a wide variety of pneumatic tools, not least of which is the incredibly useful air impact wrench, which makes light work of the most difficult of fasteners. When you've finished, clean up the workshop and clean and replace all your tools. You'll reap the rewards in time saved next time out and in tools that last much longer and work much better.

Using the latter also offers the opportunity to give a 'commentary' as well. Don't believe you'll remember everything – it's amazing how much the memory fades, even after just a week, and many race car projects take months to come to fruition.

Under the bonnet

- Make sure that the gearbox is in neutral, before starting the engine.
- Don't leave the key in the ignition while you're working on the car.
- Always remove the coolant filler cap with a cold engine. If you *have* to do it when the engine is warm, do it slowly, with a cloth for protection. Undo slightly and let the cap settle at the first indentation. This will release the pressure and steam – but remember that the steam will be even hotter than the escaping coolant.
- Keep brake fluid and anti-freeze off your paintwork. Wipe up spillages straightaway.

- Never siphon fluids, such as anti-freeze or petrol (gasoline) by mouth – contact with skin as well as inhalation can damage your health. Use a suitable hand pump and wear gloves.

General safety notes

- Take care not to inhale any dust, especially brake dust, which may contain asbestos.
- Wipe up oil or grease spillages straightaway. Use oil granules (cat litter will do the job!) to soak up major spills.
- Use quality tools – an ill-fitting spanner could cause damage to the component, your car and, of course, to yourself!
- When lifting heavy items, remember the rule; bend your legs and keep your back straight. Know your limitations – if something is too heavy, call in a helper.

- Time is a vital element in any workshop. Make sure you've got enough to finish a job; rushed work is rarely done correctly.
- Children are naturally inquisitive but don't allow them to wander around your garage unsupervised, or to get in the car you are working on, especially if it is jacked up.

Fire

The rules state that you must have a fire extinguisher in your race car, and it makes great sense to have one to hand in your workshop, too. Choose a carbon dioxide type or, better still, dry powder, but *never* a water type extinguisher for workshop use. Water conducts electricity and, in some circumstances, could actually make an oil- or petrol-based fire worse. Check the instructions for use *before* you need to use it and always direct the jet at the base of the flames.

Naked flames (when using gas welding equipment, for example) are an obvious threat, but petrol and its vapour can be ignited even by a spark. This could be caused by something as simple as a short circuit. This is why you should always disconnect the battery earth terminal before starting work. Other problem areas include sparks from a grinder or the striking of two metal surfaces against each other, the bulb in an inspection lamp or even a central heating boiler starting up.

Mains electricity

Mains power tools should be used with care outdoors (which includes a garage or workshop). Use the correct type of plug with correct and tightly-made connections. Where applicable, make sure that they are earthed (grounded). Use a residual circuit breaker (RCD) – which, in the event of a short circuit cuts the power immediately to reduce the risk of electrocution. RCDs can be purchased from most DIY stores quite cheaply.

Take special care when working in damp conditions, especially if you are using a mains extension lead. Wherever possible, work indoors and/or use battery powered tools.

Fumes

Never run your Mini in an enclosed space – the exhaust fumes contain deadly carbon monoxide and can kill within minutes. Treat all chemicals with great care, not least of which, petrol. Many cleaning agents and solvents contain highly toxic chemicals and should not be used in confined spaces or used for long periods without a break. Wear gloves when working with chemicals, and if any is spilled on your skin, rinse off with water immediately.

High tension ignition

Touching parts of the ignition system with the engine running (or being turned over), notably the HT leads themselves, can lead to severe electric shock, especially if the vehicle is fitted with electronic ignition. Voltages produced by electronic ignition systems are much higher than normal and could prove fatal, especially to those with cardiac pacemakers.

The likelihood of an electric shock is more pronounced in wet or damp conditions, when a spark could 'jump' to the nearest earthing point – which could be you! Take great care when performing a task which requires the engine to be running (setting the timing, for example) not to touch any ignition components.

Plastic materials

Working with Fibreglass and other similar 'plastic' materials, opens up a whole new area of safety awareness. It is vital that the instructions for use be followed to the letter in order to avoid a dangerous situation developing. Substances such as polymers, resins and adhesives

Always have a fire extinguisher to hand and know how to use it. There are so many things in your workshop and on your Mini that are flammable, you can't afford to be without one.

produce dangerous fumes (both poisonous and flammable) and skin irritants. In particular, do not allow resin or two-pack hardener to come into contact with the skin. Make sure such materials are clearly labelled and stored safely away from the reach of children and/or under lock and key.

The battery

Most batteries give off a small amount of highly explosive hydrogen gas, so you should never allow a naked flame or a spark near your battery. Always disconnect the battery earth terminal whenever you are working on your car, to remove the possibility of an accidental electrical short circuit. When charging the battery, remove both negative and positive leads. Unless otherwise advised, loosen the filler caps to allow excess gasses to escape.

The battery electrolyte level should be kept topped up (using only distilled water) to the point specified on the side of the battery. If any electrolyte is spilled, wipe it up immediately and wash off skin where applicable – it is highly corrosive. If you need to remove your battery, wear rubber gloves and goggles, always keeping it upright.

Petrol safety

Petrol is a highly flammable, volatile liquid and should be treated with great respect. Even its vapour will ignite at the slightest provocation. When not actually in your fuel tank, it should be kept in metal cans (or approved 'plastic' cans) and stored where there is no danger of naked flames or sparks. Cans should have a ventilation hole to prevent the build-up of vapour. If you work in a pit, extra care is required, as petrol vapour is heavier than air and will tend to build-up in the bottom of the pit. When carrying fuel in cans, remember that heat can build up in the boot and cause the vapour to 'whoosh' when the cap is opened.

Engine oils

There is some danger from contaminates that are contained in all used oil and, according to some experts, prolonged skin exposure can lead to serious skin disorders. You can offset this by always using barrier cream on your hands and wearing plastic or rubber gloves when draining the oil from your engine or transmission.

Oil disposal

Never pour your used oil down a drain or on to the ground. Environmentally it is very unfriendly and will render you liable to action from your local council. In most EC countries, including the UK, local authorities must provide free Oil Banks as a safe means of oil disposal. If you're unsure where to take your used oil, contact your local Environmental Health Department for advice or ring the Oil Bank Line on freephone 0800 663366 for details of your nearest bank. To save transporting old oil five litres at a time, use a large drum (say 25gal) as interim storage. When it is full, take it for safe disposal.

Fluoroelastomers

Many items found on modern cars (e.g. oil seals, gaskets, diaphragms, and 'O' rings) appear to be rubber, but in fact they are made from a synthetic substitute which contains fluorine. The materials are called fluoroelastomers, and if heated to more than 315°C

(599°F) they can decompose in a dangerous manner. Indeed, some decomposition can occur at temperatures of around 200°C (392°F). These temperatures would normally only be found on a car if it were to be set alight or if it were 'broken' by a vehicle dismantler using a cutting torch.

Where there is any water present, including atmospheric moisture, the heated fluoroelastomers produce extremely dangerous by-products. The Health and Safety Executive says: 'Skin contact with this liquid or decomposition residues can cause painful and penetrating burns. Permanent irreversible skin and tissue damage can occur.'

Clearly, this is important to note if your car has caught fire, even if only partially, or if it has been stolen and 'fired' by the thieves. Even more caution is required if you are searching for used parts in a vehicle dismantlers.

Observe the following safety procedures:

1. Never touch blackened or charred pieces of rubber or anything that looks like it.
2. Allow all burnt or decomposed fluoroelastomer materials to cool down before inspection, investigation, teardown or removal.
3. Ideally, don't handle parts containing decomposed fluoroelastomers. If you have to, wear goggles and PVC protective gloves whilst doing so. Never handle them unless they are completely cool.
4. Contaminated parts, residues, materials and clothing, including protective clothing and gloves, should be disposed of by an approved contractor to landfill or by incineration according to national or local regulations. Oil seals, gaskets and 'O' rings, along with contaminated material, must not be burned locally.

Raising your Mini safely

The Mini is not a heavy car *per se*, but if it drops on you whilst you're working underneath it, you'll find out the hard way, that it is far from light. You simply cannot be too careful when working under your car – 20 people die every year as a result of a car falling on them!

Under the car

- Never work under your Mini when it is supported only by a jack. Use additional support from securely placed axle stands.
- Protect your eyes and hands using goggles/gloves.
- Don't attempt to loosen high-torque fasteners while the car is off the ground.
- Tighten them back up when the vehicle is on the floor.
- Never touch any part of the exhaust, manifolds or catalytic converter before ascertaining that it is cold.
- Catalytic converters get extremely hot – don't park over dry grass, oily rags or any other material which may catch fire from the heat. Never run a catalyst-equipped engine without the heat shield in place.
- Although engine and transmission fluids should be warm in order to drain them properly, ensure that they are not hot enough to scald.
- Having removed the wheel, it's a good idea to put it under the car as a belt-and-braces measure.

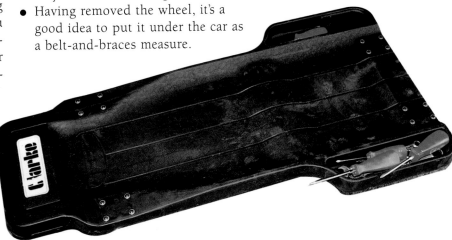

Rolling about under your car on a cold concrete floor covered in dirt and oil isn't exactly appealing. A car 'creeper' not only keeps you off the floor, but its castors make moving around much easier. (Courtesy Clarke International Limited)

This is SIP's Omega 3-tonne Pro-jack. Clearly, its safe working load (SWL) gives plenty of leeway, and it has a large (140mm – approx 5.5in) saddle, so there's little danger of it slipping. Where you are jacking on parts that might be damaged superficially, you can use the rubber protective cover provided, and its small extra 'Fast Lift' handle is very useful, getting the jack arm to the jacking point quickly. The lift height of 133mm/483mm gives a lift span of 350mm. Being of the professional style, the long main handle turns cog gears to release the pressure, thus removing the need for constantly removing a handle to turn the valve manually. The Clarke stands are heavy duty and, rated at three tonnes maximum, are easily up to coping with the weight of a stripped-for-racing Mini. Position them carefully, of course.

prior to supporting the car on axle stands. Only use the jack at the specific jacking points or certain strong parts of the vehicle – to do so elsewhere could be extremely dangerous, not to say expensive. If you're not sure where they are, check your handbook or Haynes Workshop Manual. In many cases, the jacking points will be rotten and great care should be taken in case the car slips whilst partially raised.

Using a trolley Jack

Leave the vehicle out of gear and with the handbrake off until you have reached the required height. This allows the vehicle to move as the jack 'rolls' into place. Exercise *extreme* caution during this procedure and ensure that no-one could be hurt if the car suddenly slips off the jack. Reapply the brake, put the vehicle in gear and chock the wheels remaining on the ground. *Always* use axle stands as well as the jack to support the weight of the vehicle. Once the vehicle is safely at the right height, remove the ignition keys. If you need to run the engine for any reason, make sure you put the transmission in neutral.

Ramps

When you intend working underneath your Mini, the safest way to raise it is to use ramps. Get a helper to ensure you drive up the ramps squarely and with a wheel in the centre of each ramp. Drive up to the end stops on the ramps, but not beyond. Take care that you don't ground bodywork front and rear, especially if you've lowered the car from standard. Chock the wheels remaining on the ground. A strip of carpet wound round the end of the ramps helps the wheels get a purchase on the rungs and prevents the ramps 'skidding'. Never use ramps, jacks or axle stands on a 'soft' surface, such as tarmac.

Scissor jacks

A scissor jack should only be used for *emergency* wheel changing or, at most, raising the car

Glossary of technical and specialist racing terminology

Term	Definition
A series	The redoubtable 4-cylinder engine which started its BMC life in 1951 and powered the Austin A30, A35 and Morris Minor prior to being used in the Mini.
Airbox	A box, usually hand-made from aluminium, attached to the carburettor to concentrate the air flow.
Alloy	Technically the word meaning a metal made up of two or more other metals, but actually more commonly used to mean aluminium.
Blue Book	The RACMSA Competitors' Year Book – the motor racer's bible.
Camber	This the angle of a road wheel when pointing straight ahead, plus or minus compared to the vertical. If the top of the tyre leans out, this is POSITIVE camber; if the top of the tyre leans in, this is NEGATIVE camber.
Catch tanks	Small tanks, usually home-fabricated from aluminium, fitted to catch oil and/or water from breathers.
DOT	An abbreviation used in relation to brake fluid, a Department of Transport standard, denoted by a number (e.g. DOT 3).
Dyno	Abbreviation for dynamometer – a professional workshop device for testing the power/torque outputs of a race car.
ECU	Electronic Control Unit, commonly known as the black box. A box full of complex electronics for controlling such things as programmable ignition systems.
Free	In competition regulation terms, this means that the driver has a choice over which product and specification to use and in some cases, where it should be mounted. For example, in the Mini Challenges, the battery is free and can be any type/specification and fitted wherever required.
Firewall	The bulkhead front and/or rear which literally forms a fire-proof wall between the driver's cabin and the engine/boot (complete with fuel tank).
Glaze-busting	Literally cutting through the glaze that can form on metal over time, usually referring to the glaze on a cylinder bore or on the inside of a brake drum.
Oversteer	A cornering problem where the car turns into a corner more than the driver wants it to – the effect being to hang the tail of the car out and/or cause the car to spin. (*See* also understeer.)
Pot (as in 4-pot)	Pot is the word used in tuning and racing circles for a calliper brake piston. The standard Mini braking system uses two pistons per calliper, one for each pad. Uprated callipers often use two or even three pads per piston for more efficiency, hence 4-pot or 6-pot callipers.
Psi	An abbreviation for pressure, pounds per square inch.
RACMSA	Royal Automobile Club Motor Sports Association (*see* Appendix 2).
Roll cage	A strong tubular structure fitted inside the Mini shell to prevent the bodywork collapsing in the event of a serious shunt and/or roll over situation.
Tachometer	Rev counter.
Thou	An engineer's abbreviation for thousandth of an inch (1/1000in). When working with race cars, it is a very common unit of measurement.
Understeer	A cornering problem whereby the car turns into the corner less than the driver wants it to – in other words, it has a tendency to go straight on rather than turn. (*See* also oversteer.)
Surge	The action of fuel sloshing about in the tank under heavy braking/cornering allowing the pump to draw air. Also, oil surge – where the level in the sump is low it can result in temporary starvation.
Tanks (radiator)	The top and bottom sections of a radiator, either made of copper or, latterly, plastic.

Useful conversions and abbreviations

To convert	To	Multiply by
inches	millimetres	25.4
millimetres	inches	0.0394
feet	metres	0.305
metres	feet	3.281
miles	kilometres	1.609
kilometres	miles	0.621
miles per hour	kilometres per hour	1.609
kilometres per hour	miles per hour	0.621
ounces	grams	28.35
grams	ounces	0.035
pounds	kilograms	0.454
kilograms	pounds	2.205
US gallons	litres	3.785
litres	US gallons	0.2642
UK gallons	litres	4.546
litres	UK gallons	0.22
UK gallons	US gallons	1.20095
US gallons	UK gallons	0.832674
miles per UK gallon	kilometres per litre	0.354
kilometres per litre	miles per UK gallon	2.825
miles per US gallon	kilometres per litre	0.425
kilometres per litre	miles per US gallon	2.352
pound/foot	Newton metres	1.356
Newton metres	pound/foot	0.738
pound/foot	kilogram/metre	0.138
kilogram/metre	pound/foot	7.233
cubic inches	cubic centimetres	16.387
cubic centimetres	cubic inches	0.061
Fahrenheit	Celsius (centigrade)	(subtract 32) 0.5555
Celsius	Fahrenheit	1.8 (plus 32)

abbreviations	
cm	centimetre(s)
cu in	cubic inch(s)
cu cm/cm³	cubic centimetre(s)
ft	foot/feet
gal	gallon(s)
in	inch(es)
kg	kilogram(s)
kg/m	kilograms/metre
lb/ft	pound/foot
m	metre(s)
mm	millimetre(s)
mV	Millivolt(s)
V	volt(s)
W	Watt(s)
TPI	teeth per inch or threads per inch
psi	pounds per square inch
SWL	safe working load
thou	thousandth (of an inch)